D0983666

# What Is
# Theology?

FORTRESS TEXTS IN MODERN THEOLOGY

# What Is Theology?

## Rudolf Bultmann

Edited by Eberhard Jüngel
and Klaus W. Müller

Translated by Roy A. Harrisville

Fortress Press          Minneapolis

WHAT IS THEOLOGY?

First Fortress Press edition published 1997

Translated by Roy A. Harrisville from the German *Theologische Enzyklopädie* by Rudolf Bultmann, edited by Eberhard Jüngel and Klaus W. Müller, published by J.C.B. Mohr (Paul Siebeck), Tübingen, 1984. English translation

Publication of this work has been generously supported by the Inter Naciones agency, Bonn.

---

Library of Congress Cataloging-in-Publication Data

Bultmann, Rudolf Karl, 1884–1976.
    [Theologiche Enzyklopädie. English]
    What is theology? / Rudolf Bultmann ; translated by Roy A.
Harrisville. — 1st Fortress Press ed.
      p.    cm. — (Fortress texts in modern theology)
    Includes bibliographical references and index.
    ISBN 0-8006-3088-2 (alk. paper)
    1. Theology.  2. Theology, Doctrinal—History—Modern period,
1500–  3. Theology—Germany—History.   I. Title.   II. Series.
BR85.B896313    1997
230—dc21                                      96-40256
                                                  CIP

---

---

Manufactured in the U.S.A.                                          AF 1-3088

01    00    99    98    97    1    2    3    4    5    6    7    8    9    10

# Contents

# Translator's Introduction

In 1984, Rudolf Bultmann's Marburg lectures on "Theological Encyclopedia," or introduction to theology, extending over a ten-year period from 1926, finally saw the light of day. The occasion for their publication was observance of the hundredth anniversary of Bultmann's birth (August 20, 1884). For this reason, the *Theological Encyclopedia* was but one of several publications devoted to the "Bultmann-Gedenkjahr" or jubilee. In the same year, the Darmstadt Wissenschaftliche Buchgesellschaft published a four-hundred-fifty-page assessment of Bultmann by twenty-eight theologians and philosophers from various countries (*Rudolf Bultmanns Werk und Wirkung*). Kohlhammer of Stuttgart printed Bultmann's 1912 study of Theodore of Mopsuestia (*Die Exegesis des Theodor von Mopsuestia*), which had earned him the right to teach. Together with the *Encyclopedia*, J.C.B. Mohr of Tübingen printed a new edition of Bultmann's sermons (*Das verkündigte Wort: Predigten—Andachten—Ansprachen, 1906–1941*). The Darmstadt review may have been the most significant work *about* Bultmann to appear in 1984, but it was clearly rivalled by publication of this work, originating with Bultmann himself—the *Theological Encyclopedia*, here presented under the title *What Is Theology?*

## Why Now?

The reasons why this work deserved publication in 1984 are the very same for its translation now. First of all, *What Is Theology?* is not simply one more piece by the greatest biblical scholar of this century. It acquaints us with a Bultmann unknown to us, a Bultmann not yet at zenith but in midst of development, of reexamining perspectives that had dominated theology and biblical interpretation for a hundred years and for the sake of a fresh and vital communication of the Christian message. In this formal sense, Rudolf Bultmann's *Encyclopedia* is kin to Karl Barth's 1919 commentary on the Epistle to the Romans. It shows us the young scholar in the first throes of struggle with inherited tradition. For that reason, the tone of the work is sharp, biting, in marked contrast to what we have come to know of the older, seasoned scholar.

One after another, the greater and lesser lights—Friedrich Schleiermacher, Rudolf Otto, Georg Wobbermin, Emil Brunner—come under attack from the young, forty-year-old Marburger. The easiest target by far is Ernst Troeltsch, in whom the error of interpreting faith as a universal religious feeling appears "in its crassest form." A congeries of worldviews and positions is weighed and found wanting. Everything is subject to a scrutiny softened in Bultmann's later years. One reviewer has termed this volume's description of faith as understood in Catholicism, for example, as unjust and distorted. And in fact, Bultmann does reproach Catholicism for conceiving God as an "existent thing," for ignoring the *actus* of revelation in the present, for identifying justifying faith with dogmatic faith, for insisting upon good works as a requisite supplement to faith, and for exhibiting faith as a worldview. The same reviewer appends the hope that Catholicism might be more fairly judged among us.[1] Someone might conceivably entertain the same hope respecting Protestant orthodoxy or liberalism, pietism, or mysticism—Bultmann's criticism of any one of which is equally stinging. Erich Dinkler, initial editor of the manuscript, reports that Bultmann hesitated over a final readying of the text. Add to this the fact that he no longer lectured on the topic after 1936, and the suspicion arises that he had come to adopt a certain reserve toward it. Still, Bultmann never gave up his plan for publishing the lectures.

A second reason for presenting this work to Bultmann's readership is that for all its character as "germ" or inchoate, *What Is Theology?* furnishes as clear a compendium of Bultmann's theology, and thus as useful a prolegomenon to his principal works, as anything he subsequently authored. Later, Bultmann would accent the appropriateness of a particular philosophical vehicle for the transmission of the gospel, specifically, the use to which Martin Heidegger's phenomenological analysis of *Dasein* could be put for theological explication of existence and faith. Here Bultmann's affiliation with that analysis is as evident as with the burgeoning "dialectical theology," for which Barth has been celebrated as principal exponent. But nowhere does Bultmann discuss at greater length the relationship between bibical interpretation and systematic theology than in this work. And nowhere does he indicate with greater clarity how the one discipline must be related to the other, if the one is not to degenerate into positivism or biblicism, and the other into mere speculation. And, incidentally, nowhere is the reader given a better glimpse than here into the range of education enjoyed by a generation now past and gone.

## Structure of the Work

The structure of *What Is Theology?* is simple and straightforward. Chapter 1, the briefest and entitled "The Task of Theological Encyclopedia," attempts a definition of theology through reflecting on the object which makes it what it is. In Chapter 2 theology is further defined through identification with the science of the *fides quae creditur* or the "what" of faith (*fides quae creditur*—"the faith which is believed"). Chapter 3 discourses on God as the *fides quae creditur*, adding definitions of "science" and "truth," the latter in terms of existential resolve. Chapter 4 analyzes the concept of revelation as Word of God, set in the contingent historical event of Jesus of Nazareth, alive in the church's tradition, and in contrast to "religion," which never gets beyond the question *about* God. Chapter 5 describes the *fides qua creditur* or the "how" of faith (*fides qua creditur*—"the faith by which it is believed"), and in opposition to the concept of faith as a psychic event. The closing section (§15) of the *Theological Encyclopedia* returns to the introductory question, What is theology? and serves as summary of the whole. It should be noted here that Bultmann has frequent recourse to the Latin terminology—evidence of his students' acquaintance with the scholastic nomenclature, thus of its contemporary use in systematic theological discussion.

## The *fides quae*

One reviewer's claim that the *Theological Encyclopedia*'s purpose is to justify the status of theology as an integral part of university study reflects a reading of the lectures from the perspective of the later, more mature scholar.[2] More accurately, it reflects a reading from the *reviewer's* perspective of the later, more mature scholar, that is, of Bultmann as apologist, in this instance as apologist in face of, say, "Kantian" resistance to the theologian's place in the academic procession. The purpose of the work, rather, is to define theology in light of impulses at work in Wilhelm Herrmann and Adolf Schlatter, and culminating in "the great change with Barth and Friedrich Gogarten," for which Søren Kierkegaard and Friedrich Nietzsche, the "two great town-criers of the nineteenth century," together with a host of others, furnished the "underground."

In the matter of the insistence upon God, upon the *fides quae creditur* or the "what" as the proper object of theology, and of attacking a theology that imagines it has its object in the *fides qua* or the "how," it is style or temperament, not perspective or point of view, that separates the Bultmann of *What Is Theology?* from the Barth of *The Epistle to the Romans*: "Our desire to comprehend the world in its relation to God, must proceed either from the criminal arrogance of religion or from that final apprehension of truth which lies beyond birth and death—the perception, in other words, which proceeds from God outwards."[3]

If the one could hold Schleiermacher, that "great ripe classic of modernism," responsible for such "arrogance of religion" in which we have to do "not with God as He is, but only with a god as He appears to us,"[4] the other could indict Schleiermacher for overlooking the fact that faith is such only by relation to its object, that it can be spoken of only when God is spoken of (§5). Bultmann was insistent. Schleiermacher, he said, "does not see that we come no further than the *question* about ourselves and God, no further than to a *concept* of God, but not to God. He does not see that he is not developing the *Christian* idea of God that speaks of God's *action* toward us. . . ." For this reason, according to Barth, the doctrine of the Trinity could not come at the beginning but only at the end of Schleiermacher's dogmatics. For this reason, according to Bultmann, Schleiermacher could only develop assumptions from which the meaning of the Incarnation might—subsequently—be inferred.

But this absence of the "what" or *fides quae* was not restricted to Schleiermacher. It was absent also in attempts to avoid the romanticism of the Berlin giant, in, say, Rudolf Otto's definition of revelation as consciousness of the numinous or mysterious or enigmatic. Bultmann had come to know Otto during his years in Breslau (1916–1920). Later he would concede that Marburg's invitation to Otto to occupy the chair in systematic theology spelled great gain; but he would add that he and Otto had grown far apart, to the point where even their students were made aware of the rift.[5] This volume gives insight into the public character of the rupture as well as of its extent. In these lectures, Bultmann reproaches Otto for a total misunderstanding of Schleiermacher, for assigning to him the idea of God as "given" in terms of belonging to the world, or as inherent in the feeling of freedom (§10). More seriously, Bultmann attacks Otto for confusing God with the irrational: "It is false to confuse the irrational with God and to suppose we speak of God when speaking of the irrational. If the numinous should denote more than awareness of the enigma of our existence, then not having is taken for having, and God is confused with the devil." The distance from Barth's early appraisal of Otto is minuscule: "Rudolf Otto's 'Idea of the Holy,' whatever it may be, is at all events not to be regarded as the Word of

God, for the simple and patent reason that it is the numinous, and that the numinous is the irrational, and the irrational something no longer distinguishable from an absolutised power of Nature"[6]

In a lecture long neglected and delivered at the same spot at which he had read his celebrated "New Testament and Mythology" (Alpirsbach, April, 1941) Bultmann described Schleiermacher with his concept of "absolute dependence," and Otto with his notion of the numinous (together with Ernst Troeltsch with his idea of the "religious a priori"), as representatives of a "science of religion" (*Religionswissenschaft*) in contrast to a theology of the Word of God.[7] No *fides qua* without the *fides quae*!

In the 1940s and '50s, many of Bultmann's critics would come to fault him for embracing the selfsame error as Schleiermacher and his posterity had committed—for ignoring the *fides quae* for the sake of the *fides qua*. In large measure, the criticism was fired by Bultmann's contention that the *fides quae* was not an available fact of world history and therefore could not be seen from a standpoint outside of faith. For this reason, Bultmann's references to the "historical fact of Jesus Christ," to the revelation of God as commencing with "the contingent, historical event of Jesus of Nazareth" (§11), or, as in the essay of 1941, to the word of God as the "sober, factual account of a human life, of Jesus of Nazareth,"[8] would long torment his readers. The references appear to reflect an inconsistency, a taking with one hand what the other had given, an affirmation of the "quest of the historical Jesus" on the heels of its repudiation. For some, this "inconsistency" or "undercurrent" in Bultmann would furnish stimulus for the "new quest of the historical Jesus."[9] For others, the extent to which Bultmann reduced what could be known of Jesus by means of historical research to the single affirmation of his having lived and died, laid him open to the charge of reductionism for the sake of that alleged sole allegiance to the *fides qua*. Yet the solution to the "inconsistency" seems so simple now: "We cannot understand what God is if we do not also understand what faith is, and vice versa."[10]

Here too, there was little distance between Bultmann and the Barth of the 1930s. In Barth's words:

> The inquiry about the self-revealing God, which therefore forces
> itself upon us as primary, cannot . . . be separated at all from the sec-
> ond question, how it *happens*, how it is real, that this God reveals
> Himself. Or from the third, What is the result? what is the *effect* of
> this event upon the man whom it befalls? Just as also on the other
> hand these second and third questions cannot possibly be separated
> from the first.[11]

Precisely because the historical fact of Jesus Christ does not
encounter us as other facts of intellectual history but rather in a tradition peculiar to it, that is, in a proclamation requiring faith for its
illumination, a *fides quae* in terms of the fact of Jesus of Nazareth as
a visible something amenable to investigation is not faith at all, but a
human attitude.

## The *fides qua*

But if Schleiermacher, Otto, or Troeltsch symbolized preoccupation
with the how apart from the what of faith, Bultmann was no less hostile toward concentration on the what or *fides quae* apart from the
how or *fides qua*. Orthodoxy was prey to this peril, Protestant orthodoxy in particular, with its interpretation of the what in terms of
"pure doctrine" (§6), thus its description of *notitia* (explicit knowledge of things to be believed) as a component of faith (§12). To this
notion of revelation as the transmission of knowledge, thus of faith
as orthodox belief, and wherever its home—in Protestant orthodoxy,
Catholic tradition, or rationalism—pietism supplied the reaction. For
if revelation is a reality within our existence, then the word concerning it is more than the report of an available fact of world history. It
is the disclosure of our existence, which can only mean that the
explanation of the meaning of the revelation is at the same time the
explanation of the meaning of our existence. In other words, recognition of the truth of that word involves its application to me, to the
individual (§12). No *fides quae* without the *fides qua*! Years later,
one of the principal thinkers of the Western world in this century
would write in a similar vein:

> The gospel does not exist in order to be understood as a merely his-
> torical document, but to be taken in such a way that it exercises its
> saving effect. This implies that the text, whether law or gospel, if it is
> to be understood properly—i.e., according to the claim it makes—
> must be understood at every moment, in every concrete situation, in a
> new and different way. Understanding here is always application.[12]

Theology then, that science occupied with the "conceptualizing of
believing existence," required a mode appropriate to its object, the
mode we call faith. It could not be carried on, Bultmann insisted,
"out of curiosity" or for the purpose of earning a living but as a "venture, in which we ourselves are at risk." For if God is the object of
faith and accessible only to it, then a science apart from or merely
alongside faith sees neither God nor faith (§§5, 15). Theology had to
be independent of any idea or practice of science that omitted or
ignored the mode of access appropriate to its object.

Again, the assumption that Bultmann's *What Is Theology?* was
written to justify theology's place in the university curriculum is
incorrect. The call to freedom from inherited, even contemporary theological tradition, only thinly veils Bultmann's struggle to free the
theological enterprise from subjection to the language and conceptuality of the inductive disciplines. "We define theology," wrote Bultmann, as a "positive science," that is, a science which finds its object
beforehand, an object found in no other science than in theology and
invisible apart from faith. Theology thus refuses to be subsumed
under a rational system, which being interpreted means, refuses to
allow a philosophy to prescribe its object for it. It was this fact that his
teachers did not appreciate, and which constituted the "peculiar problematic of the nineteenth century." For this reason, theology could not
inquire after a criterion furnished by another science, and for this reason the attempt to justify theology as a science before the forum of an
unbelieving culture spelled theology's surrender. Bultmann's struggle
would be continued in the battle for the "human sciences." Again,
Gadamer reflects it well: "Knowledge in the human sciences is not the
same as in the inductive sciences, but has quite a different kind of
objectivity and is acquired in a quite different way."[13]

## Revelation and the Point of Contact

But if according to Bultmann there could be no *fides quae* without a *fides qua*, there could be neither a *fides quae* nor a *fides qua* without a revelation. With his notion of a universal intuition of transcendence or "religious a priori" Troeltsch had dispensed with revelation, had relegated Christian faith to the status of a phenomenon within the history of religion, and had reduced theology to an auxiliary of sociology or psychology (§5). Still, insistence upon revelation as the origin of the how or what of faith did not exclude a knowledge of God apart from faith. On that point Bultmann was adamant. If he first said it here, he would say or write it a thousand times more: Apart from faith there is an awareness or knowledge of God, so that it is possible to speak of God, to develop an idea of God apart from faith.

When Bultmann reviewed the second edition of Karl Barth's commentary on Romans, he described it as a "straightforward—Pauline—radicalism, clear about what faith, and about what grace means," but he believed that its description of faith as lying "beyond consciousness" bordered on the absurd. Of course, Bultmann wrote, the dynamic of faith did not consist in a perceptible event of consciousness. But faith nevertheless gave to the content of consciousness its orientation or direction. For that reason it could not be detached from confession. Bultmann detected a certain Kantian transcendentalism in Barth's "purification" of faith from everything visible, perceivable. "How do I come to faith?" he asked, and answered:

> The question can only be answered by showing what faith *means*. For when the meaning of faith is made clear, it is guarded from every misinterpretation as a psychic process. . . . To the person involved in the question, How do I come to faith? no more of an answer can be given than that he reflect upon whether and where in his life he encounters the reality to which he can totally submit—must submit.[14]

If the meaning of faith could be shown, then obviously it could be shown to unbelief. But if so, then it was necessary to understand where faith and unbelief could meet, necessary to know the "broad and empty structures" of human existence within which the specific, concrete movement of faith could occur. And for that knowledge, Bultmann turned to an analysis of human existence gleaned from observing what was available to everyone: actual, everyday life as determined by the reality of things—in other words, to phenomenological analysis, and specifically, to the analysis of Martin Heidegger (§§7, 8). Neither idealism with its observation of the "inner" life of the mind, nor a science of religion as in positivism, nor Schleiermacher's science of a knowledge of God as a practical task for directing the church, could furnish this knowledge. On the contrary, these worldviews were all preoccupied with the mastery of things, not with the things themselves.

Bultmann's old teacher, Wilhelm Herrmann, saw more clearly than Barth the threat to faith in its removal from everything called "world":

> What Barth says of the contrast between world and God, applies in great measure to his contrast between nature and intellectual life (culture), so certain is he that both—nature and culture—spell "world" from God's point of view. We do no justice to the problem of culture by construing it, with Barth, as simply a product of nature. On this view, a good piece of the radicalism of the concept of faith is broken off, insofar as what applies to culture, but cannot be viewed as nature since culture has been eliminated, is now said from the point of view of God, with the result that God is identified with the world.[15]

Denial of a "point of contact" between faith and unbelief did not distinguish faith from "world"—it *identified* faith and "world." From now on, the difference between Barth and Bultmann would widen, would become a yawning gulf, and, ironically, where both were concerned, for the sake of an understanding of faith, not of a worldview. But in insisting on revelation as indispensable to faith, Bultmann was as unflinching toward Heidegger as he was toward Troeltsch, as hostile to the phenomenologist's assumption that the knowledge *about* God apart from faith involved also the capacity to know God, as he was to the historian of religion's assumption of a universal, religious a priori. This matter had to be cleared up before he advanced to the main portion of this work:

I can neither know God himself from out of the situation, since it only presents me with its claim and nothing more, nor can I find God in myself through my resolve. But this means that I cannot find God at all within my human possibilities. If there is to be talk of God, then it must be an address to the human possibility, to the moment. And such talk cannot be directed to the phenomenon of the moment, as though it were contained in it. It can only be accepted. That is, there can only be talk of God on the basis of his revelation, and the revelation can only be heard in faith. (§9)

According to phenomenology, *Dasein* lives authentically when it affirms its temporality, its "historicality," when it affirms that it is limited, when it resolves to be open to the future, to death. But faith reckons such resolution as despair. Thirty-five years ago, in a study of Bultmann's theology, Schubert Ogden would describe Bultmann's denial of authentic existence to "man as such" as a *non sequitur* drawn from his understanding of man as radically fallen.[16] For what has now been dubbed the "third" quest of the historical Jesus, assigning the capacity for authentic existence to "man as such" is short of being axiomatic—Jesus serving as an illustration, albeit the highest, of a capacity given with existence. Bultmann demurred: The idea of revelation implies that "man as such" is never authentic, that despite his freedom, man is always determined by possibilities arising from out of his past, so that he always remains the old, never arrives at genuine life. In fact, in man's unconscious search for authentic existence, he is fated to miss it, because he intends to find it on his own. As the reviewer earlier adverted to phrased it, "whoever will not be harnessed to Heidegger's cart," can still profit from the *Theological Encyclopedia*, since "Bultmann is not Heidegger."[17]

But if there was neither a *fides quae* nor a *fides qua* apart from revelation, that revelation was not something to be grasped in intuition, feeling, or presentiment. It could only be believed. For all his insistence on faith as constituted solely by the activity of God, as created by what it believes (thus his identification of the basis of faith with its object), Herrmann, Bultmann's teacher, had forgotten that faith was trust in a word, in a proclamation, not in the impression of Jesus as an experienceable fact.

Herrmann's notion of faith as retrospection on the person of Jesus was thus as absurd as Barth's description of faith as lofted beyond consciousness:

> [Herrmann's] argument is that the relation of trust toward others, a relation that is possible to us only as broken and uncertain, is nevertheless possible toward Jesus as unbroken. . . . But an analogous relation of trust toward Jesus is simply not possible. It was such only long ago for his disciples. . . . Since Herrmann's train of thought cannot result in an I-Thou relationship with Jesus, it finally ends up representing the "inner life of Jesus" as a palpable fact, though it is an absurdity to want to perceive faith or a man's love. (§14)

Barth's absurdity rendered him invulnerable to Herrmann's absurdity, and once more in agreement with Bultmann:

> What did [Herrmann] aim at upholding? The peculiar free life of the Christian subject-matter as against all human findings. . . ? Or solely the mere human claim of a romantic anti-intellectualism. . . ? We must, of course, say that the second is the answer in the foreground, just as the first is the answer in the background. . . . So far as we must say the second, Protestantism will do well not to identify itself with Herrmann.[18]

"So far as we must say the second," Bultmann did not identify himself with Herrmann.

## Politics and the Encyclopedia

In his introduction to Bultmann's theology, Walter Schmithals acquaints the reader with the Marburger's little-known and even less publicized aversion to the ideology of National Socialism, an aversion reflected in essays and sermons from 1933 onward. From these Schmithals concludes that "if there are any theologians in our country who can look back without shame to what they said and wrote in

1933 and afterwards, Rudolf Bultmann is among them."[19] 1933 was the year of Hitler's election as Chancellor, his disbanding of political parties, and his seizure of sole power in the *Ermächtigungsgesetz* ("empowering law"). All of the *Encyclopedia*'s reflection on the German political scene appears in "Draft D," composed in the same year. In that draft, Bultmann affirms a "man's link to his nation." Science and culture, viewed apart from existence, are nothing but an organized flight from the self; they require conditioning by one's relation to a nation. Awareness of this requirement, writes Bultmann, was making itself felt in contemporary Germany (§7). The power of the national movement thus lay in its consciousness of *Dasein*'s "historicity," in its turning away from idealism and rationalism, from liberalism, even from democracy—all of these engined by timeless ideas intent on giving reality to life and measuring the individual by the universal (§9). On the other hand, the national movement was in danger of going astray, its positive force traded for an ideology that threatened to obscure and destroy it. That ideology was the spawn of idealism, with its notion of God in the nation, with its identifying national spirit with the will of God. Bultmann protested: "Nation in the true sense is not a biological but an historical phenomenon. This means that our participation in it is not a question of descent but of existence." "Unequivocal, as is always the case with Bultmann," writes one reviewer, "is his rejection of the world-view of National Socialism."[20] Another, coming upon a footnote to the effect that the national character of a science is not a criterion for truth (cf. p. 207, n.5), or upon the reference to "German abuses" in Tacitus (p. 209, n.28), remarks: "Such an addition in 1933!"[21]

## Bultmann and Company

Finally, if the link to the "early" Barth proves that Bultmann was not a theological loner, greater similarity to yet another Swiss is evidence that he was part of a movement. That other Swiss was Adolf Schlatter, born in St. Gallen, student at Basel and Tübingen, pastor in Zürich, professor at Bern, at Greifswald, Berlin, and finally at Tübingen. Bultmann's loss of a brother on the German side in World War

II Schlatter could match with the loss of a son on the same side in World War I. Schlatter wrote: "I went with his coffin through the darkened land toward Tübingen, and wrote on his cross: 'None of us lives to himself.'"[22]

Schlatter had Bultmann's passion for wedding biblical to systematic theological concerns. In Berlin and Tübingen he actually lectured on dogmatics and ethics. His teachers were not those of Bultmann—Karl Müller of Tübingen, Hermann Gunkel and Adolf Harnack of Berlin, Adolf Jülicher, Johannes Weiss, and Wilhelm Herrmann of Marburg—but instead Johan Tobias Beck and Karl Heinrich Weizsäcker of Tübingen, Franz Overbeck and Jacob Burckhardt of Basel along with Friedrich Nietzsche, who treated his audience as a "despicable mob." And his friends were not Martin Rade, Friedrich Gogarten, Hans von Soden, or Walter Baumgartner, but Hermann Cremer, Adolf Stoecker, Friedrich Bodelschwing, and Martin Kähler. But however disparate their beginnings, Schlatter and Bultmann were something of a pair.

Like Bultmann, Schlatter was intent on struggling free of an intellectual tradition, a struggle echoed in a word to his students at Tübingen in 1931: "I admonish every student that he hold fast to evangelical rejection of infallibility in every situation, toward himself and every teacher, every book, every school, every party."[23]

Just as with Bultmann, Schlatter's tradition comprised unequal parts of rationalism, orthodoxy, pietism, of religion construed in terms of "feeling," positivism and the advocacy of a "religious a priori." And as with Bultmann, each allegiance came under attack. Of the "a priori and the like," Schlatter wrote that every genuine theologian is an observer and thinks on the basis of what is given, not "a priori," since what is divine can only be grasped to the extent it appears in history.[24] Of positivism, or the "atheistic method" in theology, Schlatter contended that with the choice of this method the result was already "dogmatically fixed" prior to observation.[25] He wrote of the religion of feeling given classic expression in Schleiermacher that it eliminated thinking, willing, and acting from religion.[26] Of the pietist tradition, to which he belonged by birth, and whose strongest impressions he received in Beck's lecture hall,

Schlatter wrote that it rejected the history which creates nations, states, and churches.[27] Schlatter's critique of orthodoxy, particularly of the Lutheran variety, was stinging. He spoke of its "egoistic utilization of faith to nurse the ego," its suspicion of love or work done for God, its despising of nature, its flight from community, its clericalism, and its erection of a scholastic and imperious system—all of which he saw not merely retained, but given further shape in Albrecht Ritschl.[28] After hearing Beck's exposition of Romans, Schlatter resolved to be neither Reformed nor Lutheran: "We could not saunter back into the old Tübingen, where everyone had the true, pure faith, and where a violent man sat in the chief official's house, and a thief in the house of the lower city—both, however, indubitably orthodox and Lutheran."[29] For this reason, or for all of the above, the "quest" of the historical Jesus never came within Schlatter's field of vision. He refused to distinguish between the historical Jesus and the Christ of faith.

But if there was significant similarity in what Karl Barth, Rudolf Bultmann, and Adolf Schlatter were struggling to throw off, there was similarity in what they, or at least what Bultmann and Schlatter, were led to embrace. For example, Bultmann's arguments on behalf of the budding phenomenological analysis with its accent on observing what was available to everyone—everyday life as determined by the reality of things—could have been a leaf torn from Schlatter's book: "Since we are set in midst of history, it either carries us blindly along with it, or we share in it as seeing. . . . It is our affair to see what is shown us, to take what is given us."[30] Again, "Science is first of all seeing, and secondly seeing, and thirdly seeing, and seeing again and again."[31]

Like Bultmann, Schlatter was committed to the critical method, which he also believed served the ends of faith. Unmoved in his university years by the dogmaticians or, as he called them, the "conceptual artists,"[32] and urged on to observation by Burckhardt and others, he struggled to wed the interests of criticism and faith, and for his pains was damned by the one faction as a "critic," and by the other as a pietist whose faith in the Bible rendered him unfit for scientific work.[33] "For me," wrote Schlatter, "faith and criticism never divided into opposites, so that at one time I would have thought in a Bible-believing way, and at another critically. Rather, I thought in critical fashion because I believed in the Bible, and believed in it because I read it critically."[34] Schlatter's best-known work on critical method was produced on the occasion of an article appearing in *Die christliche Welt* for 1905, and entitled "The 'Atheistic Thinking' of the Newer Theology." In it Paul Jäger, a well-known Freiburg pastor and pulpiteer, argued that theology should work only with a method as recognized in the university. Such method furnished a "photographic" picture of what could be known, and left God entirely out of play. Schlatter countered that the historian could not stand pat on the mere description of past occurrence, but was required to hand down a judgment. Perception thus needed to be combined with perspective—both subsumed under an evaluation within the context of a theory that gave them integrity.[35] With Bultmann, but in this instance also with Barth who had little taste for critical method, Schlatter would form an early twentieth-century triumvirate summoning the interpreter to a decision on behalf of the text.

But also with Bultmann, Schlatter had no appetite for Barth's situating faith beyond consciousness. In his younger years, he had attempted avoidance of the gospel with Benedict Spinoza, never with Immanuel Kant.[36] In his review of the second edition of Barth's Romans commentary, he wrote:

> The "No" which Barth sets over the entire condition of our life strikes at the act of thinking with ruinous force. Every idea turned toward God, every religious utterance shatters on the idea that God is the inaccessibly distant, the "Other." At base, every theology becomes nonsense, since it can only speak in continual self-contradictions. . . . When the thought-act is destroyed, faith does not come through unscathed, since it needs a content accessible to our perception, a content we can appropriate with reasoned judgment.[37]

But if allegiance to a "content accessible to our perception" linked Schlatter to Bultmann, that same allegiance separated them. To what degree Schlatter was aware of Bultmann's work is not clear. And whether or not he would have agreed with "the old Marburgers" that despite his demurrer, Bultmann had given such accent to the *fides qua* as obscured the *fides quae*, is not clear. What is clear, is that Schlatter wished to assign a vulnerability to that *fides quae* which it appeared to have lost with that accent. At the conclusion of the paragraph begun with the statement that we are either carried along blindly with history or share in it as seeing, Schlatter wrote: "By taking possession at one spot, everything else becomes alien territory to us. . . . Still, this is not failure." A faith linked to reality may in fact suffer shipwreck, but a faith raptured from critical testing wins immunity only at the price of meaninglessness. That word to which Bultmann held fast, the word of God as the "sober, factual account of a human life, of Jesus of Nazareth," and by virtue of his accent on the *fides qua* to the puzzlement of his critics, that word Schlatter intended to leave exposed. Now Schlatter, Barth, and Bultmann abide, but the greatest of these is. . . .

A few notes about this translation: First, since the intention has been to remain as close to the original as possible, modification has not been made for inclusive language except in minor instances. Second, the term *Dasein* often appears in the text and most simply denotes "human being" or, as per Bultmann's generation, "man." In the phenomenology of Martin Heidegger, who gave the term extensive exposition (for which reason it inched its way into English vocabulary), it has ontological weight. Third, where there is extensive use of biblical Greek, it has been transliterated and an English translation appended, according to the NRSV. Finally, as indicated in the Editor's Foreword, the various layers of Bultmann's text, added over a ten-year period, have been indicated by means of bracketed letters A–E and O.

*Roy A. Harrisville*

# Editor's Foreword

Rudolf Bultmann's literary remains include a manuscript of considerable size entitled "Introduction to Theological Study." As the list of offerings of the Marburg Theological Faculty indicates, under this title Bultmann announced a two-hour lecture for the summer semester of 1926.[1] This list also makes clear that he lectured on "Theological Encyclopedia" in the summer semesters of 1928, 1930, 1933, and 1936—evidently revisions of the lecture of 1926.[2]

On its 350 pages the present manuscript from Bultmann's hand contains the text of the lecture of 1926 together with the corrections, expansions, deletions, and changes that Bultmann continually thought were needed, and were made when he held the lecture under a new title in years to follow.[3] Further, these pages include Bultmann's notes dealing with individual stages in his revision of the text, but also with themes linked to it.[4]

From the "original draft" of the year 1926,[5] subsequent layers of the text can be lifted out with relative ease.[6] With the aid of various indices they can most often be assigned with a high degree of probability to a specific new draft.[7] The text given here refers to the various layers by means of the letters A to E added.[8] Notes on a specific section of the text, when not otherwise indicated, belong to the layer of text linked to that section. Note is taken (in the editorial remarks) where Bultmann later inserts individual phrases or ideas into an older portion of the text only when such changes help to make clear the development of his thought and theology.

The shape of Bultmann's recognizably latest lecture was normative for that of the text of this edition. For the reconstruction of this final draft the third Table of Contents with sections 1–11 offers relatively certain clues.[9] References to the last four sections appear in the manuscript's marginal notes. These notes, clearly reflecting various editorial stages and thus often contradictory, were more often written in pencil than in ink, and thus are seldom to be assigned a specific editorial stage. They are of only dubious assistance in reconstructing the final draft.

Bultmann apparently did not undertake a more thorough editing (and tightening) of sections 12–14.[10] Section 15 ("What Is Theology?") is not even mentioned in the two final drafts of the Table of Contents from his hand. Still, this section, entirely rewritten for the lecture of 1933 and later reedited, no doubt belongs to the final draft. There is some uncertainty, of course, as to whether Bultmann would have subsumed this paragraph under chapter 5 ("The Concept of Faith"), or whether he considered it a brief, summary concluding chapter.[11]

In some cases, this lack of clarity obliged the editors to use their own discretion when deciding between various conceivable alternatives. In doing so, it was naturally their aim wherever possible to offer the draft Bultmann himself would have regarded as most suitable. Within the latitude allowed there was also considerable room for deciding which of Bultmann's statements belong in the main text and which in the notes. In this instance, aside from Bultmann's infrequently recognizable intent, legibility was the norm. The basic principle was to include all Bultmann's statements—whether in the text or in the notes—that were contained in the last recognizable draft. Marginal notes that Bultmann made in pencil involve ideas most often set down in catch-words, later fully written out (thus written over in ink). These notes pencilled in the margin have also been included[12]—except for instances in which individual terms, signs, or numbers yield no sense for the reader.

Since one of the principles of this edition was to let only Bultmann himself speak, breaks in train of thought or sentence structure could not always be avoided where two layers of the text coincide.

The text as is was interfered with for only the following reasons:

(*a*) As a rule, abridgements and abbreviations were written out in full or (together with the abbreviations) adjusted to the system of abbreviations in the "Theologische Realenzyklopädie."[13]

(*b*) Quotations were researched and where necessary improved. In general, we cited the text of the work quoted by Bultmann.[14] Our procedure differed respecting Luther quotations, which Bultmann most often cited from secondary literature or from the Erlangen Edition. These were cited and referenced according to the Bonn or Weimar editions of Luther's works. Quotations from old Protestant orthodoxy[15] were proofed according to H. Schmid, *Die Dogmatik der evangelisch-lutherischen Kirche*, newly edited and examined by H. G. Pöhlmann (9th ed.; Gütersloh: 1979). Texts from the Lutheran Confessions are cited and referenced according to their authoritative edition.[16] Similarly, in every possible instance, doctrinal decisions of the Roman Catholic Church are cited according to the *Enchiridion symbolorum*, edited by H. Denzinger and others.

(*c*) Bultmann's often sparse bibliographical references to the literature he mentioned and cited are completed without comment.

(*d*) The punctuation, capitalization, and writing in lower case, which Bultmann often managed differently in various drafts of the text, has been unified and adjusted to present-day rules.

(*e*) Obvious misspellings[17] were corrected without comment. When improvements in syntax were required, Bultmann's draft was referred to in the editor's notes.

If for the first time, following the publication of smaller passages by Erich Dinkler,[18] we offer here the complete draft of Rudolf Bultmann's "Theological Encyclopedia," we carry out an intention more than a half-century old. In 1929 Bultmann signed a contract with the J.C.B. Mohr (Paul Siebeck) publishing house to edit the series "New Theological Outlines" ("Neue theologische Grundrisse"). To the series, Bultmann himself was to contribute volumes on "Theological Encyclopedia" and "Biblical Theology of the New Testament." On the 11th of February, 1930, the publisher expresses his hope the "Encyclopedia" may soon be finished as volume one of the series,[19] a hope that seemed appropriate then, as appears from Bultmann's answer written the next day.[20]

In the years that follow, the "Encyclopedia" is often mentioned in Bultmann's correspondence with his publisher. But after Hitler's "*Machtergreifung*" Bultmann appears to have relegated the plan for publication more and more to the periphery.[21] He no longer took it up, though he often dealt with the thematic of a theological encyclopedia as presented here.[22]

According to information from Bultmann's oldest daughter, Mrs. Antje Bultmann-Lemke, the "Encyclopedia" belongs to those portions of her father's estate which he hoped would be published in the last years of his life, though he felt he was no longer capable of preparing anything for publication. In those years Erich Dinkler was most intensely occupied with Bultmann's manuscript. Dinkler's death hindered publication. Naturally, his preliminary work on the text did not proceed beyond a first stage.

Appended to this edition is Bultmann's till-now-unpublished lecture on "Truth and Certainty" ("*Wahrheit and Gewissheit*") delivered at Eisenach on October 2 and 3, 1929, at the fall retreat of the Bund for Gegenwartschristentum. One of his two respondents was Friedrich Gogarten.[23] As correspondence between them indicates, Gogarten was induced to speak before this group solely on Bultmann's account.[24] In his lecture Bultmann often refers to Gogarten's response. This is the reason for its publication here, though themes and arguments in the lecture sometimes overlap with statements in the "Theological Encyclopedia."

*Eberhard Jüngel*
*Klaus W. Müller*

# 1

# The Task of Theological Encyclopedia

## §1. The Definition of Theology in Idealism and Positivism[1]

The earlier, common title "Encyclopedia"[2] reflects Alexandrian scientific terminology since Aristotle, in which the *engkyklios paideia* (*orbis doctrinae*, Quintilian, *Ins.* I 10, 1)[3] denotes all sciences in *general education*—grammar, rhetoric, music, geometry, and astronomy—that form the basis for the study of philosophy.

Technical usage of the *newer science* harks back to the seventeenth century. In that usage, "encyclopedia" denotes "a survey-like description of knowledge giving an orientation to the entire intellectual heritage."[4] The prime interest here, of course, is in the content, not the method of knowledge, hence the ideal of a *Realenzyklopädie*, gathering all the content of knowledge or a specific branch of it in alphabetically arranged articles or in monograph form.[5]

This is in contrast to the idea of a *formal encyclopedia* set up by G. W. F. Hegel: "As encyclopedia science is not set forth in the detailed development of its various parts, but restricted to the origins and basic concepts of the individual sciences."[6] [A]

On this view, encyclopedia is reflection on the nature of a science, on what makes it a science.

Each *science* has its particular object, an area of observation that is recognizable (unveiled) in it and, of course, as a coherence and a totality. And, corresponding to its area of observation, each science has its own method of describing (unveiling), of offering evidence (establishing its principles), as well as its own conceptuality.

It is clear that there can be as many sciences as there are possible areas of observation. For the person learning to know a world that first seems to be a plurality, the question unavoidably arises: Do all areas of observation make up a unity? And is there for this reason a *unity of science*?

All areas of observation do appear combined into a world unity. And if the world is not an aggregate of disconnected areas, then all areas of observation must cohere in the order of a unified world system. Accordingly, the sciences would also have to cohere within a *system of science*.

Is there a system of science? And would theology's place be assigned and its nature determined on the basis of that system?

*Idealism* believed in a system of science, on the assumption, of course, that all areas of observation, every existent thing, may be viewed as unified from a single origin and that this origin is also the origin of science. It believed that the One from which every existent thing and all thought derive is the Absolute conceived as Spirit, a Spirit beyond all division into subject or object, real or ideal. Grounded in the idea of the Absolute, the unity of what exists and the unity of science must be intelligible within their various articulations.[7] But since the Absolute is conceived as Spirit, the scientific system has primacy over that of whatever exists, and the world-system is conceived as functionally dependent upon the scientific system. The system of nature is rooted in the scientific system, for what exists is constituted by the Spirit. Accordingly, each individual science is not rooted in its object but in its origin in the Spirit. Its nature is not to be understood from a relation to its object but to be derived from the idea of Spirit, from which all conceivable objects of science (nature, history, etc.) are to be understood.

The question, *What is theology?* would thus not be answered by reflecting on its object, on God, but by its derivation from the idea of Spirit and by its ordering within the system of sciences. Philosophy would precede theology, and theology, as a branch of universal philosophy, would be the philosophy of religion.

With the advance of nineteenth-century natural science, belief in the Spirit as the power of origin begetting whatever exists is lost. *Positivism* emerges, for which the real world is the objectively existing world. On this view, the idea of the unity of the world is retained, since all spheres of being are reduced to an existent that can be mastered mathematically, reduced to what is measurable, calculable. Within this reduction to what can be mastered mathematically, one science corresponds to the unity of the world. It is one because at bottom it has only one area for its object: the world as nature, researched with the methods of mathematical-mechanical natural science. In this world the human is viewed as a natural phenomenon. History, the sphere of human life, is researched via the method of natural science. The human thus becomes the object of psychology, sociology, biology.

From this perspective, the question *What is theology?* is to be answered in such a way that its object is humanity insofar as the human thinks about God. These thoughts are not considered from the person's relation to God, but from the person's religious need. The object of theology is religion; that is, theology becomes absorbed into the science of religion. Insofar as Christian theology asserts that it is the science of God as the human's counterpart, the result of positivism is the dissolution of theology as well as of faith, the reduction of faith to a psychological, sociological phenomenon. Ludwig Feuerbach drew this conclusion[8]—rejected, of course, within the discipline of theology—that is, that theology is to be reduced to anthropology. In face of positivism, theology as a systematic discipline seeks to cling to the idealistic tradition. But positivism is encroaching more and more upon historical theology, especially in the field of "comparative religion." But the more systematic theology is engaged in the psychology of religion, the more it too falls prey to positivism. [D]

## §2. Schleiermacher's Concept of Theology

*Friedrich Schleiermacher's* undertaking corresponds with what we have outlined above. In his first semester at Halle, in 1804/05, he lectured on "Encyclopedia and Methodology." Then, in 1811, on the basis of this oft-repeated lecture, appeared his *Brief Outline of Theology as a Field of Study*. A second, revised edition appeared in 1830.[9] [A][10]

Schleiermacher's approach appears to be different. In the *Brief Outline*, §1, he defines theology as a *positive science* "whose parts join into a cohesive whole only through their common relation to a particular mode of faith, i.e., a particular way of being conscious of God. Thus, the various parts of Christian theology belong together only by virtue of their relation to 'Christianity.'" If this sounds as if theology takes its positive character from an object that cannot be derived from the idea of Spirit, Schleiermacher's exposition immediately betrays the opposite intention: "A positive science is an assemblage of scientific elements which belong together not because they form a constituent part of the organization of the sciences, as though by some necessity arising out of the notion of science itself, but only insofar as they are *requisite for carrying out a practical task*."[11] According to §3, this practical task is *church leadership*. Section 5 thus defines Christian theology as "that assemblage of scientific knowledge and practical instruction without the possession and application of which a united leadership of the Christian church, i.e., a government of the church in the fullest sense, is not possible."[12]

Accordingly, the *positive character* of theology as science is in no way constituted by its *object*, but by its *purpose*.

Accordingly, therefore, scientific knowledge becomes theological knowledge when it serves the practical aim of church leadership. To the question whether there is any scientific knowledge as such that is theological, that is, by virtue of its peculiar object, §6 replies in the negative.[13] Thus, insofar as theology is a science, that is, with an object and a method of research, it has no churchly character, in fact, does not at all comprise a unified science. Rather, its propositions belong to other sciences.

Naturally, what first belongs to such science is the *"essence of Christianity."* The understanding of that essence belongs to theology as the embodiment of knowledge required for church leadership. This knowledge as such is not theological. It is not, since the essence of Christianity is recognized only in relation to other types of faith, and these in turn only "in relation to all the other activities of the human spirit" (§21)![14] And, of course, Christianity and the religious communities must be demonstrated to be "a necessary element for the development of the human spirit" (§22)! A definition of the essence of Christianity thus assumes the philosophy of religion (§23), and for this reason results in *philosophical theology* (§24). Such, then, would be authentic theology, based on the assumption of the unity of the Spirit differentiating itself in historical phenomena, so that each phenomenon must be understood from the concept of the human spirit. Philosophical theology is actually a *philosophy of history*. Just as Christianity as a religious community must be understood on the basis of the unity of the human spirit and its development (§22),[15] so must "theology" in its unity with the knowledge of the unity of the Spirit, thus *within the system of sciences*. Philosophy is the authentic science (§28).

Theology, then, does not at all begin with itself, that is, with its particular object. Its object is only an occasion for recourse to philosophy.

On this subject refer to Schleiermacher's *Ethics*, §1: "If a particular science is to be exactly described, then it may not begin just with itself, but must be linked to a higher, finally to a highest knowledge, from which each individual detail must proceed."

Note also *The Christian Faith*, §1.1: "Since the preliminary process of defining a science cannot belong to the science itself, it follows that none of the propositions which will appear in this part (in the 'Definition of Dogmatics')[16] can themselves have a dogmatic character."[17]

But this means that the definition of a science, thus also of theology, derives from elsewhere than from its object. Since "philosophical theology" has proven to be part of the philosophy of history, what theology is becomes clear only from the study of ethics,[18] "the science of the principles of history" (§29).[19] By way of the church construed as "religious community," and thus as a particular instance of religious communities per se, theology is again incorporated into the system of sciences.[20]

According to Schleiermacher, along with "philosophical theology," *historical theology* also belongs to theological study as its authentic corpus. For "leadership of the church also requires a knowledge of the whole community which is to be led: (*a*) of its situation at any given time, and (*b*) of its past, with the realization that this community, regarded as a whole, is a historical entity, and that its present condition can be adequately grasped only when it is viewed as a product of the past" (§26). Historical theology thus comprises "knowledge of the entire previous career of Christianity" (§82), and (a logically prior) historical knowledge of the present moment. To the latter Schleiermacher assigns "dogmatics" and "church statistics" (thus, say, "symbolics"). Here too, the object of science and its methods is not specifically theological. Rather, "Insofar as it forms a theological discipline, the historical knowledge of Christianity is, first and foremost, the indispensable condition of all intelligent effort toward the further cultivation of Christianity; and in this connection all the other parts of historical study are strictly subservient to it" (§70).

And, naturally, knowledge of the history of Christianity is in turn guided by the results of "philosophical theology," which first lays "a foundation for the properly historical perspective on Christianity" (§65).[21] [C]

## §3. The Definition of Theology Based on Its Object

(*a*) With the loss of faith in "Spirit" in the idealistic sense, faith in scientific system has vanished. The power of positivism as a worldview has been broken. Today there is absolutely no system of science or of a worldview that could claim to understand every existing thing on the basis of Being.[22] Of course, there are all sorts of attempts at such a worldview and linked to all sorts of strident claims. Note the National Socialist "worldview." But what does it say? That race, for example, is the principle of its worldview means at best that race should be viewed as the supreme value toward which all action is to be directed. But the question of being as a whole cannot be answered on the principle of race, as the following examples show. Neither mathematics nor science can be understood as an expression of race, since it cannot be the basis for posing or answering the question about truth. In fact, one must "reduce" the question about what is true to the question of what race requires.[23] But this means being stuck fast in positivism, in its American pragmatic form.

Actually, inquiry into being as a whole can only turn to the objects themselves and strive to see them as they show themselves. In philosophy this is the principle of *phenomenology*, that is, an appeal to the things themselves.

This turning away from a worldview with its mastery of things in the direction of the things themselves, given systematic elaboration in phenomenology, is not to be construed only as an immanent development of logical thought. It is based on the fact that the reality of life determined by the reality of things has made itself felt in the various spheres of life. Theological and philosophical work are thereby closely linked in a variety of ways.[24]

*Søren Kierkegaard* (1813–1855) furnishes a starting-point for both. He heaped scorn on Hegel as the philosopher who forgets that he exists. *Friedrich Nietzsche* (1844–1900), like Kierkegaard, sees that the reality of existence is experienced only in existing, and not on the basis of spectator thinking. He sees that human reality is neither "spirit" nor merely "body," but historical existence. These are the two great town-criers of the nineteenth century. They gave birth to a new thought and have had decisive effect today in Martin Heidegger and Karl Jaspers.

Time was needed before they could have effect. The impulses at work in them are also making themselves felt in others. They are at work in philosophy, in *Wilhelm Dilthey* (1833–1911), whose correspondence with Paul Graf York von Wartenberg (1877–1897)[25] indicates the similarity of motifs in philosophy and theology. In addition, note *Jacob Burckhardt*'s (1818–1897) *Force and Freedom*,[26] which renounces all philosophy of history in order to make human being in its reality the object of research ("man suffering, striving, doing, as he is and was and ever will be"); "hence our study will, in a certain sense, be pathological in kind."[27]

There are impulses at work in poetry, in *Carl Spitteler* (1845–1924), whose "Prometheus and Epimetheus" (1880/81) appeared before Nietzsche's related "Zarathustra" (1883–85); in *Stefan George* (1868–1933), and in *Rainer Maria Rilke* (1875–1926), more significant than George,[28] though George at first had greater influence in the study of literature (Gundolf)[29] and of history.

In *theology* such impulses are at work in figures such as *Wilhelm Herrmann*[30] and *Adolf Schlatter*. In New Testament exegesis, Schlatter distinguished biblical thought and its conceptuality from Greek thought, which had come thoroughly to dominate modern interpretation, and in 1906 (2d ed., 1910), in *Die philosophische Arbeit seit Cartesius*, battled idealism in theology. Then occurred the great change with *Karl Barth*[31] and *Friedrich Gogarten*.[32] Barth came from the school of Wilhelm Herrmann[33] (whom he has interpreted more and more according to his Schleiermacher side), and under the influence of Kierkegaard and Nietzsche.[34] Gogarten came from the school of Ernst Troeltsch. Strongly influenced by Dilthey, he struggled for a new understanding of history and was likewise under the influence of Kierkegaard and Nietzsche. In addition, both Barth and Gogarten were influenced by Fyodor Dostoyevsky.[35]

Everywhere, experiences of World War I had an effect, although they did not furnish the primary foundation. (Note the earlier movements of life reform, the youth movement, etc.) [D]

(*b*)[36] In any event, we define theology as a *positive science*. And just as no positive science can allow a philosophy to prescribe its object for it, but finds that object beforehand in the life-relation to it, so also theology. As every positive science is the elaboration of a prescientific knowledge already given in relation to the object itself, so also theology.[37] *What is its object*? [C]

According to the meaning of the term, *God* is obviously the object. But can God be made an object of scientific research?[38] Or, in what sense could God be such? But does actual theology—the biblical, historical disciplines, etc.—treat God as an object? [D]

*How is the object of theology to be defined*? How is it to be discovered?[39] Is it not simply to be read off from the actual work of theology,[40] that is, if theology consists of investigation into a specific sphere of objects? But how is it with *the* theology? Where is it located? In which of the disciplines into which it is splintered should we search for it and its object?[41] And would it perhaps be possible that in the actual doing of theology it would have lost its true object; in fact, that it would have no object at all, but would be a phantom, the residue of a primitive science, whose object has long since become an object of the secular sciences?[42] Can one simply say that Christianity is the object of theology? One may, perhaps, say so, but in what sense? [C]

How does one obtain possession of God? By treating *faith* in God and thus "bracketing" God? In that case, the object of theology would be "Christianity."[43] [E (perhaps also D)][44]

What is to be posited: *Christianity as a historical entity*, a historical occurrence, an item in the history of religion, of the spirit, of culture, in the visible past and present in institutions and doctrines, cults and ecclesiastical societies? And would theology be the science of what is posited, this spiritual- or culture-historical phenomenon?[45]

The answer is, clearly not; for theology is still and all a phenomenon that is part of this very Christianity. It belongs to the whole of Christianity and its history. It is borne by it and in turn defines it. It cannot stand above it, for as a history or philosophy of culture it would then have no *real* object. There would be something to be posited there, but not what establishes theology as a particular science!

The result would be a *philosophy of culture* making theology its object, which then would either relapse into an idealistic doctrine of science, or on the basis of a *naturalistic or historicistic empiricism* would construe theology as the ideology of particular sociological phenomena, explicable in terms of historical development. And here, as in idealism, the case would be prejudiced, since it would be assumed that there is but one existent—the world of the tangible, and but one science—natural science, biology, or sociology.[46] Here, of course, the object of all the other sciences would not be assigned them as in the idealistic system. They would be explained as ideologies which actually have no object at all.

If we reckon with the possibility that this applies to theology, then no prior settled assumption can substitute for theology's proof of identity. *Whether or not theology has any object must be demonstrated within theology itself.* Its object is not Christianity as historical phenomenon but what makes Christianity what it is, thus, what constitutes Christianity and theology itself. Or, put formally, the object of theology is that which constitutes what is Christian. What constitutes theology as such, and the manner in which it constitutes and articulates it in its specific character as science—this is what *encyclopedia as the self-reflection of theology* must show. Certainly it cannot do so from the outside as a science antecedent to theology but as a theological work itself, a work in which theology risks itself in the question whether it has an object peculiar to it and if so, whether that object can in fact be defined by theology in its work.

Theological encyclopedia is thus to be defined as *the answer to the question, What is theology?* And, of course, it is to be defined as a *theological task, in which theology reflects on itself regarding the object that constitutes it.* [C]

# 2

# The Object of Theology

## §4. The Question of *fides quae creditur*

Every[1] science is based on a prescientific relation to its object. It does not produce that relation but finds itself within it, explains it, expands it. [D]

Since[2] theology must originate in its object, or in its relation to the object as already given, then this object must be apparent when the question is raised concerning *the purpose* for doing theology. For theology does nothing else than explain in reflective fashion the prescientific relation to the object, and, in the interest of just that relation—as does every genuine science. This is its purpose. Its object is therefore not to be read off from the actual doing of theology—this may have gone astray—but from its why, its purpose. *How does this purpose appear in our actual situation?*

Theology is in the service of a church whose task is in any event proclamation, preaching, teaching. Students prepared in theology should be able to preach and teach. Theology would thus be the science of *right teaching*. So it is according to Piper and Barth.[3] According to Piper,[4] with this definition of its task theology is fundamentally distinguished from all other sciences. These sciences *seek* the truth, ever their task, while theology is already given the truth in the teaching of the church, and is merely to give it utterance corresponding to the time.

This is a *self-deception* resulting from the *ambiguity of the concept "truth."* If truth denotes disclosure of the object, and if the object of theology is disclosed once for all, then the task of *giving it timely expression* is not a scientific task at all, but an aesthetic, rhetorical, or practical-pedagogical one.[5] But if it is a serious scientific task—and this, of course, is what Piper intends—then what it makes clear is that its object is not at all disclosed but hidden, that theology certainly does not possess the truth, but searches for it as does every science.

Another explanation for Piper's opinion is that he overlooks the fact that "*the truth*," the "right teaching" he has in mind is *the object of theology*, not its result, its product. Theology asks, What is the correct teaching? It does not seek to produce it, but to render it intelligible.[6] The possibility of doing theology assumes an object and a relation to it just as does every other science. Just as *theology in a certain sense must already possess the so-called truth* in order to speak the truth about it, so natural science in a certain sense must already be in possession of nature, and historical science in possession of history, etc., in order to be able to say something true about it. In any event, every science seeks a specific, concrete truth, seeks to disclose a specific sphere of objects already disclosed in a prescientific way. The fact that the sphere of theology may be designated as "the truth"—or better, as right teaching—does not at all mean that theology as science already possesses its scientific truth.[7] *It seeks the truth concerning the "truth,"* concerning right teaching.

This then is clear: *Pure doctrine is not the correct theology*, but is rather its object to be discovered. The correct theology is not the pure doctrine, but must seek it, discover it. It does not "teach," but says what must be taught—and it can only do so because it is already instructed.[8]

If we wish to say of other sciences, of philosophy, for example, that they teach, then science and teaching are in that case identical. The correct philosopher would be the correct teacher. But what is odd here is that the object of theology itself is the "teaching." If, in addition, we wish to describe theology's scientific work as "teaching," then as teaching what is pure doctrine.

The situation becomes clearer when we keep in mind that the method of teaching in the church is proclamation, *preaching*. Theology thus searches for the pure doctrine by seeking to determine what should be preached. The sum of what the church or preaching proclaims may be formally described as faith, in terms of the *fides quae creditur* (the "faith that is believed"). Preaching clearly states: You must believe *this*! and the hearer asks, *What* should I, *what* may I believe? Theology would therefore have as its object the pure doctrine as the *fides quae creditur*, and it would be the task of theological encyclopedia to explain more precisely what this means, and how, on the basis of this object, the task, the basic concepts, and the articulation of theology are determined. [c]

On this view the *fides quae creditur* is not seen as an historical phenomenon to be established by the historian of dogma by bracketing the question of truth. Theology does not inquire into the *fides quae creditur* for purposes of orientation but in order to know what I should believe. Its intent is to understand what gives material support to the *fides quae creditur*, that is, to understand the *fides quae creditur* in its relation to its object. Thus, in order to understand it in that relation, it must also understand what is believed. [E (and D?)]

So then, does theology presuppose faith? Yes and no. Yes, since without faith theology would be meaningless. No, since faith is something that cannot be taken as a datum, a proposition.[9] If faith is determinative of existence, then it cannot be assumed to be something that can be controlled, for the purpose of which theology could be carried on. *Are* we then the justified, the reborn, the new persons, the new creation? Yet, genuine theology can only be done where faith is alive in it. But precisely because faith is evidenced in it, theology cannot assume faith as a datum. Faith can only be evidenced when and by venturing theological work.[10]

In any case, the result is that theology cannot be carried on as something we do out of curiosity or to earn a living, but as a work, a venture, in which we ourselves are at risk. But when done in this way, then it is certain that our existence must gain clarity and truthfulness through it. Then it is a work in which, by putting ourselves at risk, we gain ourselves in one way or another. If we fail as theologians, that must not simply mean theology is not for me (as when one fails at any other profession), but rather that there is no theology, and our work was a stage on the way toward truth. Still, it may be that in the work we will be assured that there is a theology, since we are theologians.

So again the question, What is theology? and in this sense, Is there a theology? "Encyclopedia" is a self-reflection that raises these questions and deals with them. [A]

## §5. Theology and Faith in Modern Theology

As the "pure doctrine" of theology, faith is clearly conceived as *fides quae creditur*, a doctrine that theology does not first produce or discover by dint of researching an object, but which is to be unambiguously established and interpreted in face of confusion with heresies, that is, a doctrine that is to be rendered intelligible to each generation so that proclamation in the church is possible. The[11] faith as *fides qua creditur* ("the faith by which it is believed") is thus dependent upon theology, which in turn is linked to the *fides quae creditur*.

Thus emerges the problem of theology and faith! What does *Johannes Wendland*[12] mean when he defines theology as the attempt to lay hold of the divine revelation in our thought-forms? He adds: "Religious faith precedes theology[13] and brings it about." In this definition, "religious faith" is clearly the *fides qua creditur*. In a typically modern way, Wendland wants to render faith independent of theology. Theology is added later,[14] and in essence is motivated by practical concerns—by the need for agreement among Christians,[15] or by interest in mission and apologetics.[16]

On this definition, theology views the believing subject as the object of analysis. It construes "faith" as a human attitude and works out a purely formal concept of faith with which Christianity and all religions agree. In this regard, Wendland unabashedly states that apologetics and the philosophy of religion must first show why religious faith is at all essential, necessary, and normal to human existence. Next, he states that through demonstrating a development, that is, through a comparison of religions and types of faith, it must be shown why Christian faith is superior to all other types.[17]

But if theology does not in essence belong to faith, what sense is there in doing it, since the practical reasons for it are obviously not sufficient? Theology becomes a science *about* faith, while it was once a science *for* faith. And as science *about* faith (the *fides qua creditur*) it no longer involves the *fides quae creditur*. It no longer establishes what true belief is but rather what true believing is.[18] [A]

While for Wendland the question of truth is actually eliminated from theology, for Wilhelm Bruhn[19] it makes its entry, but not, however, to be acknowledged as a question of the faith theology must serve. It appears as a question of the thinker who in an urge for self-preservation needs a unified worldview and would like to know whether as believer he may also be permitted to believe what he believes, who wants to have what he must experience confirmed by what he must think![20]

What is typical in all this is that when theology is no longer a science of the *fides quae creditur* and therefore has lost the question of truth, other sciences concern themselves with it—according to Wendland, the comparative study of religion; according to Bruhn, philosophy.

What an odd faith this assumes! It has an experience of God but has not yet broken through to God himself! It doubts, conceivably, though its doubt gives evidence that it is not faith at all. Such faith is surely not a real relation (of the person) to its object! This faith is only a worldly phenomenon, an experience as an object for thought, for the purpose of establishing whether something objective matches it. And on this view Bruhn already assumes what he intends to prove, that the experience of God actually achieves God, since he assumes that what is basically human is directly rooted in the divine.

But if we are actually speaking of God, then the mode of access appropriate to him must be conformable to him as the object of experience, the mode we call faith. If God is the object of faith and accessible only to faith, then a science apart from faith or *alongside* it can see neither God nor faith, which is what it is only by means of its object. For Bruhn, thought apart from faith attains the object of faith in a more authentic fashion than faith itself! For him, thought yields the evidence for truth. If there should be a science which speaks of God and faith, then it can only be a science from the perspective of faith. In a certain sense Bruhn's science is of course such a science, to the extent it assumes the divinity of the human. [c (perhaps also b]

On this view, the *fides quae creditur* is simply forgotten. Or, the objects of faith are interpreted on the basis of the *fides qua creditur*, just as in the rational system scientific objects are interpreted on the basis of the thinking subject. But we may still ask, Is the faith that is at issue here served by such a theology? Does not faith actually inquire after the *fides quae creditur*, that is, after whether it is actually related to what it believes, to God and Christ, as it does or should believe? It does not matter to me that my faith is the relatively highest. I want to know whether it is right, that is, I do not want to know whether my attitude may properly be described as religious faith, but whether I believe in what is right.[21] And the question is whether modern theology, oriented to the philosophy of religion, has any right to look condescendingly upon orthodoxy and rationalism, even upon catholic theology, which seriously concern themselves with proving that what one believes is true, that, for example, there *is* God, freedom, and immortality!

What then is apologetics supposed to do? If it should really give reasons for faith, then the question whether faith has a right to exist lies within its competence, and faith is dependent on it.[22] And from where does apologetics derive such right? From faith? In that case, faith is pulling itself up by its own bootstraps (which, by the way, it actually does in all apologetics). But if apologetics is rooted in a science apart from faith, how can it establish faith? [a]

Friedrich Schleiermacher wants to avoid the error of rationalism, of speaking scientifically about God apart from faith as the only possible mode of access to him.[23] He recognizes that God is given only to faith and for this reason speaks of faith. But since he assigns only faith[24] (and its effects[25]) to theology as its proper object, he overlooks the fact that faith is faith only by relation to its object, that faith can thus be spoken of only when God is spoken of.[26]

This is already indicated by the fact that in place of "faith" Schleiermacher uses the term "*piety*," so as to protect the religious character of piety from intellectualistic misconceptions.[27] And he takes pains to describe piety as a purely human attitude without relation to its object.

*Piety* is "*a modification of feeling, or of immediate self-consciousness.*"[28] Feeling is distinguished from knowing and doing by the very fact that it is deprived of relation to an object,[29] that its intentional character is denied. It is

> not only in its duration as a result of stimulation that it is an abiding-in-self: even as the process of being stimulated, it is not effected by the subject [so that the subject would be objective to itself and thus emerge from out of itself, R.B.], but simply takes place *in* the subject, and thus, since it belongs altogether to the realm of receptivity, it is entirely an abiding-in-self.[30]

Naturally, *piety* can stimulate a *knowing* or *doing*, but it is neither one. Knowing and doing hark back to a motive based upon a determination of self-consciousness, a feeling.[31] In fact, there are pious feelings that are pure states[32] "without regard to any knowing or doing that proceeds from them."[33]

According to Schleiermacher, all *self-consciousness* contains two elements: (1) consciousness of the self, and (2) consciousness of a variable state of being, thus a self-caused element, and a having-by-some-means-come-to-be. And, of course, in every outward-tending self-consciousness the element of receptivity, in some way or other affected, is the primary one.[34]

At the stage of "sensible" life subsequent to the life of the lower animals or the child, human existence lives in an alternation of the *feeling of freedom and dependence*, lives in the consciousness of this opposition. A feeling of absolute freedom is not possible, since every independent action assumes something given, independent of freedom. But there is also no absolute feeling of dependence, since one is conscious of a counter-influence upon every object in some way given to us.[35] In fact, *consciousness of absolute dependence* would mean that we would have to be conscious of all our spontaneous activity as "from a source outside of us," just as we know that what is given and affects our receptivity is "from a source outside of us." But over against any single part of the world as well as the world as a whole we know we are both dependent *and* free.[36]

The feeling of absolute dependence does not exist in a single moment as such, because such a moment is always determined by what is given, toward which we have a feeling of freedom:

> But the self-consciousness which accompanies all our activity, and therefore, since that is never zero, accompanies our whole existence, and negatives absolute freedom, is itself precisely a consciousness of absolute dependence; for it is the consciousness that the whole of our spontaneous activity comes from a source outside of us in just the same sense in which anything towards which we should have a feeling of absolute freedom must have proceeded entirely from ourselves.[37]

At the highest stage of human self-consciousness this feeling accompanies all other awareness of the antithesis of dependence and freedom, that is, the feeling that absolute freedom and thus freedom as such are denied us. This does not mean that as individuals who exist in this particular way we are dependent upon any other individual being, but rather *that we are individual finite existence*, so that in this feeling of absolute dependence all antithesis between one individual and another is done away.[38] But this feeling is always actualized in each moment of sensible self-consciousness, a consciousness aware of the antithesis of dependence and freedom.[39]

This feeling is an *original and innate tendency* of the human soul, and requires only development toward clarity.[40] It is the feeling that we do not exist on our own; it is alive *in the question concerning the whence*, our origin, a question, however, that cannot be answered by reference to the world, toward which we are of course both dependent *and* free.

This feeling is rather *the general and truly negative feeling of the whence as such*. For it is roundly denied that in this feeling we recognize someone else over against us. "God" is merely a name for the "*Whence* of our receptive and active existence, as implied in this self-consciousness."[41] For this consciousness no prior knowledge of God is required. The idea of God is "nothing more than the expression of the feeling of absolute dependence . . . the most direct reflection upon it." Self-consciousness—to which each person can and should arrive independently—includes the consciousness of God:

> The feeling of absolute dependence becomes a clear self-conscious-
> ness only as this idea [of God, R.B.] comes simultaneously into
> being. In this sense it can indeed be said that God is given to us in
> feeling in an original way; and if we speak of an original revelation of
> God to man or in man, the meaning will always be just this, that,
> along with the absolute dependence which characterizes not only
> man but all temporal existence, there is given to man also the imme-
> diate self-consciousness of it, which becomes a consciousness of
> God. . . . On the other hand, any possibility of God being in any way
> *given* is entirely excluded, because anything that is outwardly given
> must be given as an object exposed to our counter-influence, howev-
> er slight this may be.[42]

This corresponds with Schleiermacher's intent to understand the church as a religious community and as such to conceive it as "a necessary element for the development of the human spirit."[43] Reli-gious communities are understood as associations of individuals deriving from their generic consciousness. What is inward in the individual turns to the outside and becomes perceptible. The expres-sion of feeling

> does indeed at first arouse in other people only an idea of the person's
> state of mind. But, by reason of the consciousness of kind, this pass-
> es into living imitation; and the more able the percipient is (either for
> general reasons, or because of the greater liveliness of the expression,
> or because of closer affinity) to pass into the same state, the more eas-
> ily will that state be produced by imitation.[44]

Thus there is no appreciation for the historicity of human being and of life in community, and no possibility of understanding the "Word." [C]

Schleiermacher's analysis of the feeling of absolute dependence is not simply false.[45] He does, in fact, see *that God is not "given"*— neither a given of that type of world toward which I know I am so dependent that I oppose it in the feeling of freedom, nor a given within the feeling of freedom, in regard to which I may speak of the "*deus in nobis*" (as does, say, Bruhn).

Schleiermacher sees that we can only speak of God when we speak of our *existence*, and that this is given us only in the question, that is, is not really *given*. Of course, he does not see that we come no further than the *question* about ourselves and God, no further than to a *concept* of God, but not to God. He does not see that he is not developing the *Christian* idea of God that speaks of God's *action* toward us, but merely developing the assumptions from which the meaning of the Incarnation as the encounter of God with our world can be theologically understood. [E]

The theological development of the nineteenth and twentieth centuries carried through this concept of Christianity as religion, and of course as a spiritual, psychic, or cultural phenomenon. The disciplines of church history and the history of dogma view the pronouncements of church doctrine as individuations of Christian religious life under concrete historical, that is, causally intelligible, conditions. The history of religions treats Christianity as an instance of general religious history, occurring according to psychologically intelligible laws. All religions exhibit the same features,[46] for example, the formation of churches with rites and ascetic or moral regulations, with sacred scriptures, priesthood, and theology. In fact, they exhibit many of the same theologoumena, for example, creation and divine recompense, satisfaction, the doctrine of the dying and rising divine savior, eschatology, etc.

Thus Ernst Troeltsch (1865–1923) can construe theology merely as a branch of the science of culture, just as he can construe Christianity merely as one phenomenon within the history of religions. Religion, of course, based on the religious a priori, belongs to the life of the human spirit. But religion is an eternally evolving entity. Not even Christianity need be its final form, since it is not a unified phenomenon, but assumes very different shapes within the various cultural epochs. Even the gospel is a temporal entity, "nonetheless till now and indeed for a long time effectively the impulse of the weightiest, most adaptable, to a certain extent also the simplest and clearest religious movement history has produced."[47]

On this view, theology has a threefold task:[48] (1) historical-psychological understanding of Christianity in the framework of its developments and all of religious history; (2) the religious-philosophical elaboration of its experiences and concepts in connection with all elements of spiritual life, particularly with the highest ideas and convictions attainable in philosophy. Along with such a task theology would have to demonstrate the religious a priori and thus prove its right. (3) And finally, the task would involve critical fusion of the motifs of the Christian worldview with the worldview of the given culture, or of natural science, thus the elimination of old dogmas linked to an ancient geo- and anthropocentric worldview.

The romantic-pantheistic belief in the deity as immanent in cultural events helps transcend the otherwise inevitable conclusion that religion and Christianity are merely functions of human spiritual life.[49] Common to all religions are certain experiences of a mystical sort, in which the deity witnesses to itself with direct, tangible force. Whether everyone is conscious of this force is open to question. Believers are certain of it as a living experience; but it is irrational, a certainty only for the "trusting" spirit, a matter of dispute for whomever will not allow for it. And "the effect of deity on the soul is always combined with the total content of the soul or spirit in the given cultural situation."[50] [A]

Georg Wobbermin (born 1869)[51] wishes to avoid the consequences of this view by way of the *religious-historical circle*.[52] According to him, the *fides qua creditur* points toward the *fides quae creditur* and is only to be understood together with it, or, the former is to be understood on the basis of the latter. In this way the *fides qua creditur* is seen as the act or experience of faith that comprises one pole in an alternation, the other pole of which is the *fides quae creditur*, thus actually, God. But since God is not directly accessible (in God's transcendence), but rather is accessible only in his immanence, that is, in the historical revelation or the scripture,[53] theology, instead of attempting to understand God, must understand the objectivizing of religious life, researching the alternation between it and the subjective experience.[54] Thus, just as the *fides quae creditur* is taken to be a worldly phenomenon seen apart from faith, so also the *fides qua creditur*. Only then can the *fides qua* be understood as a "pole" in a reciprocal action,[55] for as the faith which believes, it is in fact itself the person's relation to God. "Our own personal conviction and experience of faith" are made the object of scientific investigation, so that by "taking them into consideration" the object of faith can be investigated,[56] while at the same time only faith itself sees that object.[57] If faith is made the object of scientific investigation and its "objective content" worked out, then this content is not its object. It can only be a complex of notions or ideas in a philosophical system.

Correspondingly, "the nature of theology as science . . . is conditioned by its position within the total scientific system."[58] "Its claim to being scientific can only be established with reference to the context of the sciences and on that basis."[59] Further, nothing is to be gained by conceiving the nature of science in "purely formal fashion," by limiting it to the form of scientific work.[60] For, beneath the individual sciences, and uniting them into a system, stands philosophy as logic (and epistemology), and over them again stands philosophy as (epistemology and) instruction in a worldview.[61]

According to Wobbermin, theology is on the one hand a separate science that must investigate a specific component of human life and history, that is, religion, and the Christian religion in particular. But beyond the scope of a separate science it must "pursue the interest of the Christian religion in a worldview"[62] and thus competes with philosophy.[63] "Theology's place in the system of sciences is thus indicated by the fact that it is a separate science within the human sciences, as well as a theonomic instruction in a worldview."[64] Theology is "the science of the Christian religion in its significance for religious life as such, or otherwise expressed, it is the science of the Christian religion with its claim to absolute truth."[65] [c]

## §6. Liberalism and Orthodoxy

The question, What is theology? is itself a theological question, or can only be treated theologically.[66] It is not to be answered apart from knowledge of the object of theology, which cannot be known apart from theology. Who else should supply the answer? Obviously not another science, any more than mathematics furnishes ethics its object or vice versa. Not even such a fundamental science as philosophy should do so. To say what theology is, it would itself have to be theology.[67]

Theology, therefore, can be defined only on the basis of its object, and its object is found in no other science than in theology. This object, clearly, is God, in some sense or other.

We cannot dodge the issue here and say that a science does not manifest this object, that it is rather life that furnishes it. That is correct, insofar as science naturally does not beget its object. But it does not mean that the object is inaccessible to a particular (that is, theological) scientific reflection. It is true of every science that it finds its object beforehand in a life-relation to it.[68] But here the question arises, Who readies the object for scientific discussion, who *speaks* of it? Moreover, the relation of science to life may not be prejudged. So, who says that life does not furnish it, if science does? The only question is whether science itself is a life-possibility.

Thus to deal with the question, What is theology? already means to do theology. And the peculiar problematic of nineteenth-century theology derives from the fact that it did not appreciate this. This is why it wants to subsume theology under a rational system, that is, wants to let philosophy tell it what it is. Or rather, in doing so, it does not define itself on the basis of its object but in purely formal fashion as a function of the human spirit. And in so doing it loses its object, an object that philosophy—which it allows to assign it its task and method—cannot see at all, since it has another object.

But if theology has lost its object, then it searches for another. It regards itself as its object, to the degree it intends to be a "doctrine of faith" in terms of an explicit development of the Christian worldview. That is to say, it regards as its true object the *fides qua creditur*, and of course distinguishes theology from faith and takes some pride in doing so.[69] To that extent it is a subsequent reflection upon faith, which it finds ready-made, as are other world-phenomena. It treats faith in, say, historical-psychological or religious-philosophical fashion, turning theology into a philosophy or an interpretation of history, an interpretation that proves to be theological by the fact that in it faith is conceived as an "essential, necessary, and normal" function of human existence. Now, to the extent that by so doing theology for its part develops a so-called worldview, but on the other hand construes faith as a motif within a worldview—a motif made explicit in theology as scientific inquiry or corrected by it and taken up as an ingredient into that worldview—and in this fashion "establishes" faith, to that extent *theology sets itself in the place of its object*.[70] Then it is itself "pure doctrine," a doctrine that demonstrates the right to believe, and thus confuses itself with its object.

If by this means theology has lost the *fides quae creditur*, it also misconstrues the *fides qua creditur*. It regards the *fides qua* as a human attitude to be examined without respect to its object. That is, it analyzes a false because purely formal concept of faith. The *fides qua creditur*, however, is what it is only with reference to its object, to the *fides quae creditur*. It does not *exist* by *itself*, as a human attitude, a human function, but solely as faith *in*, that is, in its object (this is its intentional character!). Let us say that the *fides qua creditur* has no object—something that would have to be determined by researching the problem of the *fides quae*. If that were true, it *would not exist* at all. Or, essential to the *definition* of the *fides qua creditur* would be *this*, that it is related to *nothing*. The problem, therefore, cannot arise from, say, elaborating on the nature of faith (for example, as numinous feeling, pious disposition or the like, and in neutrally descriptive, perhaps quite "phenomenological" fashion, tantamount to a pseudophenomenology), then asking whether it has any right to exist. Or, the problem of the relation of reality to the truth of faith cannot arise,[71] since the two cohere, just as the question of the reality of the perceived external world makes no sense, since perception is not a state of mind but perception of something or other.

The *fides qua creditur* is thus what it is only when understood as a relation to its object,[72] when it is not understood as a "capacity" or an

"attitude," something formless and timeless, but as a concrete historical attitude toward a particular object. When this is ignored, faith
becomes an object of psychology as a pious disposition or numinous
feeling, or an object of philosophy and the like as an ethical stance.
Basic theological concepts such as revelation and miracle are then
dissolved.

If, then, the question, What is theology? is a theological question,
since theology is defined by its object, by the *fides quae creditur*,
then what theology is can only be stated by reflecting on the *fides
quae creditur*. But if this is so, another danger threatens, signalled in
the description of the *fides quae creditur* as "pure doctrine." Then
there is danger of confusing "doctrine" with "doctrine," kerygma
with scientific theory, and[73] a doctrine appears as the object of faith
just as it is an object of study, that is, of theology.[74] In this instance,
theology has not confused itself with its object but confused its
object with itself. By making a theology of the *fides quae creditur,* it
does not set itself where its object belongs but sets its object where it
belongs, as in orthodoxy.

Theology confuses its object with itself when, for example, it
attempts to give a proof for faith (the *fides quae creditur*),[75] whether
by means of a natural theology, by arguing from reason, or from
authority, the scripture. For in so doing it renders faith a matter for
discussion, makes it a theology, the tenets of which can be discussed
in scientific fashion. In fact, it already does this when it refers to the
truths of faith as universal (not visible only in faith), as in the doctrine of the divine attributes or in the proposition that God created
the world. Orthodoxy also is accustomed to speak of a Christian
worldview,[76] but for it, that worldview is not a philosophy of history
or of religion but a sort of ancient metaphysics, of no value to anyone (for example, proof of miracles).[77]

Above all, theology confuses its object with itself when it uses the
*fides qua creditur* to require agreement with correct doctrine in terms
of specific ideas served up from somewhere or other,[78] without anyone's being able to generate or comprehend them on his own.[79] But
the orthodox position is especially clear in its rejection of criticism
in theology, thus criticism of scripture or dogma. From this derives

the lack of appreciation for science, which is by nature critical.[80] Now, since the *fides quae creditur* obviously cannot be accessible to scientific criticism, opposition to criticism indicates that the *fides* has been confused with theology. Otherwise, one would have to know that scientific criticism cannot at all reach the object of faith.

In its attitude toward biblical criticism, orthodoxy is especially concerned with proving the originality of scriptural teaching, as well as with contesting dependencies, for example, respecting the commandment of love. In this fashion it proves that it finds doctrines (equal to universal truths) in scripture.

But most of all, by confusing its object with itself, orthodoxy misconstrues the *fides qua creditur* by turning it into a resolve never to regard as true ideas that make sense.[81] This is in fact impossible, since wanting to believe that something is true is never the same as actually believing that something is true.[82] The *fides implicita* of the Catholic church is more honorable, since it admits this fact and believes in the authority of the church, which can involve real trust in the church. In orthodoxy the *fides quae creditur* becomes a human attitude, an abstract and formal thing, not at all related to its object. In fact, it *cannot* be related to a scientific doctrine, since one can only know (in the critical sense) but not "believe" a scientific doctrine. In orthodoxy, however, "faith" is required, with the result that it is not faith at all, since it is not a relation to its object but only the resolve to submit to a doctrine.

This aspect of orthodoxy is clearly expressed in the old Protestant doctrine of faith as *notitia*, *assensus,* and *fiducia*, whereas Melanchthon, "in treating the concept of faith in the *Apology*, could limit himself to the aspect of *notitia* or knowledge of the content of the doctrinal tradition, and to the aspect of *fiducia* or trust in this content."[83] The doctrine of the threefold nature of faith is an admission that *fiducia*, actual faith, is not an actual relation to its object.[84] If it were, it would also be the primary mode of access to the One who is disclosed to it as reality.[85] But when the *fides quae creditur* is no longer the object of faith but a scientific doctrine, then, of course, *assensus* must be interposed between *notitia* and *fiducia*.[86] Then the entire "theological" discussion is nontheological, since *fiducia* is added as an extra something to the knowledge and acceptance of pure doctrine. The result is that pure doctrine in theology is not developed as visible only to faith, thus within theology, because faith is not an element in it, and the object of faith is not determinative.

Hence, the two paths of liberalism and orthodoxy are in error because they are nontheological. In both the object does not determine theology, and for this reason both lose their object altogether.

The path of liberalism is in error because it imagines that it has the object of theology, subject to scientific analysis, in the *fides qua creditur*. The path of orthodoxy is in error because it imagines that it has its object, the *fides quae creditur*, apart from the *fides qua creditur*, thus because it imagines it can develop the *fides quae creditur* as universal truths.

The *fides qua creditur* can only be understood in relation to the *fides quae creditur*, otherwise it has no object and is not what it is. And the *fides quae creditur* can only be understood in relation to the *fides qua creditur*, since the *fides qua* is the only possibility of access to it. If it were not, if a theology *prior to* the *fides qua creditur* were the primary access to the *fides quae creditur*, then the *fides qua creditur* would in fact be superfluous. Then its object would not really be the *fides quae creditur*, but a theology or "pure doctrine" that requires its *assensus*, on which it must rely.

The task, therefore, is to define the nature of theology on the basis of its object, and within its only possible mode of access, on the basis of the *fides quae* and *qua creditur*. What God is cannot be understood if faith is not understood, and vice versa. Theology is thus science about God, since it is science about faith, and vice versa.[87] [C]

# 3

# Theology as the Science about God

## §7. Science and Truth[1]

In idealism's "theory of science," science is an awareness of self as knowledge, as spirit, not an awareness of something. It is a function of reason, not a being directed toward an object that yields disclosure.[2] By deriving all possibilities of knowledge from the idea of reason, since even those of being are thus derived, all objects are actually eliminated, understood on the basis of the subject, and being itself is derived from consciousness. By this means, then, science is a system of propositions, and truth an attribute of what is thought. And the motive for knowing, in this case no longer for knowing something but only oneself, is obviously a notion of existence that finds its authentic possibility in knowing.

Clearly, however, this is not the original meaning of knowing. The original meaning is that one wants to know *something*—since one lives in a world that is not reducible to "spirit"—and also that truth means disclosure of the object. The original purpose of knowledge is clearly guided by concrete occasions, by a purpose, for the sake of which one desires to know,[3] by the concern which motivates life.[4] [A]

*The concept of science* should not be *deduced* (reason) from a concept of spirit (reason) but gleaned from the observation of *Dasein* (human being), from the observation of self available to everyone and, of course, not from observation of the "inner" life of the mind but from that of actual total, everyday life, for the emergence of knowledge is a continual occurrence. Science is explicit knowledge given expression, raised to consciousness, a knowledge already present in converse with the given object. [c (perhaps also b)]

The human being exists as one who acts, who is responsible, and as such exists in the community as a *zōon politikon*. Science must thus have "political" significance. Naturally, the concept of the political may not be too narrowly conceived: (1) It must embrace the total sphere of activity in community. (2) It must embrace direct and *indirect* political activity.[5]

The question whether a science is political is thus not the question of its direct political usefulness. Usefulness is no criterion of truth.[6] [d]

In science knowledge is more and more loosed from its purpose, first of all by its being detached from its immediate purpose, so as to be available as general knowledge, and at any given moment made to serve some concrete purpose. The result is that science as a whole is guided by one purpose: the science of law on behalf of the state, medicine on behalf of the physician, mathematics and natural science on behalf of the technical professions.

This detachment can proceed still further.[7] Purpose is originally defined by a person's involvement, and through a person's concern. The occasions on which he wants to know are not mechanical impulses, as in a machine, but concrete life-situations in which he exists as alive and involved. Since it is within such concern that he gives shape to his world, in performance or in work, and learns to furnish means for eventual needs, it is possible for him to confuse concern for himself with concern for the world, and instead of caring for *himself* to care for his work, supposing that he is caring for himself. He understands himself on the basis of what he makes or achieves.[8] As a shoemaker takes his name from making shoes, so a scientist from creating science, writing books.[9] Science has become an end in itself, and if one wishes to understand or give a reason for it, one calls it a cultural value. On this view, culture is conceived as the total work, the person's total achievement. It has become an idol, because it devours his real life, and the question, To what purpose? is answered by referring to an abstraction, to human-*ity*.[10] Knowledge is then a something, which, when it has lost its relation to life, understandably also loses its objects, since these are given only for life itself.[11] And with this has occurred a misunderstanding of one's own existence, to the extent that life is viewed as something over which one has control, something to be secured through cultural work, made independent of event. Objects are seen merely as standing still for observation, not as they first encounter us, not as the plurality of possibilities for my acting and suffering, for my deciding.[12]

The act of *observation*, of course, has its basis in the nature of *Dasein* as originally motivated by authentic concern. Compare the way in which a botanist observes a plant with that of the owner of a garden. To a degree, the first type of observation is already contained in the second; and since there are conditions under which interested observation requires the entire scientific apparatus, science is clearly rooted in *Dasein*.[13] But in such instances *Dasein* can be led by what it makes, and science is thus loosed from its purpose. Then science no longer has interest in the factual, the contingent, but in the universal, and construes the individual as an instance of the universal. [A]

The *concern* that motivates *Dasein* is the primary impulse of science as well as of culture per se.[14] When concern is applied to work, one's concern for himself becomes concern for his work, the purity of concern is destroyed, and that genuine concern with which the person should come face to face is lessened. Without further ado, *concern for culture* is taken to be legitimate; and when genuine concern—even if only primitive—awakens, the human is directed toward culture.[15] Past the person, human-*ity* is to be made happy.[16]

Actually, *culture* is not for all, since it cannot be. But one should not be deceived about the fact that *civilization* is for all, which in turn makes "culture" serve a purpose,[17] as it honestly should. Even the person who does not share in a culture has something of civilization—the worker, for example, who can go to the cinema instead of the pub, etc.

Where there is genuine concern, the person does not need culture. But he does need civilization, since the principal concern is
to preserve his life.[18] The possibility that culture may originally
have emerged from genuine concern is another matter.[19] [C (perhaps also D)]

This development is heightened by the fact that detachment of
knowledge from its purpose also occurs where it allows itself to be
ruled by curiosity. Here too we arrive at knowledge for its own sake,
at Wagner's confession, "I know much now, but I fain would know
all."[20] That idea of "knowing everything" makes the misunderstanding of one's own existence most evident, insofar as our existence is
actually never complete, but historical, for which reason our knowledge can never be complete. Here too it is clearest that there is no
longer any life-interest in the factual, the contingent, for what is factual can never be known in its entirety. Hence, the ideal of "knowing
everything" can only be held up when a person imagines he is standing securely outside of life, life then passing in review for his observation, and thus where he is buried alive, though only in books.[21]

Such curiosity, already observable in the child or the primitive,
stems from the same impulse as the transfer of self-understanding
from living existence into work, that is, from the flight from oneself.[22]

Thus organized science, culture, as soon as it is taken for an idea
that is beyond life and master of it, is the human's organized flight
from himself.[23] Science is an entity over against the person, toward
which he takes flight or to which he yields. In such science, truth is
the universally binding character of its propositions, a universality of
no concrete concern to anyone who does not use it for practical purposes, that is, in a technical interest.

The relation of this science to its objects consists in observing at a
distance.[24] The person, standing outside of life, looks about, as it
were, for what he can manage scientifically, or he lives uncritically
by the tradition from which he extracts the alleged "values" of art,
science, etc. [A]

What is making itself felt today—and often still unclear—is the
awareness that the relation to things, thus science and culture as

such, is and must be conditioned by *one's link to one's nation*.[25] This is correct, insofar as a person normally grows up in a family and national community, and insofar as this community gives the person a relation to things.[26]

For example, one obviously studies German history to understand himself and the possibilities and necessities of his action. History as abstract science knows nothing of such limits. But concrete science is bound to its purpose. Thus, the study of foreign history, of Greek history, for example, is required to the extent it explains the current situation. The concept of nationality interrupts the purely abstract and endless inquiry of science. Of course, one should not wish to regulate this through statutes, but must allow the tension to exist. For example, there is considerable debate as to whether the study of early German history is essential to a knowledge of German history in the service of Germany today.[27]

Further, the idea of nationality may not be counterfeited in romantic or historicistic fashion. That is, a more precise definition of nationality may not be gained by comparing it with other nationalities. We can surely say that to be German means to be true. This is not an empirical statement but a summons. We can never make being German a criterion for action, only for being true.[28] One should strive for freedom, truth, justice, purity, nobility on behalf of one's nationality. But this goal is a requirement for members of other nationalities as well. It is obvious that something specifically German derives from German activity; it cannot be manufactured. The question of the national character of science must also be considered from this point of view.[29] [D]

Our natural science and thus our concept of "nature" have been shaped to view the world around us *insofar as* it is perceived through our observation, but not in itself. The shape given this observation has then led to regarding humans and their life as a part of nature, or as a natural process. This is true not only of materialism, to the extent that history is consciously construed as a natural process, but even in the human sciences, to the extent that history is interpreted as the great nexus of cause and effect in, say, psychological or economic fashion, or when it is treated biologically or morphologically.[30]

Conversely, what Goethe knew derived from his life-relation to an existing thing: "We learn to know only what we love, and the deeper and more complete that knowledge is to be, the more powerful and vital love, yes, passion must be." Max Scheler[31] parallels Goethe's word with a line from Leonardo: "Every great love is daughter to a great knowledge."[32] He contrasts these words, affirming the deepest relation between life and knowledge, though in opposite ways, with the "specifically modern bourgeois[33] judgment that love renders one 'blind' rather than seeing, that consequently all true knowledge of the world . . . can rest only on the extremest repression of these emotions and on the simultaneous disregard for the differences in value between the objects." To this, Scheler opposes a word from Pascal: "Love and reason are one and the same."[34]

The view of the relationship between knowledge and love differs among Indians and Greeks. But it is alike in this respect: Ontologically, values are functions of being; noetically, love is a dependent function of knowledge.[35] Love is thus construed intellectualistically. The reverse is true in Christianity. There, love establishes knowledge, a thought never developed in a clearly systematic way in "Christian" philosophy, not even in Thomas; at best in Augustine and Augustinianism (Malebranche, Port Royal, Pascal). Whereas for *Thomas* every function of the appetitive capacity (the *vis appetitiva*) must be preceded by an act of understanding (the *vis intellectiva*); every arousal of desire by the presence of a *species sensibilis* in sense perception; and every volition by an act of purposeful knowledge that seizes hold of the conceptual nature of a thing—so that love and hate are described merely as variations on the *soul's* capacity for *striving*—for *Augustine* both knowledge as well as aspiring and willing are rooted in love. "*Volo ergo sum*," according to which "*volo*" denotes love and taking an interest as the most elemental tendency of the human spirit.

There can only be genuine knowledge where it is defined by its object,[36] where truth spells disclosure of that object. But being defined by the object belongs to knowledge only where knowledge is not appended to life as an added reflection but is itself grounded in the person's relation to the object. Or, this relation is a being *togeth-*

*er with*, the relation to the object thus becoming apparent in the person and made explicit through knowledge. For in fact, knowledge is not something that begins abruptly at some time or other. Rather, *Dasein* is always astir in a provisional, vague knowing that is involved in any relation to some thing. *Dasein* itself can make this provisional discoverability of the world its own by applying itself to knowledge. Knowledge is genuine, however, only when it[37] is not absent from *Dasein*'s relation to the existing thing. But knowledge is always *Dasein*'s knowledge, since it is historical, not a natural event making its way through the here and now. The beast has no knowledge because it lives only in the here and now, passes through time, without itself being temporal. A man's here and now can be determined by past and future. This possibility is given in knowledge of himself and his world, that is, when the content of his here and now becomes objective in knowledge and can be held to and related to what is to come.[38]

But if the aim of knowledge is to disclose the object in this relationship, and thus to have truth, objectivity, it is clear that objectivity (as such) may not be defined by *any* specific science with its specific relation to specific objects, thus by any mathematical-mechanical[39] natural science.[40] Objectivity means something different at any given moment. Or, it means that *truth generally* has *the meaning of claim*, the claim of the object upon us. Not mathematics but appropriateness determines precision.[41]

True knowledge is thus not something added subsequently to life, but part of life itself. Materially, then, science is not something only a few possess. It is an attitude of *Dasein* directed toward a particular purpose.[42] It cannot be constructed outside a living relation to objects as some universally valid method toward which all knowledge of an object would have to be directed. Rather, its method denotes its appropriateness to the object, hearing the claim of the object. Thus, where genuine knowledge is involved, *a contrast between living and knowing* does not exist. Where it does exist, there is false knowledge, a knowledge no longer aware of its object, be it empty speculation or a tradition uncritically accepted, thus a seeming knowledge, so long as it is not critically tested by the object.[43]

Conversely, *life* can go astray in "business," for example, and communal life (in traditions and conventions) can distance itself totally from genuine community, even while knowledge can contain a genuine relation to the object, so that even knowledge can critique life.

From the outset, however, knowledge can distance itself from life by lifting what exists and encounters us to the sphere of the objective. By this means it preserves it and "knows" it, even when there is no longer any actual relation to it. Knowledge is thus handed on, and is in turn always in need of criticism from the viewpoint of the object. But knowledge itself does not function in answer or address, only in general propositions. [A] The criterion of truth is not given in individual, subjective relation to the object, but in the object itself.[44]

Precisely for this reason science can critique "life," in which judgments tested by the scientific examination of objects have become fixed through traditions. For science, "truth" is not what is decisively won but rather the claim of the object. This is the "liberalism" inseparable from science![45] [D]

But this is the shape of the question that arises as to purpose: What is truth? In this shape, the intent is not to know about truths but *the* truth. Since science assumes responsibility for this question, it in fact subjects *Dasein* and its understanding to the same detached examination as its other objects, as though apart from *Dasein* it could examine it from outside. In such fashion it ignores the fact that *Dasein*'s concern is at base a concern for the here and now, that the question about the truth is the question as to how I understand myself, and of course, since *Dasein* is temporal, historical, the question as to how I understand the moment.

Clearly, an empirical science cannot answer the question, What is truth? It can put this question only with respect to its sphere of objects. But the meaning of this question takes on clarity from another aspect. If every science has its truth because it has its sphere of objects, and if truth always spells disclosure of the object, then there are as many truths as there are possible spheres of objects.[46] None of them answers the question, What is *the* truth? because this question is always raised and can only be answered by *Dasein* itself.

All truths are only in the service of the one question concerning *the* truth, insofar as *Dasein* intends to understand its world—that object over against it—in order to understand itself.

*But* the question *cannot even be put* by these empirical sciences, since, rightly understood, the question is always *Dasein*'s question concerning its here and now, a question that cannot arise within the compass of any science whose propositions are timeless. It is an error to ask of natural or historical science, What is truth? and *Dasein* errs if it thinks it can master the question put by the here and now by means of timeless truths.[47]

In general, *truth* denotes *the disclosure of the object.*[48] This implies that truth is "universally valid," that is, that everyone who sees the object under discussion must see it *just as* I do,[49] must speak of it *just as* I do, assuming we are seeing and speaking of the *same* object. Naturally, one can see the object from various aspects or can accent what is different in it. But if there is a difference attaching to that object, then what is determinative or essential in it, what it is, must be seen; whatever is different must hold true of *it*, be understood of *it*.

By itself, however, *universal validity* does not mean that each must see the object in question.[50] Such validity is not an empirical fact; it does not consist in everyone's seeing the object. Rather, it denotes the fundamental fact that all *who* do see it, must see it as it is.

*Mathematical propositions* are universally valid truths for all who can think mathematically. Obviously, mathematical thought does not have its object in what is beautiful. *Propositions concerning the beautiful* or a work of art, if true, are also universally valid; otherwise the work of art is not seen for what it is.[51] We should not allow ourselves to be deceived by the fact that very different things may be said of, say, a statue. But apart from its being a work of art, a statue can be seen in still another regard: As an object available for use, whose proportions can be evaluated mathematically, its material chemically or economically. In that case, another object is seen (constituted in the seeing). Even aesthetic judgment may differ, but when, for example, a classicist or romanticist judgment of a Greek statue differs from an impressionist judgment, it is due to the fact that in the one or other instance the work of art is not seen in its true essence—or it is not seen as a whole, which means that it is constituted a new work of art within a new aesthetic perspective. It may be that the work of art is no longer entirely accessible, but in any case, judgments that see it as it is agree.

So too, *judgments of faith* regarding its object do not differ from scientific judgments because they are "subjective," so that in contrast to the scientific concept of truth that concept would be relativized in the thinking of faith.[52] At bottom, the truth of faith is as universally valid as the truth of science, and the "subjectivity" of judgments of faith can only mean that the object of faith is not "universally" accessible, or not accessible to methods to which earthly phenomena are not[53] visible. If God is not made accessible through physical research, the knowledge of God is no more "subjective" than the knowledge of "history," which is also closed to physics. But this does not mean that any and all statements about God are true.

If in its universal validity the truth of knowledge rests on the object's being seen as it *is*, then we can say that "*truth*" as disclosure of the object makes a *claim* on knowledge: In order to know an object, I must recognize it as it is and as it shows itself. Hence we may speak of the *claim of truth* since in fact the question concerning the object always arises from *Dasein*'s being motivated by concern. Because *Dasein* acquires knowledge through such motivation, it indicates that it is dependent on the self-disclosure of objects; that it does not have itself at its disposal, but is dependent upon its world, and must hear its claim in order to understand its situation in the moment. The claim of every truth becomes audible in the claim of the moment. And the disclosure of the moment can be described as *the* truth, in the interest of which I will or must always know a truth.

There are as many truths as there are objects or spheres of objects that can be disclosed. The question: *ti estin alētheia* (John 18:38) is not about the truth of a sphere of objects and is not answered by pointing to something true. The question, What is truth? is raised as soon as *Dasein* is rendered insecure in its naive understanding of self and the world, when it sees that an understanding of the here and now does not dawn with knowing some individual thing with which

it is dealing. The question, What is truth? indicates that in a certain
sense truth belongs to *Dasein* itself. *Dasein* inquires about truth,
because it must understand itself in order to be with itself, to arrive
at its authenticity, and this also means—since *Dasein* is always
action—in order to know whatever it is I should do. It does not
inquire after truths, but after the truth: *A pollē spoudē* is awakened,
*to alētheias idein pedion hou estin.*[54] That is, *Dasein* inquires after a
view that discloses to it an uncluttered sight of the world and life as
they really are.

Does *Dasein* find *the* truth by finding *all* truths? by gathering
from them a picture of the world as a whole? This was the procedure
in the *Enlightenment* and in *positivism*. It makes sense that *Dasein*,
in order to understand itself, should first turn to the world to understand *it*. From the outset, *Dasein* lives in a world and must understand it, so as not to stand blindly in it. So we can appreciate the
notion that one must know as much as possible, and everything if
possible. If we know everything, then we can no longer err, hit a sour
note. On this view, human action is conceived as a technical skill
that assumes thorough knowledge of the material and the rules, and
is carried out with confidence. And all activity is understood as "producing something," not as an activity in which the I *develops* or
comes to itself. It is rather assumed that the I is always with itself,
exists authentically, and that science can see and understand this
*Dasein* from the outside. [C (perhaps also B)]

In the Enlightenment and in positivism, the question about *the*
truth is basically eliminated, since *Dasein* is no longer aware of the
question concerning its authenticity. In that case I do not need
knowledge to understand *myself* but in order to know something.
The question, What is truth? can then only be raised as a question
about some particular truth. It is the question concerning what is
practical, what ensures success, success then is no longer subsumed
under the question about the truth. [D]

In the Enlightenment and in positivism, the question of *alētheia* is
the question concerning the condition of what is available for use,
even of myself as available for use, with specific attributes, and when
knowledge of such truth is expanded and completed, the here and

now has lost all problematic. I know why I do what I do. But I no longer ask, What should I do?[55]

But the original meaning of the question, What is truth? as related to the claim of the moment, is the question, What should I do? assuming that now it is I who am involved, that I become something through my acting. The *whole* truth, *my* truth, is in question. I want to understand *myself*. Thus in *Hellenism* and in *idealism* the question is of *alētheia* as the norm for individual life. In light of *alētheia*, of the disclosure of world and life, individual life should be lived in accordance with unveiled reality. Here too *Dasein* turns first to the *kosmos* but under the assumption that it is understood, so that one need not know all possible truths but only *one*, the truth that makes the *kosmos* a *systēma* and in this way gives to it as well as to me its reality. And, of course, the question of *alētheia* here is guided by the assumption that I have the *alētheia* in me, and must look into myself to find it: *gnōthi seauton*—know thyself. For what gives to the world as well as to me its reality is the *logos*, reason, spirit. To know it, I need not know all truths, but only one, from which all truths derive, a truth that gives to all being, even to my own, its reality.[56] The *alētheia* that is to determine my individual activity is, on one hand, the disclosure of my own authentic being, thus of that which I in fact intend; on the other, it is embraced in the *logos*, in thought. Thus for Hellenism as for idealism knowledge of *alētheia* and the activity that corresponds to it are so intertwined that where there is knowledge, action necessarily follows. *Alētheia* is finally the disclosure of my own *Dasein*, under the assumption, of course, that this disclosure is communicated to me in the *logos*, that in it I should and am able to arrive at authentic *Dasein*. But my truth is revealed in the *logos* in such a way that turning to the world the *logos* views it as a unity, as springing from an *archē*. To understand the world as unity, then, means to know its meaning, and this meaning is also mine, for I am a part of the entire *systēma*, of the *kosmos*.

In Hellenism and in idealism, the *logos* speaks in all speaking but arrives at self-recognition in science. Science thus takes on responsibility for the question, What is truth? Indeed, not the empirical sciences, not empiricism, but philosophy. Philosophy claims it can answer the question concerning the claim of the moment and must therefore lift the moment from the sphere of the finite and temporal into the sphere of the eternal, the timeless, into the sphere of the idea.

The Greek and idealistic answer can hold true only so long as *the I* is understood *as a phenomenon* of the *kosmos*. Then the question, What is truth? can be answered by pointing to a timeless truth, to a timelessly valid law, or it can be eliminated as meaningless, since "everything" is true, because everything that happens must happen.

But if *Dasein* is *temporal-historical*, always involved in the here and now, and in that here and now does not choose one among the possibilities offered to it, but (in doing this also) is always seizing hold of its own possibility—if for this reason, *Dasein*'s existence is an existence that is *able to be*, since each here and now is in essence new; and, if in this very moment *Dasein* takes on meaning, that is, through deciding, thus not from some timeless interpretation of the world—then the question of truth has meaning only as the question of the *one truth of the moment*, my moment.

Science therefore cannot answer the question, What is truth? Or is there a science that can do so, a science such as *philosophy*? Does it not ask, *What is being human*? and is not this question finally synonymous with, What is truth?

On the other hand, is not *theology* such a science, if it is to treat the *question of God*, if *God* is to be its object?[57] For what else is the query about God if not the question, What is truth? If the question of truth is put as a question concerning the moment, can it be anything else than the question about God, who, if thought of at all, is thought to be the power in control of the here and now, the claim audible in the here and now?

These questions shall be dealt with first by clarifying the question concerning theology as the science of God and by explaining its relation to existence-philosophy.[58] [C (perhaps also B)]

## §8. God's Unknowability

If the question, What is truth? is a question about God, then God cannot be the object of an empirical science which, based on *Dasein*'s primary relation to its world, elaborates the understanding given in this relation, and sets down and furnishes knowledge of its object in general statements. If the question, What is truth? is the question of the claim of the moment ever stirring in it, then it can only be answered by me in the here and now, for the claim is always new.

Thus, where science is concerned, God is unknowable. This unknowability does not mean that "God" as object would be too vast for our knowledge, too comprehensive, too incalculable, that *our knowledge would be "inadequate."*[59] Let there be no frivolous talk of God's unknowability![60]

God is not a whole or partial *X*, so that our ignorance of God would have the character of an ignorance of certain hidden things, of a certain world behind or above. In that case, knowledge of God would at bottom be conceived as knowledge of the world, and the insufficiency of our knowledge of the world would be confused with knowledge of God.

Questions such as how God makes or has made this or that, why this or that is such, misconstrue the idea of God and search for an intelligible world-principle, an *archē*, which renders the world intelligible. But a world-principle is itself a world. And when we do not find such a principle, and the world remains entirely obscure, this does not indicate a lack in our knowledge of God, but in our knowledge of the world. [D]

Further, what is *"unconditioned"* can only imply a world-principle,[61] and, of course, the question concerning the unconditioned (thus not concerning an unconditioned truth, requirement, etc.) does not imply the question about a reality but about an idea. The idea of the unconditioned is an abstraction or limiting concept. In fact we only know that what is individual and conditioned is real; and insofar as we know we ourselves are conditioned, we arrive at a limiting concept of the unconditioned. This concept is actually nothing more than the negation of ourselves and the attempt to construe all that is conditioned in its totality and unity as unconditioned. It is also the attempt to understand ourselves as unconditioned, to the extent we are taken up into the totality.[62] To the extent we do not have the idea of the all or unconditioned in sight, but have it merely as a logical concept, the idea of the inadequacy of our knowledge can re-emerge. But it means nothing more than that we have no experience or sight of the unconditioned, and has nothing to do with a knowledge of God. [A] It means that because we ourselves are world we cannot get "behind" the world, cannot get a sight of it as a totality. [E (perhaps also D)] Another term for the unconditioned can be the *eternal*. This term is likewise available to us only as a limiting concept, since we know only temporal creatures to be real.[63] The idea of the eternal would merely express the opposite of what we are and would not be.

Of course, if we understand the *idea of the unconditioned or the eternal as expressing a summons*,[64] then we are aware of being under the summons to abandon a life driven by instinct in the isolated here and now, to be independently and freely something for ourselves. If we understand it as the idea of our responsibility as that of the here and now in face of the future,[65] then, of course, we grasp the reality of our existence. [A (perhaps also D)] But this only means that we are under a summons, not in control of ourselves, no more in doing than in thinking. But this does not yet have God in view.

The idea of the unconditioned as an *unconditional requirement* is also a merely *formal idea*. It means that we are aware of being unconditionally summoned at any given time, that what we are answerable to is unconditioned.

In the idea of the unconditioned nothing is said of a concrete summons or responsibility. And it is useless to want to make what is unconditional visible as a "highest good" or "highest value." We experience the unconditional summons in our *conscience*. But conscience does not give us any visible, ethical principle or table of values. In each moment it tells us that we should do what we have come to know is good, or that we should recognize what at any given time is good, is required. [D]

At any rate, it is[66] a mistake to hypostatize the idea of the unconditioned and eternal lodged in our awareness of that summons, and to regard it as God.[67] "It is not the eternal that saves us, but God who is master of the temporal and eternal."[68] [A]

Thus, insight into the impossibility of our understanding the world as a totality is still not an awareness of God, if it means the impossibility of our laying hold of destiny or our admission that the world is a mystery because we distance ourselves from nature and yet are woven into it (hunger and love, sickness and death); because we shape history and yet are trapped in it (fate); because we will the good and yet are entrapped in guilt. [E]

This mysteriousness is not God, and the anxiety threading through our life is not fear of God. If "terror" is "humanity's best part," it is because humanity can have in it a deep grasp of itself, but not of God.

Then too, the *irrational* is not identical with God.[69] For again, it is only a limiting concept.[70] If it should simply mean that God is not the object of rational knowledge, then it is of course correct. But the irrational is a purely formal concept and refers to nothing else than the unknowable.[71] There is no reason or justification for calling it God. But to the extent it denotes more than something merely formal, it indicates the riddle we ourselves are. And if we pass off this *X* as God, then the devil really has us by the throat. For the qualities of the *tremendum* and of the *fascinosum* suit the devil as well as God. [A]

The frequent, popular expression (stemming from mysticism) that God is the incomprehensible, inexpressible One, etc. overlooks two facts:

(1) The concept of the incomprehensible, inexpressible, etc., is by all odds a concept of something thought. To be able to think of the incomprehensible, etc., what is comprehensible, etc., must be thought along with it, and God simply conceived as its negation. So it is meaningless to speak of God without qualifier as the incomprehensible One. What this means is that he is not primarily accessible through reason, that "by way of reason his actual essence can neither be fathomed nor his right confirmed."[72] [Again Heidegger:]

This can in fact be what is incomprehensible and never accessible through reason, but at the same time need not rule out its being conceived. On the contrary, if incomprehensibility as such is to be appropriately disclosed, then this occurs only by means of proper and comprehensible exposition, that is, an exposition that also thrusts toward its limit. Otherwise, incomprehensibility to a certain extent remains mute.[73]

(2) Barth:[74]

> Do not let us think poorly of thought; do not let us share in the anti-
> intellectualism of these days! We cannot act without thinking! The
> great demand that the mercy of God imposes on us is primarily the
> demand of right thought, of a knowledge out of which then the right
> action must come! Repentance means: Effect must be given in our
> thought to the knowledge—which puts our will in motion—that we
> have to be thankful to God.

So, regarding talk of God's incomprehensibility, we must ask,
How is it meant?[75]

(1) Is it to be taken as the incomprehensibility of an available substance? Then it is meaningless, since God is conceived as world, and
hence is not spoken of at all.

(2) Is it to be taken as the incomprehensibility of the idea of God?
Then it is just as meaningless, for whatever is spoken of must in
some sense be understood. So we are either speaking of incomprehensibility as such—in which case we are not speaking of God—or
we have already conceived the incomprehensibility of God precisely
as God's.

The question, What is truth? is no more a question about *a* truth or
truth as such, and not of the truth of the moment, than God's incomprehensibility is the incomprehensibility of something or as such,
and not of the incomprehensibility of the moment!

(3) Is God's incomprehensibility to be taken as the incomprehensibility of the present moment in its whence, why, and wherefore?
Then it is taken correctly! But such incomprehensibility is not what
is usually meant in talk of God's nonrationality. Mysticism actually
wants to avoid awareness of God in the concrete, temporal here and
now. It wants to divest the present moment of its temporality. [B]

The fact that science cannot speak of God, cannot make God an
object of research and knowledge, simply means that *God cannot be
made an object of our conduct.*[76] We can no more act directly upon
God, making him an object of our activity, than we can make him the
object of our thought. God does not "hold still," as it were; he *is not
at our disposal.* God is no longer God when conceived as an object

apart from thought or over against it. When we think of God in the authentic sense, we think of the Almighty who determines our existence absolutely, or we do not think of him at all. Then, to be able to think of him, we would also have to be able to dispose of our existence, take a position over against it.[77] But, of course, we also exist in such an act, or in the imagining of it.

This character in God, that he *cannot be disposed of or controlled*, is thus not an accidental quality, as of some existent thing that cannot be mastered.[78] This fact *also* spells *one's inability to master oneself.* The human being is subject to God; he is not his own master.[79] He is never free of God, never left to himself so that he could make himself his object. He *is* only as existing.

But this means that he is his own object only insofar as he is also his subject;[80] that is, *he must always seize his existence* in the decision of the moment. In the moment that summons him, God summons him. God's unknowability does not result from the faulty organs of human knowledge, but from human *temporality*. The riddle of the moment is that I *do not know the future.* But not knowing the future is not like not knowing some dark, unexplored space. For the future is *my* future; the time is my temporality. The future brings me to myself as lost or won. Man *is* temporal and does not allow temporality to run past him like a room through which he strides.

It is in the *stoic* concept of God that knowing God means to be master of the moment. [E]

Actually, on this view, the *Stoa* supposes it has an adequate knowledge of God, since it thinks it knows what answer each moment requires. It is aware of eternity, of course, that is, as the timeless nature of Spirit. To decide in favor of this Spirit, and that means in favor of inner freedom toward whatever one encounters, is the meaning of the moment which is ever the same.[81] In a formal sense, both the Stoa and Christian faith could say:

> Nothing can happen to me,
> but what he has ordained,
> and what is good for me.[82]

But in each case the meaning is different, since for the Stoa there can never be encounter with something new. What is specific in the moment is reduced to the universal. I always know how I must decide (*anechesthai* and *apechesthai*) and can encounter nothing new. In Christianity the question of the moment is always new. It has dawned on me that the idea of my inner life as at my disposal is false. This coheres, first, with that other concept of the Thou, always encountering me in the moment, and second, with the concept of freedom—which for the Stoa means that I can master my inner life, am independent of something other than myself, while for Christianity it is precisely *this* freedom that is called into question.[83] [D]

The question, however, is whether the Stoa really understands human existence. It is mastery of the moment that actually eliminates what is specific in the moment. In *mysticism*, too, knowing God means to be master of the moment, since it wants to possess eternity in the moment. But by divesting the moment of its temporality and thus annihilating it, it robs it of its character as moment.

The knowledge of God is the *knowledge of the summons of the moment*. Its call becomes audible as the moment's summons to us. God is invisible to the objectifying research of science.

Is God visible in the summons of the moment!? Here, of course, is where God *should* be visible! But *is* he?[84]

Can we clearly hear the summons of the moment? We know that we are summoned by the moment. But the voice of *conscience* tells us only *that* we are summoned, whereas it is in wagering that we must discover *what* it is to which we are summoned. And we cannot ourselves judge whether we have chosen rightly. A "good conscience" is only the absence of a bad conscience, not a positive phenomenon.[85] The "bad," accusing conscience remains, or there is continual uncertainty.

The fact that the truth of the moment encounters us in conscience as a summons, as a "thou shalt!" as an appeal that calls us back to ourselves from being lost to the world, indicates that we are not open to the truth of the moment but must continually seek it in conflict with ourselves.[86] In the desire to possess a conscience the human

decides to be himself on his own responsibility; he decides to prepare for guilt.[87] But this means that he recognizes the obscurity of
the moment and even in this darkness dares to be himself. In the
moment he does not hear God but himself.

Precisely since it is in conscience that the human is called back to
himself, he does not hear God. The call of the moment is indictment
and summons, not comfort and fulfillment.[88] Actually to become
aware of God in answering the summons of the moment is an idealistic notion. It is Christian conviction that God is not heard in the
summons. Or, the summons of the moment as *God's* could only be
the summons openly to receive the *grace* of the moment. The truth
of the moment could only be its intelligibility as *gift*. An attitude that
is open to God could only be what Christianity calls *faith*.

This is likewise clear when we consider that the call of the
moment is not only to action but also yields *destiny*. As such a
moment, it asks whether we can affirm this destiny as our own, can
receive it as gift through which we come to be, whether we meet it
with reservation, with selection, criticism, rejection. It would mean
to see God in the moment, when our willful self would be silent and
we let ourselves be brought to ourselves by God alone. This would
assume a total surrender of ourselves: *hē gar dynamis en[89] astheneia
teleitai . . . dio eudokō en astheneiais, en hybresin, en anangkais, en
diogmois kai stenochōrias, hyper Christou, hotan gar asthenō, tote
dynatos eimi* (For power is made perfect in weakness. . . . Therefore
I am content with weaknesses, insults, hardships, persecutions, and
calamities for the sake of Christ; for whenever I am weak, then I am
strong; 2 Cor. 12:9f.).[90]

By nature we do not allow destiny to encounter us in this way. We
encounter destiny with continual desiring and striving. A life that
would always see God in its moments would be a life in joy. Ours is
a life in perpetual change, a life that in joy knows of the threat to joy,
knows that all desire wills eternity but does not achieve it, a life that
can never say to the moment: "But stay, you are so beautiful."—Our
life is one of care and complaint, of discontent and unrest, of anxiety,
whether open to reality or benumbed.

The *unknowability* of God is thus:

(1) The unknowability of the truth of the moment by way of objective examination, because this truth is grasped only in resolute seizure of the deed required and the destiny offered; it is grasped only in existing itself, not in standing by as an observer.

(2) It is further the impossibility of understanding the moment as in fact God's call, since God's call is drowned out by the voice of one's own willing and wishing, by sin. [E]

## §9. God's Knowability in Existence through Revelation

If God is thus unknowable, how then can God be spoken of at all? Have we not already spoken of God by speaking of God's unknowability? This would have to be true, if the topic is to be *God's* unknowability, and not unknowability as such. And it is precisely this we should be clear about, that to speak of the nonrational does not mean to speak of God.

In fact, God's unknowability is in a certain sense limited, should we be able to speak of it at all.[91]

It is the same phenomenon as our being able to know and speak of thankfulness and trust, friendship and love, though we can never have these things in general, but only in the concrete instance. Science can never discover a friend, faithfulness, or love. Such is discovered only in the wagering surrender.

Still and all, there is knowledge of it. And this is because our temporality consists not only in the moment's encountering us as new, but because we preserve time in our remembrance, bringing the past along into the here and now, and because the character of the moment consists precisely in questioning us who are qualified by our past.[92] For this reason, too, the enigma of the moment differs for each, since each has *his* or *her* past. But this means that it is the moment that demands an accounting of our experiences and requires that we objectify them to ourselves. We are aware of their significance; we can know and speak of them. We do not possess them in our knowledge—in our very knowing they can be lost to us. But in experiencing them we also have knowledge of them.[93]

We do not *possess* our experiences by knowing or speaking of them. In the last analysis we do not even know or speak of them but only of the idea of them.[94] It is true that the idea of God can be grasped apart from faith. And apart from faith the meaning of God's unknowability is apparent, to the extent it denotes science's inability to know the truth of the moment. This means, therefore, that apart from faith there is knowledge of God. And for this reason, of course, it is possible to speak of God apart from faith, possible to develop an idea of God, since each *Dasein* is moved by the question of truth. In the question about God, *Dasein* apart from faith is aware of God.

This corresponds to the fact that even apart from love, friendship, etc., talk of love and friendship can be understood—in yearning, for example. In fact, it is possible that its meaning can be made clearer in the question about it than in a life-relation to it.

*Luther* assumes that the human being has an idea of God, that is, that he has it in his question about God.[95] He writes that it belongs to man to hang his heart and rely on a power to which he assigns all good,[96] that man as such knows of his being directed toward. . .

Luther also assumes the possibility of a philosophical concept of God, adding, of course, that the God of philosophy does not concern us.[97] But he also teaches a natural knowledge of God, and in fact a knowledge of God that to some degree does concern us: Through the law the knowledge of God is known to reason; it is aroused in the conscience, and is thus the knowledge of being summoned.[98] "All Turks, Jews, papists, Tartars, and heathen say there is a God, Creator of heaven and earth, who will have this or that done or not done, if we should live."[99] [E]

What more does faith know of God?[100] First of all, it contests the right of unbelief to speak of God other than of the question about God. Second, it recognizes the radical impossibility of knowing God. Third, it speaks on the basis of God's revelation, that is, on the basis of God's word that interprets the situation: The conscience as the call of God, the forgiveness of sins (*pecca fortiter, sed crede fortius:* "sin boldly, but believe more boldly still"), the world crucified. [O]

Should there be talk *of God*, then it is of course clear that there can be talk of him only as Lord, that is, as the one who sends the

moment and makes his claim in it, as the one whose claim is heard
precisely in the claim of the here and now.[101] There would have to be
talk of him as one whom conscience obeys, who is experienced in
the world that enslaves, though he is the Almighty.

But it may not simply be said *that* the claim of the moment is
God's, *that* the voice of conscience is God's, *that* God is Lord of the
world that enslaves, or the Lord of the reality that encounters and
favors us.[102] In that case, the simple fact of being claimed in the here
and now, and of being enslaved or favored,[103] would be called God
without any reason or justification, and God would be only a name
for phenomena that are apparent even apart from God.

Can *the claim of God* encounter us *among other claims*? as, for
example, the claim of this or that particular person? Clearly not.
God's claim would then be alongside others, and the question concerning the truth would have to aim at God at one time, and at something else at another. In *every* question concerning truth *God* is
inquired after; in *every* claim of the here and now *God* is encountered. The question and the claim are always concrete. In *every* concrete situation, therefore, *he* must be Lord. But what does this mean?

It cannot mean, of course, that the mere facts of the question and
the claim get a special name, that they are "religiously" transfigured
through experiencing their weight. And it cannot mean that from
them we *infer* someone or something behind them. In that case the
ultimacy of the claim would be missed, a claim not simply legit-
imized by something behind it. Actually, we hear nothing but the
claim, and God is not an hypothesis.

The moment is always my moment and always new. If God discloses himself in it, then *what God is is not at all to be defined in
general terms*. Rather, God is the one who is always speaking to me
and always speaking anew. But what sense is there in saying that
*God* speaks in each new moment of mine? *What more do I know*,
when I know that God speaks to me in the moment?

I know that when I hear God in the moment, then I *correctly*
understand that moment; then I know the *answer* to the question
about the truth.[104] Apart from God I know that the moment is decisive for me, that I choose myself in it. Apart from God I know that I

can find or lose myself in it, seize or miss my authenticity. I can also define my authenticity in a formal way, thusly, that I am authentic only in decision. But I never know whether I have really decided or not, whether or not I have fled from the decision. For the decision assumes total clarity about my situation, and I never know whether I have hidden it from myself out of frivolity or anxiety.[105] For this reason it is conscience that intrudes and says to me: In this way or that I must acknowledge I am guilty.

Thus I can neither know God himself from out of the situation, since it only presents me with its claim and nothing more, nor can I find God in myself through my resolve. But this means that I cannot find God at all within my human possibilities. If there is to be talk of God, then it must be *an address to* the human possibility, *to the moment*. And such talk cannot be directed to the phenomenon of the moment, as though it were contained in it. It can only be accepted. That is, there can only be talk of God on the basis of God's *revelation*, and the revelation can only be heard in *faith*. Now we have arrived at the themes of investigation to follow.

These themes can only be elucidated to the extent as results from what precedes. What must be held to is that God can be spoken of only as the *how of our existence*, that is, as the one who always encounters us anew in the moment. But to hear God in my moment it would have *to be determined by a fact*, by something actual, so that in it, that is, spoken into it, I encounter the revelation—from the standpoint of philosophical analysis an accidental, historical fact.

*But this fact must be of a special kind*, that is, it must be different from other facts that constitute my situation, and different in this respect: that it does *not* establish the situation as human, historical, does not first create the claim (in the here and now even *without* it), does not first unveil the truth inquired into, but first renders the situation audible in its claim, in its truth.

So this fact must have *its special claim, its special truth* in addition to the situation, yet only in such fashion that it makes clear the claim and truth of the situation.[106]

This word cannot be a speculative theory, a universal truth; otherwise it would of course not be the word in the moment and heard

together with it. And from where should it come? It can only be the
accidentally historical word that always encounters me now, a word
with meaning only for this moment of mine toward which it is
aimed. If the idea of the moment is to be held to as the claim of
God—and it must be—then of course it contains its own truth ever
anew. The word of revelation may not take this truth from it but can
only allow it to be recognized. This means, however, that in a certain
sense the word of revelation must also be understood ever anew (better, heard ever anew);[107] otherwise it would annul the historical character of the moment. [C (perhaps also B)]

The situation is not significantly altered when the objective world
shaping the individual through his participation in it is no longer
understood in idealistic terms as the world of spirit, as the timeless
world of morality, of science and art, the world of the good, true, and
beautiful, but rather in romanticist terms as the world of irrational
life forces from which the individual emerges and which give him
his reality.

The so-called worldview of the National Movement[108] is in danger of going astray here. The truly positive force of the movement is
raised to consciousness in an ideology that threatens to obscure and
thus destroy it. Its power springs from latent knowledge of the historicity of *Dasein*, of the fact that concrete historical givens with
their claim, as well as concrete historical decisions, make up the
reality of life. This is the reason for turning away from idealism and
rationalism, from liberalism and democracy, insofar as in these
movements timeless ideas would challenge and give reality to life,
and the individual would be measured by the universal. Negatively
and positively this movement is in a line that made its first great
attacks against idealism and romanticism in Kierkegaard and Nietzsche, that struggles for clarity in the critical historical observations
of Jacob Burckhardt[109] and the "life philosophy" of Wilhelm Dilthey
and Count York,[110] and is gaining influence in the phenomenology of
Heidegger and in dialectical theology.[111]

But in the reaction to idealism and rationalism there is great danger of slipping into romanticism and a materialistic biology. Those
concrete givens of life that make up our reality can do so only as *his-*

*torical*. The historical moment and its claim are always defined by what is concretely given. But as historically given it can never be unequivocally defined as ready to hand. This is true even of what is called nationality. Nationality is[112] never something unequivocally given as ready to hand, but is always and at the same time something surrendered. Everything given us from the past or from nature is rendered problematic in face of the future, and only in this way can be genuinely appropriated. Nationality that makes up our reality, is not a natural, biological entity, but an historical one. When in his address as rector[113] Heidegger summoned us to submit to the might of our origin if we truly desire to be, and said that this origin is humanity's setting out toward itself, beginning with the philosophy of the Greeks, the nation "nearest" us, then it is clear that his concept of nationality is not biological, but historical, and for which one decides through historical reflection. And when Heidegger states that this origin is not something lying behind us but rather ahead of us, a distant disposition that has penetrated our future, then this means that nationality is not something merely given that realizes itself in the resolve to seize it.

But this means that the *deus in nobis* of idealism may not be interpreted as God in the nation, according to which national spirit and the will of God are equated. Nation in the true sense is not a biological but an historical phenomenon. This means that our participation in it is not a question of descent but of existence. God is not given in the nation but is encountered in the nation's destiny when by existing we join in establishing it.[114] [D]

# 4

# The Idea of Revelation

## §10. The Concept of Revelation in the Church and Its Disintegration

*The general concept of* revelation[1] is of a disclosure of what is hidden, an unveiling of what is veiled.[2] In this sense revelation is spoken of in a twofold differentiated way:

(1) *Revelation is a mediating of knowledge* (through the word). It is instruction, by which what is previously unknown is made known, and known from now on. In this sense, instruction can mediate a revelation. For someone a book or a lecture can be a revelation.

(2) *Revelation is an event* that sets me in a new situation, brings to light possibilities previously veiled from me,[3] including, of course, the possibility of knowing (that is, of knowing about them), without regard to whether this knowledge becomes explicit. In a crime, for example, the abysses of human nature are disclosed to me. Through an experience my "eyes are opened" to this or that, to myself or some state of affairs. One is "revealed" to the other through an act of love, of friendship, or even of hate, of meanness.

*In the area of religion* revelation is referred to in both senses,[4] assuming that the knowledge mediated or the state of affairs disclosed in it is inaccessible to humans as such but that its disclosure is absolutely decisive if humans should achieve "salvation," authenticity. In this case, revelation is the disclosure of God. Talk of revelation betrays an understanding of *Dasein* as aware of its limit and wishing to exceed it. The question is, which of these two conceptions defines the idea of revelation, and how are the human limit and exceeding that limit by revelation seen. [c]

This idea is to be explained by a survey of the history of the problem, a history marked by the question of the relation between reason and revelation.

(*a*) In *medieval Catholicism*,[5] only a few represented a *thoroughgoing rationalism*: John Scotus Erigena (head of the school at the court of Charles the Bald); Abelard (1079–1142), and Raymond Lull (+1315, intent on proving the truth of Christianity to Muslims).

According to Erigena there can be no contradiction between faith and knowledge. The *recta ratio* (proper reason) and the *vera auctoritas* (the teaching of scripture and the tradition) stem from the same source. The true religion is thus identical with the true philosophy. Abelard takes the same position: *nihil credendum, nisi prius intellectum* (nothing is to be believed unless it is first understood). Faith is a preliminary stage that is secured only when its content (the doctrines) is grasped by reason. The goal is *intelligere* (understanding).

In Duns Scotus, William of Occam, and partly in mysticism, *irrationalism* is opposed to rationalism.[6] *Duns Scotus* (+1308) distinguishes truths of reason and of revelation. Though certainty in theology is greatest, because it is established upon God's truthfulness, it still has no genuinely scientific character, since it is not constructed upon evident principles and gives no total insight into the doctrines of revelation. The latter intend to give the one destined for the supernatural goal of the *visio dei* the *doctrina supernaturaliter addita* needed for it, a doctrine that instructs one concerning one's goal and its attainment. At the same time, proof of the credibility of the revelation is adduced from prophecies fulfilled, from miracles, from the agreement among the biblical authors, from the continuance of the church despite persecutions, and from the agreement of Christian doctrine with sound human reason. What is arrived at here is thus not a basically different point of view. Skepticism toward the extent of rational proofs, not toward human being *as a whole*,[7] determines the view of the relation between them. The limit that revelation exceeds is thus merely that of knowledge.

The case is similar with *William of Occam* (+1349). Occam is skeptical of reason that cannot give compelling proofs for the existence and attributes of God, for the noneternal character of the world, and for the existence of an immaterial soul-substance. Since, where the unbeliever is concerned, the tenets of faith lack probability, to say nothing of being able to be rationally resolved, there follows the meritoriousness of faith. Mysticism teaches the extinguishing of reason and the grasping of the abyss of the divine in feeling.

The actual standpoint of the church is a *half-rationalism*, as Anselm, Albert the Great, and Thomas represent it.

*Anselm* (1033–1109) alters the Augustinian "*credo ut intelligam*" to read that rational comprehension need not precede faith's understanding of the doctrines of revelation, but that it follows it,[8] since reason must establish the fact of the revelation and above all give speculative proof for dogmatic content.[9]

From the doctrines that can be proved, *Albert the Great* (1193–1280) separates those that are inaccessible to reason (e.g., the Trinity and the resurrection of the flesh). Their sole source is revelation or the supernatural light stemming from it. For theology, revelation is the source of knowledge, for philosophy, reason and experience are. But philosophy can furnish a subsequent confirmation of the tenets of faith, so that they are more credible. Since both theology and philosophy have their origin in God who cannot contradict himself, they also cannot contradict each other.

*Thomas* (+1274), in company with Arabian scholasticism, distinguishes a twofold truth of reason and revelation,[10] not, of course, in the absolute but only in the relative sense, since theology and philosophy both stem from God as the one Truth. Reason, however, does not attain to its goal because it is prey to error. Above all, it does not because this goal is supernatural, beyond the means of human reason.[11] Thus even faith in incomprehensible mysteries is humbling and meritorious.

Basically, revelation and reason on this view are seen as stages; *fides*, which knows no doubt, is lofted above *mere opinio*. But only *scientia* gives inner insight. In fact, by itself reason can recognize a portion of the revealed doctrines: The *praeambula fidei* which precede faith. The existence of God and the fact of revelation are not only recognizable *lumine divinae revelationis*, but also *lumine naturalis rationis*. Of course, such doctrines have also been revealed as *prima credibilia* for the sake of the weak. The real mysteries of faith are not to be discovered by reason, but are *only* revealed, the Trinity for example, and the beginning of the world in time. But reason has its object even in these mysteries, since by way of apologetic it proves the absence of contradiction in them as well as their possibility. In each case, the goal is *intelligere*, and in the *visio beatifica* the *contemplari* will follow the *credere*.

Everywhere in medieval catholicism, therefore, faith is a kind of knowledge, and revelation its mediation. [A] Of course, intended in the idea of revelation here is the general sense of an event transcending human limits, an event decisive for man. But the limitation is understood as a limitation on what can be known, and insofar as knowledge of revelation can be regarded as decisive, it is assumed that in such knowledge one comes to oneself and is with God. [B] This means that insight is conceived throughout as humanity's highest possibility. It is *the ancient ideal of theōria*. Contemplation (*visio*) is not only the highest and authentic form of knowledge but the highest mode of existence. It joins the contemplative to the highest and authentic being, to God, the *ens perfectissimum*. The *visio* is pure contemplation, pure possession of what is present. Unlike willing, the attitude of contemplation does not point beyond itself but is fulfilled, whereas willing is unfulfilled.[12] The Christian life is thus the *bios theōrētikos*.

The assumption here is that *God is an existent thing, an object of knowledge*. What is also clear, of course, is the nature of the proofs for God: God is construed as world, for God's existence is proved from the world, as in the Stoics. God is the rationally intelligible world-principle or world-all. In Session III of "On Revelation," canon 1, the [First] Vatican Council (1869/70) states: "If anyone says that the one, true God, our creator and lord, cannot be known

with certainty from the things that have been made, by the natural
light of human reason: let him be anathema."[13] In this sense also an
innate idea of God is rejected and the need for proof of God's existence expressly maintained, an existence, naturally, that can be
proved a posteriori (from the given reality of the world).[14]

To this are added proofs from what is above nature: the fulfillment
of prophecies, the miracles of the Old and New Testaments, Christ
and his work, thus proofs from history. But these are fundamentally
rational proofs, as are the proofs from nature, that is, the adducing of
proof rests on the law of causality. Proofs from history (from "what
is above nature"), however, are more important, since the mightier
deeds allow us to infer a more perfect cause.[15]

The proofs for God from what is above nature are also *praeambula* for supernatural faith in God's existence, so that the problem arises as to how faith and knowledge may be directed to the same object.
The object is the same,[16] but knowledge rests on evidence, and faith
on authority.[17]

(*b*) The view is the same in *orthodox Protestantism*:[18]

> The Theology of the Way is twofold, natural and revealed (supernat-
> ural). The former is that according to which God is known both by
> innate ideas, and by the inspection of created things.[19] The latter is the
> knowledge of God and of divine things, which God communicates to
> man upon earth, either by immediate revelation or inspiration (to
> prophets and apostles), or by mediate revelation or the divine Word,
> committed to writing.[20]

The difference between *revelatio generalis* and *specialis* is further defined. *The former* is the "*natural manifestation*, by which God
makes himself known both by the innate light of nature and by the
effects conspicuous in the kingdom of nature."[21] To this belongs
"that common conception concerning God engraven and impressed
upon the mind of every man by Nature, and hence from the womb,"
that is, through conscience and the works of God in nature.[22]

*The latter* is *supernaturalis*: "The external act of God, by which
He makes Himself known to the human race by His Word, in order
that they may have a saving knowledge of Him."[23]

Here, then, we encounter the same misunderstanding as in Catholicism, only in more grotesque form, since the concept of faith is of another sort, that is, the true possibility of human existence is no longer seen as residing in knowledge. And to the extent that here too the revelation is viewed in general propositions, the rationalism abolishing the supernatural revelation is thoroughgoing. Orthodoxy, of course, intends to take seriously the element of communication, but what is communicated makes nothing evident. Rationalism clings to the element of revelation, insofar as it possesses comprehensible doctrines, but these doctrines are not communicated; they are rather produced.[24]

(*c*) In orthodoxy, then, *the revelation* is altogether *a communication of doctrines*, doctrines grasped in a knowing—first of all, in a knowing that is imperfect, made more perfect through speculation or in the hereafter. Authentic human existence is seen as residing in knowing. The rationalist standpoint is *thoroughgoing*, and the real meaning of the revelation is lost absolutely, when the need for it requires special proof (in the weakening of natural knowledge through the fall). [A]

In a time when *reason* becomes aware of itself, it does not recognize a human limitation *here*. That is, it correctly sees that reason does not reflect human limitation, but human infinitude. And it is understandable that once the limitation of reason—thought to be man's real limitation—fell away, there was no longer awareness of any human limitation. The concept of revelation thus becomes superfluous or loses its real meaning. When rationalism speaks of revelation, then of "natural revelation," a *contradictio in adiecto*; for revelation as such is supernatural. [B]

The "*supernatural*" *character of the revelation* is actually set aside when the doctrines of revelation are set in direct relation to rational knowledge. Schleiermacher was correct: "If a system of propositions can be understood from their connexion with others, then nothing supernatural was required for their production."[25] If by the aid of revelation the totality of the world were really made clear to us, it would be only the world.

If, on the other hand, the accent is on *opposition of the doctrines of revelation to reason*, then revelation is merely a private concept, that is, doctrines have revelatory character only insofar as they are rational in nature (with the minus sign).[26]

If, accordingly, the accent is on the resolve of the will to believe, then salvation depends on one's own performance, quite apart from the fact that one cannot decide to believe some unintelligible thing in the sense under discussion, that is, cannot regard that thing as intelligible after all. One can only decide not to contradict it. The result is that the idea of omnipotence is impaired. And tracing the resolve to the aid of the Holy Spirit is no corrective,[27] since he is conceived as a magical power. "The idea that the powers of faith and love worked by God exist beyond consciousness as mysterious qualities," means "to speculate like an Augustinian and live like a Pelagian" (Herrmann).[28] If the Spirit's working is not understood as an event of one's own existence, then we are certainly *not* speaking of existence. *"Fidei opus et esse videntur idem esse"* (the activity and nature of faith are seen to be the same; Luther).[29] There is no such thing as an *esse fidei* behind the consciousness-(existence-)event (the *opus fidei*).[30] If there were, then we would be speaking of a faith

> begotten in the soul before it has won redemption through the things which it will now make its own as God's gift. By such faith the unredeemed man thinks he is doing a work that God commands, that through it he might gain redemption. . . . The faith that is to be one's own as a hand or vessel for receiving the divine gift, even before this gift itself has been given his to share—such faith is a performance by which one initiates communion with God on his own. The idea that the power for such performance originates in the hidden working of the means of grace can very easily be linked to this notion. And despite all, that interior event still remains a communion with God that the person himself initiated. But everything that you begin by yourself is sin.[31]

Above all, doctrines cannot be revelation. Otherwise the term "revelation" would merely mark the (failed) attempt to characterize its origin, but would not characterize the revelation itself. Revelation is not revelation because of its remarkable origin (in history and for the individual). Rather, *revelation remains revelation*:

To begin with, all will at once agree that the word "revealed" is never applied either to what is discovered in the realm of experience by one man and handed on to others, or to what is excogitated in thought by one man and so learned by others; and further, that the word presupposes a divine communication and declaration.[32]

This is true, but if doctrines are regarded as such a communication, then God simply assumes the role of discoverer or inventor. A revealed doctrine that is further handed on, *is* no longer a revelation. [A] In that case, for natural reason the revelation has the character of mystery as the not-yet-known. But once known (by way of a communication of knowledge through supernatural arrangement), the knowledge of revelation is like any other; the not-yet is over and done with. Its supernatural character is limited to its origin, and its origin, once known, lies in the past.[33] [B]

Revelation is the way which is also the goal: *egō eimi hē hodos kai hē alētheia kai hē zōē* (John 14:6). He *is* the way, he does not *show* it; he *is* the truth, he does not *teach* it; he *is* the life, he does not *mediate* it. Jesus does not lead to somewhere where one is, or to something one has. He is not involved *with* but *as* revelation. But this also means that there can be no short cut to knowing the truth.[34] The possession of truth is not secured by its one-time discovery, to be passed on in abbreviated form. Each must go the way toward truth; for only in doing so is the truth disclosed. Thus Jesus *is* the truth, he does not *speak* it.[35] There is thus no revelation that may be regarded as doctrine or even accepted through resolve, such that the teacher (= the revelation!) is eliminated. And the believer does not *know* or *possess* the revelation. Rather, he "is of the truth." Just as each must always begin from the beginning in Christianity on his own, so also there is no history of Christianity within human history, a history of development, for example, or of problems, a history that would move stage by stage, solution by solution. Each generation has the same original relation to the revelation.[36]

Revelation thus remains revelation. It does not become something revealed. Otherwise God would become an idol. There is thus no speculation on what is revealed (no *theōria*). Rather, *revelation* is *marked by its character as present*; it is *in actu* or not at all. Its content is thus neither nature nor a history of which one may be aware, since there is no knowledge of it. It is not perceptible as world. It is not a *ginōskein*, but a *gnōsthēnai* (Gal. 4:9; 1 Cor. 8:2f.; 13:12). Or, *gnōsis* is merely the eschatological possibility of *pistis*.

Then too, of course, revelation is not a fact to be interpreted, so that one would have to distinguish manifestation from inspiration in it, "the former a series of miraculous historical facts and events, and the latter the illumination facilitating authentic exposition of the divine manifestation."[37] This is absurd, since then, of course, revelation would first have to be revealed! The believer's relation to revelation does not consist of "the interpretation of signs" and the like. God remains a mystery in revelation, and is never rationally knowable, because God remains the Thou.[38] [A]

Naturally, this holds true not only when "doctrines" regarded as revelation have come into the world through[39] supernatural arrangement but also when they are arrived at by rational thought, by speculation, as a result of which theology, with its interpretation of nature and history, becomes a philosophy of religion.[40] It holds true against *every* type of rationalism. It makes no difference whether the ideas are called "God, freedom, and immortality" as in old-time rationalism, or whether the notion of development is taken up and the ideas by which the human spirit interprets itself and its existence in the world are viewed in their historical sequence as an automatically unfolding revelation and traced back to a religious a priori. Through such knowledge the person would be aware of himself, that is, of his idea, but not of God. In this instance the revelation is a "natural" one, thus not a revelation.

(*d*) If the concept of revelation in Catholicism, orthodoxy, and rationalism is untenable, a genuine concept seems to reappear with the recognition that human life is not founded upon reason; when one sees life again within its limitations, and understands the event that bursts it as revelation—thus the *concept of revelation in romanticism*. Romanticism is aware that God is not possessed in doctrines that are intelligible or can be owned; it recognizes that revelation must remain revelation and that it is marked by its character as present. [B]

Together with the orthodox and rationalistic or idealistic concept of revelation, however, the concept of romanticism is also to be rejected, a concept that is not oriented to what is revealed or to the Revealer, but to the recipient of the revelation. [A]

There is precedent for the romantic concept in *pietism*, to the extent that in pietism "religious inwardness" is a reaction to the dogmatic faith of orthodoxy. Pietism sees that the human limitation is not that of knowledge, and that revelation is marked by its character as present. But instead of inquiring strictly after the One who is over against it, it seeks the revelation in its own experience. It separated subjective, personal piety from the church's

> supernatural institution of grace, and rendered it independent even of the Bible in a personal communion with God merely guided by the Bible. In fact, the radical pietists located the supernatural in religious exaltation to such degree that there was but a step to recognizing the same supernatural quality in all religious experiences, even apart from the Christian, and the principle gulf between Christianity and non-Christianity was bridged.[41]

Basically, human limitations are perceived in the things of every day, in limits burst by human earnestness and enthusiasm. [C]

In romanticism, revelation is not something grasped in thought but in intuition, feeling, and presentiment. But what is grasped is only the world as a totality, as a universe.[42] The reception of revelation is the perception of the world as a creative whole, and of course it is not grasped in thought as unconditioned but rather in feeling, so that this intuition is disclosed in and through the particular: "To accept everything individual as a part of the whole and everything limited as a *representation* of the *infinite* is religion."[43] At issue here is an aesthetic contemplation, as Schleiermacher's illustration by way of Greek religion makes especially clear: "They intuited the ever-active, ever-living, and serene activity of the world and its spirit, beyond all change, and all the apparent evil that only stems from the conflict of finite forms."[44] Accordingly, the human being is a member of this work of art:

Religion wishes to see the infinite, its imprint and its manifestation, in humanity no less than in all other individual and finite forms. . . . Religion breathes there where freedom itself has once more become nature; it apprehends man beyond the play of his particular powers and his personality, and views him from the vantage point where he must be what he is, whether he likes it or not.[45]

For this reason the question of truth also disappears, for every such intuition of the universe is "true": "In the infinite everything finite stands undisturbed alongside one another; all is one, and all is true."[46] The universe is thus viewed as a work of art; God is actually the artist, and in this sense the reference is to the irrational and creative.

At the same time the human being is also the artist, and in him the creative, irrational, and immediate is alive in religious intuition; and this intuition as a being overwhelmed, and as a creative act is nothing but the expression of "poetic geniality":

The same actions of the universe through which it reveals itself to you in the finite also bring it into a new relationship to your mind and your condition; in the act of intuiting it, you must necessarily be seized by various feelings.[47]

Its [religion's, R.B.] feelings are supposed to possess us, and we should express, maintain, and portray them. But should you wish to go beyond that dimension with these feelings, should they cause actual actions and incite you to deeds, then you find yourselves in an alien realm.[48]

But if human expression and action is only "portrayal," what else is it but aesthetic behavior? Schleiermacher's description of the religious experience points very clearly in this direction:

A manifestation, an event develops quickly and magically into an image of the universe. Even as the beloved and ever-sought-for form fashions itself, my soul flies toward it; I embrace it, not as a shadow, but as the holy essence itself. I lie on the bosom of the infinite world.[49] At this moment I am its soul, for I feel all its powers and its infinite life as my own; at this moment it is my body, for I penetrate its muscles and its limbs as my own, and its innermost nerves move according to my sense and my presentiment as my own.[50]

This romanticism is certainly still genuine, and in it as well the question of religion comes to clear expression.[51] It sees that to intuit the world as a unity would not be to understand God, and that there can be no direct action upon God or realization of the divine through purposeful activity.[52] It sees that to intuit the world as unity requires the idea of God's omnipotence,[53] and that the intuition of this omnipotence can only be given. But it confuses the gift of this intuition with aesthetic vision, a vision that of course does not spring from reflection or intention but, for all that is still a human attitude. It overlooks the fact that to intuit the unity of the world and to construe evil as mere appearance is an impossibility for the actual person.[54] It does not recognize human existence as insecure and historical.[55] It does not see that faith believes *despite* appearance, that to faith corresponds the offense. Finally, it sees God in what is human.

This romanticism is genuine insofar as it actually proceeds from aesthetic vision, from the experience of the artist. But it becomes spurious and tasteless in its *modernizing and trivializing* by conceiving the world and man without further ado as revelations, since the decisive idea that the revelation is experienced in the moment of creative activity has been eliminated, and one imagines one can document the creative as something tangible in the world and history.[56] If, experiencing unity with the universe in intuition, *in* and *for* the creative impulse, the human ultimately appears as recipient of the revelation as well as revealer, then he is straightaway regarded as creative; then, every personality is held to be a nonrational and immediate entity that supposedly reveals God, with the result that the revelation may be mediated through the historically intuited portrayal of a personality (especially the religious personality!), or, intuited history itself is taken to be revelation.[57] The *historical pantheism* of liberal theology is thus a murky mixture of romantic and idealistic motifs.[58] One speaks of the powers of the true, good, and beautiful, as such alleged to be divine. History is said to be a unified, meaningful struggle, in which these powers gain the victory, a struggle in which humanity shares by being borne along by these powers, thus from bondage to nature becomes a free personality with its inner riches.[59] In these powers, visible in moral endeavor and cultural creation, lies the meaning, the divinity of history. Particularly in the personalities, in the bearers of these powers, God reveals himself—thus also in the personality of Jesus. Moreover, in the context of historical phenomena Jesus is viewed from the teleological perspective.[60]

When this historical pantheism no longer suffices, then the romantic-aesthetic motifs more strongly reappear. [A]

The real reason for the question about revelation cannot be repressed. There is the vague awareness that revelation must still be something that bursts human limitations, not something flatly obvious. And, with great modesty, of course, experience is called revelation, the experience in which one becomes aware of what is creative in the world and in history, especially in encounter with "religious personalities"; the experience in which one is raptured from the things of every day and one's own limitations, and senses being in the flood of a greater, divine life.[61] [B] *The experience* itself appears as revelation, and accordingly one no longer knows what revelation or the reception of revelation is, what is actually revealed and who reveals it. The thoroughly general notion dominates that where something irrational, creative, or immediate is sensed, there there is revelation. The result is that the object of revelation no longer plays any role, nothing is any longer revealed.[62]

The counterpart to the Catholic and orthodox view has thus come to full term. There, revelation is limited to what is revealed, and the *actus* of the revelation in the present is ignored. Here, one believes he may speak of a revelatory act without anything having been revealed. But one may speak of revelation only when he can say that something is made manifest in the act of revelation, in other words, when there is reference to God as Revealer.[63] [A]

The theological (and generally religious) position that seeks to avoid the modern-liberal mixture of romanticism and liberalism, conceives the *irrational* as divine revelation.[64] In contrast to Schleiermacher's romanticism, however, it does not define the experience of revelation as an aesthetic contemplation of the universe, but as the consciousness of what is mysterious and enigmatic, of what is seductive and attractive all about us. Awe in the presence of the numinous with its aspects of the *tremendum* and *fascinosum*, the sense of self as creature yet the feeling of being seized by God and drawn to him, is the experience of revelation.

The negative aspect of this view is correct, that the reason can say nothing about what is beyond human limitation, cannot sketch what is beyond. But it is false to confuse the irrational with God and to suppose we speak of God when speaking of the irrational.[65] If the numinous should denote more than awareness of the enigma of our existence, then not having is taken for having, and God is confused with the devil. In the numinous the human being is not aware of God but of himself. He is deceived with palming off the mysterious for God, for he is not taking seriously the enigma of his existence at all.

The real error in the theory of the "numinous" is that it detaches experience of the numinous from the understanding of the moment. My experience is authentic only when I am aware of what is mysterious as *one* who lives in a concrete situation, is linked to others, and now must act—one for whom what is mysterious puts everything at risk and renders what he is and can do problematic. If the relation of the mysterious to the moment is forgotten, if what is mysterious as such is stared at, actually quiveringly enjoyed, it has become the devil. The question of the truth of the moment has then been struck down, become of no account. In that case the mysteriousness is no longer *mine*.

For such a theology, moving from rationalism to romanticism to the most recent irrationalism, there arises the *problem of the absoluteness of Christianity*. [B]

(*e*) If the content of revelation is God, thus God's accosting word in the here and now, then God is always subject in it. Then a *gnōsthēnai* never becomes a *ginōskein*; the accosting word never loses its character as address, and thus the revelation never becomes something one may happen upon. So there is *no religious-historical development of revelation*, by which its individual acts construed as tangible events would be arranged within an evolutionary context, in such fashion, say, as to reveal a timeless idea. Rather, revelation is always the activity of God, and this activity does not become a fact in hand.

But the claim is binding. In it God is encountered as the One over against me.[66] There can be no asking, Where else? Otherwise the one over against me would be misunderstood, just as if I were to ask, Where else can I have this love, this trust, where else can I say father, etc. than in my concrete, historical situation? That others may ask means nothing to me. The fact of their having been addressed is not mine, and I understand it only from the viewpoint of my own. I can call "father" any father at all, but I can say "father" to only *one*, *my* father. Father as a generic concept does not automatically include my own, for there is no such thing as "my fathers." God and God's revelation are not a generic concept. Otherwise my God would be a "divinity." My being claimed is misunderstood when I look about me to see whether God has revealed himself apart from Christianity. For the non-Christian this question is meaningless from the outset. For the Christian it is totally pointless. In Japanese *sola-fide*-Buddhism, for example, I can *see* a human attitude, but an attitude that can only caution me against confusing *my* attitude with my *faith*, against ignoring the intentional character of faith as faith in the concrete and contingent revelation.[67]

The question whether God's revelation is present elsewhere simply makes the revelation something ready to hand, human. If it is a claim made upon me, then it can never be confirmed as something on hand. The question whether others are also addressed in this way, cannot be raised as a scientific question. Only as one addressed can I hear the claim. [A]

The antithesis to expanding the idea of revelation in the philosophy or history of religion cannot read: *Ready to hand* only here. For the uniqueness of a fact that is ready to hand is always a question, and at best accidental. It involves what is solitary, not what is absolutely unique. Uniqueness must also be such by nature.

To use an analogy: My friendship or love is unique as to its intention; it has its quite peculiar questions and gifts. But as one "instance" among others, as an "occurrence" in human culture, it is only one among others.

Emil Brunner most strongly emphasizes the *uniqueness of the revelation*.[68] He writes as follows: In *the philosophy of religion (idealism) and mysticism*, revelation is a singular, and of course, a universal thing, that is, "the emergence of the eternal basis of all phenomena into consciousness. . . . Revelation as the objective element, and religion as the subjective element, are fundamentally everywhere one and the same."[69] In *popular religions*, on the other hand, there are revelations aplenty, theophanies and oracles, miracles of all sorts; events in which the deity manifests itself. In *Christian faith* revelation is (1) a happening, an event, and, of course, an event that has already occurred. Not the metaphysical, but the historical saves. Christian faith is indissolubly connected with an historical fact, the fact of Jesus Christ.[70] (2) But this event is singular, unique; and *in essence*, of course, it is unique. "The fact that this revelation has taken place once for all does not constitute an arithmetical difference, but a positive difference, a difference in quality."[71] Only as unique is the event decisive.[72] "The decisive is unique." The serious nature of the decision is identical to the uniqueness.[73]

But Brunner does not sufficiently explain the *concept of uniqueness*, and the question is confused by (correctly) denying that uniqueness is an aspect of natural events (in nature there are only individual examples of the genre), by reserving it for history, but by stating that history only tends toward it, that the truly unique and decisive is not to be found in history. This is not correct. The decision to cross the Rubicon is absolutely unique. The decision to marry, the decision on behalf of one's calling is absolutely unique. After the decision, one is different and can never be the same.[74] The question cannot be decided as long as the dispute is merely over the *formal* concept of decision. That for which the decision is made is all important. And it is not yet enough to call it a decision for God, since it is not clear why the question of deciding for God should not be put more often, in encounter with the neighbor, for example, in whom, as the Christian believes, God also reveals himself—this, of course, only because God has revealed himself in Christ. But just for this reason the meaning of the uniqueness of the revelation in Christ as asserted by faith must be explained.[75] And as long as it is merely asserted that the historical fact of Christ is the revelation, but it is not indicated to what extent, then the contrast with idealism is clear, but the uniqueness is not substantially explained.

Now, when the Christian affirmation is that Christ is the only revelation of God, that only by this means does God reveal himself to us elsewhere (in the neighbor, in fate), so that at bottom Christ is everywhere the revelation, then it is clear that Christ cannot only be seen as an historical fact available in the past, but that this fact can be present in a peculiar way. How? In the preaching! To be sure—-but to what extent is preaching more than a report concerning a fact of the past? In what way does it make Christ present?

If Christ is revelation, not as an available fact of world history, but as present, then this means that he is a reality within our existence. If preaching is more than a report, then this means that it discloses to us our existence by speaking into it. But then the meaning of revelation cannot at all be explained if our existence is not explained as well—just as it was already made clear that God can only be spoken of as a how of our existence.

Brunner does not sufficiently explain this:

> For an event to belong to the "wholly other," in principle, would be an event in "super history"; it would belong to that kind of history whose end lies outside history altogether; it would be absolutely final and unique. The issue is clear: either this fact is unique and absolute, or it is only relative; either we are confronted with an absolutely incomparable new fact, or rather a new category which transcends history and is thus no longer history at all, the fulfillment of time in the midst of time; or it is something which is within the sphere of history, and which therefore can only be distinguished from the historical sphere in a purely relative sense.

Indeed, but how is this to be understood?[76] As forgiveness, perhaps? Yes, but only as forgiveness for guilt, not for sin. Toward the neighbor one is only guilty, not sinful; one is sinful only toward God.[77] But in that case, the task of existence-analysis or anthropology re-emerges. And, if the revelation is to consist of an event of history, and if the forgiveness of sins is to be its content, then the relation between sin and history must be explained by an analysis of the historical.[78]

We may put it in this way: Christology (for this must surely be at issue in revelation) can only be outlined or understood from the ethical perspective, if it is not to be mired in speculation. If revelation is the breaking through of our limitations, then the question first of all is, Where does the problem of our limitations become acute? that is, Where is the human truly human? And the answer is, in acting, in history. And if Christ as Revealer is *Sōtēr*, then the question is, For what is he *Sōtēr*? And the answer is, for sin.

This is not clear in Brunner; the unity of faith and love comes only at the conclusion.[79] But faith cannot be understood apart from love. And in §6, 2 of his *Dogmatics*, under "The Possibility of Hearing,"[80] Barth commits the error of characterizing the human as trapped in self-contradiction, without ever explicating this condition, so that the "neighbor" appears out of the blue, *post festum*,[81] while it is certain that without understanding him sin cannot at all be understood! [B]

From the point of view of faith, *the question of a universal concept of religion*, to which faith itself belongs, perhaps as its highest stage, cannot at all be raised.[82] If it could, faith would be deprived of its intentionality, its relation to God, and would be a phenomenon of this world, a human attitude (cf. Troeltsch).[83] That it is this *too* always raises a critical question for the believer, the question as to whether he knows what faith in faith is. Just as the fact that love is a phenomenon of human spiritual life—and that one may, for example, write a history of the relation between the sexes—can only raise a critical question for the lover. The result would be to show that Christian faith, to the extent it is a "religion," is a worldly phenomenon, that the awareness of religion as a necessary area of human spiritual life does not portend security for the believer. One may have one's security only in relation to God, that is, as a response to God's deed, to God who is the crisis of all human spiritual life, thus also of religion.[84]

For the believer, *the fact that there are religions* can of course be a *revelatio naturalis*, insofar as for the believer every religion is a *quest* for God. But it is a question *as well*, insofar as it asserts that it has the answer. As a question about *God*, every religion, even the Christian religion, is seen from the viewpoint of *faith*, which alone can know of God and the question about him, while apart from faith every religion misunderstands itself. But it is seen from the view-point of faith, to the extent that the question (the "homesickness," the yearning beyond what is given and perceivable) expresses human uncertainty at God's hands, or announces human sin.[85] The definition of religions as question leads beyond the psychological or the idealistic to the existential putting of the question and yields an understanding of Christianity as "religion," without reducing faith to an "instance" of the religious life.[86]

Now, insofar as historical-psychological analysis finds the content of all religions to be *awe in the presence of the numinous or irrational*, there is actually the possibility of grasping more clearly the meaning of that question about God. For in the irrational or the numinous the human does not lay hold of God, but rather the riddle of his own existence. He sees himself by recognizing himself as a "creature." To the extent he identifies the irrational with God, he has only the devil. Discovery of the irrational as the content of all religious faith corroborates the ancient Christian view that all non-Christian religions are of the devil, in saying which no disrespect is paid them, since the devil is actually a respectable entity, of which[87] one ought not think too little.

Seen from the perspective of faith, that question and the under-standing of the irrational, of the riddle of human existence, is in fact proof that God has not left himself without a witness. It is a kind of *revelatio naturalis*, and the question of the *absoluteness of the Christian religion* is settled. If the question is construed as an attempt to assign rank to religions including Christianity, apart from faith, then it is meaningless. Such an attempt merely results in what is relative, not absolute. In theology the question of the other religions can only be meaningfully put on the basis of faith, in which case the question of absoluteness is already decided, since faith is the answer to the revelation.[88]

One human being among others cannot perceive more than "religion," more than a question about God, and if one knows the answer as a believer, he can only proclaim it, wherever the question is raised. To reflect on its relation to other answers, however, means to surrender one's own. [A]

## §11. Revelation as Historical Event

[89]On the basis of our explanation of the historicity of *Dasein* and the character of the here and now,[90] we must now show in what sense *revelation* can be *the word addressed to the moment*,[91] a word that makes evident the truth of the moment and thus gives evidence of God.

The phenomenon of the "word" is not to be gleaned from an analysis of the moment as historical, present.[92] But it must be defined so that *it is intelligible to the person who is open to the question of the moment*; otherwise it would of course not be spoken *into* but rather *alongside* the moment. The fact that a person is what he or she is only in the moment would be missed.[93]

But it also means just this, that the accosting word promises the person *forgiveness* or *life* from the dead. For if it is the word of *forgiveness*, then it is assumed a person can relate the word to himself, as he comes out of the past into the present. Then it is assumed that it is a needed word that answers the question urging him on, the word to which he is directed. If it is the word about *life*, then it is assumed he was in death, but that means that *Dasein* had the needed link to life,[94] in relation to which death first becomes death.[95]

It is therefore also assumed that *Dasein under revelation is continuous with Dasein apart from revelation*, insofar as revelation first moves *Dasein* to what it wants to be and what it should be. If the revelation of God bursts the limitations of human *Dasein*, then not in terms of something appended to the *Dasein*, as if it received a plus so as to complete its knowledge. Rather, revelation bursts the limitations in such fashion that *Dasein* first comes to itself. Its limitations are not accidental, fixed from the outside, but have emerged from *Dasein* itself, are given with it. They are limitations that make *Dasein* what it is.[96]

The idea of revelation implies that *the Dasein, just as it is*, by itself, *is never authentic*. If, according to philosophy, *Dasein* exists authentically when it affirms that it is limited, when it takes over the situation in a resolve prepared for death, faith says that such resolution is despair, which makes absolutely clear that *Dasein* is not what it wants to be or should be.

Both philosophy and faith are aware of human limits, and of the quest for authenticity engaging *Dasein*. The difference is that faith denies that a person can achieve authenticity through taking over the situation in a resolve for death. But it can deny it only by affirming that *Dasein may* not gain its authenticity in such fashion, since God wills to have the person otherwise. *Faith* cannot possibly engage in discussion with *philosophy* at this point, otherwise it would itself become a philosophy and allow the choice of believing existence to appear as a free choice. Faith can judge the choice of philosophical existence only as an act of the self-creating freedom of the person who denies being bound to God.

But if faith denies philosophical existence, and if it maintains that the *Dasein* achieves authenticity only through God's revelation, then *faith* must speak *intelligibly*, so that the question, Philosophy or faith? becomes a genuine question for decision. Faith speaks intelligibly when it speaks of revelation in a way that makes clear the answer to the same question of limitation and authenticity as philosophy in its own way intends to give, but in such fashion that the decision becomes a decision of the will.

Since faith describes revelation as the word of *forgiveness*, it maintains that prior to revelation *Dasein* was under sin, that the decisions a person always encountered were false, and the claim of the moment was misunderstood. The revelation assumes (1) that the human is a *creature* who has his being from God, and should be for God who is for him; (2)[97] that from the beginning the human lived under the *requirement of love*, that therefore, trusting in the Creator and[98] in love, he should always hear the claim of the moment in order to be aware of the truth of the moment and thus of God.

By this, of course, revelation assumes, (1) that *the human is able to perceive God the Creator*, that he can understand himself as creature; (2)[99] that the *"natural man" can perceive the requirement of love*, that he is capable of a loving decision in the moment. If the revelation were not to do this, it could not speak of human sin, and could not be understood as a word of forgiveness. The New Testament also makes evident this assumption by maintaining (1) the possibility of a knowledge of God (Rom. 1:18ff.; Acts 17:27f.; 14:17; cf. John 1:4: *kai hē zōē ēn to phōs tōn anthrōpōn*), (2)[100] by stating that the commandment of love is nothing but the sum of the law (Gal. 5:14; Rom. 13:8-10), and also by assigning to the Gentiles a knowledge of the law (Rom. 1:32; 2:14f.; cf. Phil. 4:8).[101]

Philosophy too can see the possibility of love. It sees that *Dasein* exists only in community and that in such community the moment can require concern for the other. It too is aware of the phenomena of thanks and trust, etc., in which the requirement of love is heard and love becomes actual. But:

(1) Philosophy sets the appeal to the human being *to be himself in decision*, as well as the requirement *to love the other*, in a relationship which contradicts the divine requirement. For if *philosophy and faith* are both aware that the person himself is at issue, that he is to come to himself in the decision of the moment, *faith* nevertheless states that in the question about himself he must look away from himself, in order to be for the other from the perspective of the other. It states that being a self can only be given in surrender of the self. For *philosophy* the requirement of love does not dominate *Dasein* and determine each decision in the moment. It is rather one possibility among others, in which the possibility of being oneself may be realized at any time. For philosophy, to be a self is an act of freedom, not a gift of the other.

The possibility of a division here between faith and philosophy is actually rooted in the fact that in the deed of love *the act of freedom and the reception of the gift of the other* are really a unity. But all depends on which of the two establishes the other. Faith says that even the freedom to act is given. Philosophy says that my freedom enables me to receive the gift.

This difference is rooted in a second contrast:

(2) Faith says that I receive love *always as one who does not love*, and that this not-loving is guilt, *hate*. Just as the reception of love in the concrete always shames me because I am unworthy of it, so the

requirement of love discloses that I live in hate; otherwise it could not encounter me as a "thou shalt." Because the requirement of love encounters me as a "thou shalt," it leaves the moment to obscurity. True love would see the truth of the moment. The *requirement* of love, not realizable through any clear *ergon*, leaves a man in the uncertainty of decision. If he were a true lover, the requirement of love would be the revelation of God for him; it would in fact no longer encounter him as requirement. As summary of the law, the requirement of love does indeed reveal God, but by revealing the judgment, the wrath of God. The law works wrath.

*Thus God is manifest in the requirement of the moment as the requirement of love.* But God becomes manifest as *God* only when not only the requirement but also the possibility of its fulfillment is manifest. And this occurs in the word of forgiveness spoken into the moment. It tells me that in my present moment I am one who is loved and as such am free for love.

This is what this word does, since it discloses to me *my* past as determined by not loving, and, as regards the radical understanding of the requirement of love, that means *by hate*.

Since the word of forgiveness, calling from me the confession that I am a sinner, means to understand in a radical way the requirement of love that extends over my entire *Dasein*, it teaches me to see *that my Dasein is always open to the question of being determined by love or by hate*. No existence with others would not be existence in love or in hate. All forms of human *Dasein* in state, society, and culture have emerged from love or hate and can either serve the will to self-assertion or love. No action and no omitting to act is without significance for this either-or.

But precisely because the radical requirement of love teaches me to see this, it teaches me to see that in fact *my entire past is an existence in hate*, that I always move into the present as one defined by hate. The requirement makes me aware of this by encountering me as a "thou shalt," and it thus opens my eyes to the fact that my history is in fact marked by hate. Not as though I could document acts of hate here or there in my past. Over against such acts I could, of course, also document acts of love. The requirement opens my eyes in this way, that I see that the conditions of my present activity that have emerged from my history leave me in perplexity in face of the requirement of love. In what should an action of love be carried out? The *ordinances of the*[102] *state* are an ordering of *justice and force*. I understand that they are necessary, otherwise humanity would be annihilated in the struggle of all against all. But I see first of all that in these ordinances nothing at all is done in love, that through them one person is distanced from the other, since these ordinances secure one against the other, and thus remove the mutual relation that belongs to a loving decision. Through his "But I say unto you . . ." Jesus must first make us aware that legality can be a cover for self-ishness, that obedience to law does not yet fulfill the obligation to love. With our heritage in legal ordinances we are first led to con-ceive our relation to others impersonally.

But the need for the state and for justice indicates that self-will, the struggle of all against all, does in fact rule our life with one another, and that we are all led first to seek our own. We first encounter our fellow human beings with an attitude of wait-and-see, that is, with mistrust, that is, with hate. And they encounter us in the same way. We live in the state of being hated. We know well what love is, for love has encountered us all. We understand the command to love, because love is a possibility of our *Dasein*. But love is pos-sible only as conquest of self-will. That is, we actually live in hate, have a history of hating and being hated, a history in which the phe-nomena of love are exceptions. And we all contribute to the fact that this history abides as a history of hating and being hated.

*The word of forgiveness* thus compels us to recognize that we live in evil. It assumes the requirement of love and maintains it as a word of forgiveness. It makes clear that the requirement of love does not illumine the moment, does not signal its truth, because we enter the present moment as hating and hated. Only if I were to enter the pre-sent moment from a history of love would the commandment of love point out to me that moment's truth. Positively, the word of forgive-ness states *that I enter my present moment as one who is loved*, that all the hate from which I come is already purged through God's for-giveness, that I need not begin by loving, but that I receive love as a gift.[103] *En toutō estin hē agapē, ouch hoti hēmeis ēgapēkamen ton theon, all' hoti autos ēgapēsen hēmas kai apesteilen ton hyion autou hilasmon peri tōn hamartiōn hēmōn* ("In this is love, not that we loved God but that he loved us and sent his Son to be the atoning sacrifice for our sins"; 1 John 4:10). [D]

The revelation of God's love in forgiveness, however, also signifies a disclosure of the world as creation and thus human liberation from an anxiety that denies the Creator. Here it is clear that the human being's hate is rooted in his anxiety. He does not give himself to the other for fear of losing himself. In Romans 5:1-11, Paul takes pains to show that *zōē* is given with *dikaiosynē*, so that one need not live in anxiety but can live in *elpis*, certain of the future as the one whom God has forgiven.

Cf. Rom. 8:32: *hos ge tou idiou hyiou ouk epheisato alla hyper hēmōn pantōn paredōken auton, pōs ouchi kai syn autō ta panta hēmin charisetai* ("He who did not withhold his own Son, but gave him up for all of us, will he not with him also give us everything else?"); 8:15: *ou gar elabete pneuma douleias palin eis phobon alla elabete pneuma hyiothesias* ("For you did not receive a spirit of slavery to fall back into fear, but you have received a spirit of adoption")—this grounds the admonition not to live after the flesh, but to put to death the *praxeis tou sōmatos* (deeds of the body; 8:12f.), thus to let go every desire to secure the self. Cf. 1 John 4:18: *phobos ouch estin en tē agape all' hē teleia agapē exō ballei ton phobon, hoti ho phobos kolasin echei, ho de phoboumenos ou teteleiōtai en tē agapē* (There is no fear in love, but perfect love casts out fear; for fear has to do with punishment, and whoever fears has not reached perfection in love). [E]

This is the peculiarly Christian proclamation, that *in Jesus Christ God* gives *forgiveness* and has freed us for love; that the requirement of love no longer encounters us as law but is the fruit of faith active in love (Gal. 5:6, 22). The present moment in which I live is marked by love. This does *not* mean *that in that past from which I come there once lived a loving man, Jesus*, whose love of sinners is evident in individual stories about him.[104] The perception of acts of love or of a loving personality can inspire or shame me, or both, but does not make me one who is loved. His personal love does not apply to me at all. A love that has to do with me cannot be documented as a phenomenon of the past but can only meet me in the present.

Thus, that God so loved the world in Christ does *not* mean *that Jesus disclosed the insight that love* belongs *to the idea of God*, to the effect that the word about love in the preaching consisted of a pure idea of God, having been understood as an attribute of God. Such an insight could only make me aware of my distance from God.

The Christian proclamation affirms that *what has occurred in Christ is the deed of God's love* that forgives my sin, a deed, therefore, that interrupts the human history of sin, a deed that no longer leaves history to itself so that my present moment is no longer to be understood from *Dasein* left to itself, but from the forgiveness that occurred in Christ. This is what the New Testament means when it states that Christ was sent when the time had fully come (Gal. 4:4), that in him *the new aeon has broken in*; that the old has passed away and all become new, so that whoever is "in Christ," is a new creation (2 Cor. 5:17); or, that Christ is *the* crisis *of the world*, that with him light entered the world, and by that very fact the crisis has occurred, according to which people come to the light or flee from it (John 3:18f.); that everyone who believes in him has already passed from death to life (John 5:24f.).

This means that *the historical fact of Jesus Christ* does not determine history and our own present time as do other events of intellectual history. It does not determine it in such fashion that I am clearly under its spiritual effects and come to a decision in expressly appropriating these effects within the context of my sinful life. Rather, it determines it in such fashion that through this historical fact the entire context of my life is rendered problematic.

This fact determining my present moment does not encounter me as other events of the past encounter me in the historical tradition, and to the shaping of which all contribute, but in a tradition peculiar to that fact, in the *church's proclamation of the word*.

In the *church's proclamation* a fact of the past is always made contemporaneous for me.[105] Use of the proclaimed word belongs inseparably to the event that occurred in Christ. God through Christ has reconciled the world to himself, and given the *diakonian tēs katallagēs*, the *logon tēs katallagēs* (ministry of reconciliation, the message of reconciliation; 2 Cor. 5:18f.). Thus, since the proclamation is a word that accosts us, the here and now is the eschatological now: *idou nyn kairos euprosdektos, idou nyn hēmera sōterias* ("See, now is the acceptable time; see, now is the day of salvation"; 2 Cor. 6:2). Thus, since the proclamation is a word accosting us (John 5:25), each present moment is the eschatological moment, the *hōra* when the voice of God's Son is heard.

So we come *from out of a history of love*, insofar as in Christ the divine forgiveness has become reality, can ever become reality in the church's proclamation, and does so in the faith that makes it its own. Since Christ, the word of forgiveness stands over all that has occurred and still occurs. It meets us as the legitimated word of the church's proclamation, a word that with divine authority promises us forgiveness and thereby frees us to love. *God's revelation as historical event is thus Jesus Christ as the Word of God*, which begins with the contingent, historical event of Jesus of Nazareth and is alive in the church's tradition. The fact of Jesus Christ is not of concern as some visible thing apart from the proclamation but as something that encounters us in it, is made contemporary by it. He is the word.[106] As Christology, theology has the task of explicating the doctrine of Christ as Word of God and thus the doctrine of the church and its tradition. In doing so, the word must be understood in its dual character as a command to love and as the promise of forgiveness. Only in this way can it be understood as addressed to the moment. Faith in forgiveness is genuine only when it is the light that illumines the requirement of the moment, so that I as lover can discover the what or content of my action. Faith cannot be isolated against love, just as love is impossible apart from faith.

Forgiveness is, of course, not a fact to be documented, something ready to hand. It is actual only by being received in the moment in which it is spoken, the moment for which the requirement of love exists, a requirement confirmed in forgiveness and for which one is set free. The *Christian "ethic"* is rooted in revelation, an ethic that is not a system of ethical principles but rather the command to love, or rather it is the love that must always discover the what or content of its activity. *The new aeon* is a reality *in the present as always coming, an aeon that is at hand in its coming.* It is always a *coming* aeon, insofar as the future in which love is to be realized is always ahead of the moment. *It is at hand* insofar as the love that lays hold of the future is rooted in faith that apprehends the revelation that occurred in Christ and is made contemporary in the Word. We must now explain the significance of this faith. [D]

# 5

# The Concept of Faith

## §12. The Concept of Faith in the Church and Its Disintegration

(*a*) According to the *Catholic view*[1] justifying faith is dogmatic faith, theoretical assent to the truths of revelation[2]—exactly what Protestant dogmatics describes as *fides historica*. The Protestant concept of the *fides fiducialis*[3] is rejected, a concept described as subjective faith in one's own justification. *Fiducia* is of course indispensable "in the matter of justification," but only as the *result* of a particular act of assent to the fact that the sinner is justified by God's grace.[4] "Consequently, it is church dogma that genuine justifying faith is not to be defined *qualitatively* as 'fiducial faith,' but as *dogmatic* or theoretical faith in the revealed truths."[5]

On this view, revealed truths are regarded as universal truths, and the problem arises as to *how much of them must be believed*, or how much must be believed with the *fides explicita*, and how much with the *fides implicita* ("I believe from the heart all that God has revealed," or "I believe all that the church believes and proposes that I believe"—that is, even though I am not aware of it in detail).[6] The discussion turns on whether six points comprise a minimum of the *fides explicita*: (1) The existence of God, (2) recompense in the beyond, (3) the Trinity, (4) the Incarnation, (5) immortality of the soul, (6) the need for grace.[7] Of these, numbers 5 and 6 are held to be superfluous, since number 5 is already contained in number 2, and number 6 is already contained in number l, since the need for grace belongs to the dogma of divine providence, which in turn belongs to the divine recompense. Numbers 3 and 4 are probably also superfluous, since a supernatural act of repentance in and of itself may be inferred from mere faith in God's existence and in the providence of grace (recompense), and since this faith implicitly contains faith in Christ (and the Trinity)as a faith of desire (*fides in voto*).[8] Numbers l and 2, however, are indispensable as part of the *fides explicita*, and of course *necessitate medii*, thus as faith in the supernatural revelation and not as mere rational faith.[9]

This *faith, however, is indispensable for justification*, while if need be the sacraments may be done without.[10] But *faith alone does not suffice*. It must be supplemented by good works, or by other supplemental acts of disposition, acts that prove faith is effective through love and completed by it. That is, faith must develop from a *fides informis* to a *fides formata*. According to the Council of Trent, the process of justification normally occurs in four stages: (1) from belief to fear (*timor servilis*), (2) from fear to hope (*spes*), (3) from hope to initial love (*diligere incipiunt*), (4) from initial love to true repentance with the intention to better one's life (*contritio cum proposito novae vitae*).[11] In this process *fides informis* becomes the *fides formata* which justifies.[12]

The following sentence most aptly indicates how on this view justification is made to depend on one's own performance:

> But now every movement assumes a *terminus a quo* which is left behind, and a *terminus ad quem*, which is aspired to; consequently, moral movement toward God apart from faith requires the voluntary *retreat* from sin (repentance, resolution) and the voluntary *advance* toward righteousness (hope, love, desire).

Then Thomas, in the *Summa Theologica*, II-I, Question CXIII, Article 5, is cited in support:

> The justification of the ungodly is a certain movement whereby the human mind is moved by God from the state of sin to the state of jus-

tice. . . . Hence the human mind whilst it is being justified, must, by a movement of free choice withdraw from sin and draw near to justice. Now to withdraw from sin and to draw near to justice, in the movement of free choice, means detestation and desire. . . . Hence in the justification of the ungodly there must be two movements of free choice—one, whereby it tends to God's justice, the other whereby it hates sin.[13]

(*b*) By contrast,[14] *Protestant dogmatics* following Luther taught justification *apart from works*.[15] The radicalism of this view is especially clear in the assertion that even *faith itself is not a human work* that one may produce by his own strength,[16] since the "natural man's" distrust of God can only be overcome by God himself. Faith is thus to be viewed as a work of God himself effected through word and sacrament. The *Formula of Concord*, Solid Declaration III, 11, reads: "Faith is a gift of God whereby we rightly learn to know Christ as our redeemer in the Word of the Gospel."[17] And John Gerhard writes:

> We are so corrupted and depraved by sin, that we not only need redemption, the pardon of sins, the gift of salvation and eternal life, but that we also cannot of ourselves and from our own power produce even faith through which to become partakers of divine grace and heavenly blessings. God, therefore, pitying us, acted as a faithful physician, who not only carried medicine to the patient to cure him, but in addition, if there be occasion, and the invalid cannot do it, attends to the administration of it himself.[18]

For this reason a *fides implicita* is also *rejected*, for it contradicts the idea of revelation. *Fides* can only be *explicita*, if it is *fiducia* in God's saving deed. If the saving deed is not manifest, then it cannot be genuinely believed; there can only be a decision to believe something, if need be.[19] But true faith, the *fides specialis*, is that

> by which the sinner, converted and regenerated, applies to himself individually the universal promises in reference to Christ the Mediator, and the grace of God accessible through Him, and believes that God desires to be propitious to him and to pardon his sins, on account

of the satisfaction of Christ, made for him and all men's sins. It is therefore called special faith, not because it has any special promise as its object . . . but on account of the application by which, under the universal promise of the grace of God and the merit of Christ, it reaches him individually.[20]

In this way the subjectivity of faith is likewise to be averted,[21] just as on the other hand the misconception that faith is an assent to universal truths. Faith is actually a laying hold of grace. Assent to scripture and all the doctrines has meaning only to the extent grace is laid hold of in them:

> The promise of grace is the proper object of justifying faith. But as the sum, end, scope, and goal of the entire Scriptures is Christ in His mediatorial office, so faith, when it assents to the entire Word of God, regards the scope of the entire Scriptures, and refers all the other articles to the promise of grace.[22]

*Fiducia* as trust in the *promissio* is thus not conceived as a human attitude of soul. It rather is understood in its intentionality as faith *in*, that is, in God's saving deed, as much as it is also trust.[23] This comes clearly to expression first of all in the distinction between its *three components*: *notitia*, *assensus*, and *fiducia*. What is false in the Protestant dogmatic is merely its description of *notitia* as a component of faith. But reference to it indicates that the historical character of human existence as well as of the revelation is to be maintained. Faith is a human possibility only in a specifically historical situation, in which a specific proclamation is transmitted. It is neither an a priori of the human spirit nor a universal attitude of soul such as optimism or peace of mind and the like; it is not a "disposition."

Originally, *assensus* was not distinguished from *fiducia*, but denoted "the human's inner surrender to the gracious will of God becoming manifest to him."[24] Luther writes: "*assentimur cum apprehendimus promissionem. . . .*"[25]—we assent when we lay hold of the promise. Article 4, ¶48,[26] the *Apology of the Augsburg Confession* reads:

That faith that justifies, however, is no mere historical knowledge, but the firm acceptance of God's offer promising forgiveness of sins and justification. To avoid the impression that it is merely knowledge, we add that to have faith means to want and to accept the promised offer of forgiveness of sins and justification.

In Article 4, ¶81,[27] the *Apology* reads: "In this way we are reconciled to the Father and receive the forgiveness of sins when we are comforted by trust in the mercy promised for Christ's sake."[28]

But this distinction between *assensus generalis* and *specialis* (identical to *fiducia*), reflects a wrong turn. For the *promissiones* cannot at all be seen to be "true" without the *applicatio* to me.[29] Otherwise they become merely *universal truths*. And when *assensus* in this sense is added to *notitia* and *fiducia*, the illusion arises that the saving deeds must first be assented to before they can be the basis for faith, though they become visible as saving deeds only *in faith*.[30] Orthodoxy is prey to this illusion. The result then is that theology establishes itself as the object of faith[31] by demonstrating the truth of the saving doctrines. Then it is no longer God's saving deed mediated through the *notitia* (or the word), but pure doctrine which is regarded as the object of faith. And scripture appears as a compendium of doctrine, the acceptance of which on authority is secure only so long as scriptural authority (inspiration) is undisputed. And faith is misconstrued as assent to *pure doctrine*, in certain instances by means of a *sacrificium intellectus*.[32]

(*c*) *Pietism* is a reaction to this view of faith as orthodox belief. Naturally, it loses the intentionality of faith by reducing it to a human attitude. Further, the entire modern view of man in *idealism* and *romanticism* is a reaction, a view that can also construe faith as a human attitude. Finally, there is reaction in the relevant theological and anthropological insight that God and God's activity cannot directly be made the object of scientific reflection, as was the case in orthodoxy. To this is added a critical biblical research that has finally demolished belief in inspiration and with it the formal authority of scripture as a book of doctrine.

In *modern development* two tendencies can be distinguished in the understanding of faith: first in rationalism, second in romanticism, and linked to it a skeptical naturalism.

From rationalism, consistent with the tradition in Catholic and orthodox tradition, derives the understanding of faith as a *worldview*.[33] By this is meant a theory about the unity of the world, or about humanity and the world as a unity; about the origin and purpose of the world. The worldview would be religious or Christian if it did not imagine it could conceive the origin and meaning of the world without reckoning on a deity as a principle transcending the world or immanent in it. But if the world is rendered intelligible on the basis of an idea of God, then one has just an idea, not God, and what is called God is a principle, which is itself (say, as *prima causa*) the object of reflection, of thought, a principle that is world and is proved to be such by the fact that it is the basis for understanding the world.

A worldview is expressed in *universal truths*, whose universality does not depend on how many affirm it. It is established by the fact that the propositions are true, irrespective of the actual historical situation of the one who states them; by the fact that they are timelessly valid—propositions in which God and humanity are subjected to timeless reflection, to self-orienting thought as something ready to hand. A worldview is thus opposed to faith. Grounded in a general understanding of world and humanity it intends to understand the moment[34] as an instance of the universal.[35] For this reason it sees right past my historical existence, past the reality in which I live. Hankering after a worldview can be construed as a flight from oneself, as a striving to fortify oneself with universals, while it is uncertainty that characterizes my existence as human-historical. Just when I become aware of my uncertainty, a worldview aims to relieve me of decision. In cases of conflict, say, by an ethical theory, or in the case of destiny (death) by a cosmological theory.

At the same time it is of no great consequence whether the worldview is developed from rational principles, from judgments as to value, or from dogmatic tradition.[36] Even when founded on experiences, as is, for example, an aesthetic worldview, its rationalistic character is not surrendered. It is given with the claim of its propositions to timeless validity.

So conceived, the idea of *God's omnipotence*, for example, is not a thought that derives from faith if construed as manageable and even intelligible, an idea by which world occurrence is understood and my destiny comprehended as one instance of it. In that case, it is only a limiting concept, only the notion of a power raised to the infinite, or the notion of a causality conditioning everything, or the notion of the origin of regularity in the world.[37] As an idea that belongs to faith, omnipotence affirms that God can do anything God wants: "Our God is in the heavens; he does whatever he pleases" (*kōl 'asher-ḥāphēts 'āsāh*; Ps. 115:3); "Whatever the Lord pleases he does, in heaven and on earth, in the seas and all deeps" (*kōl 'asher-ḥāphēts yhwh 'āsāh*; Ps. 135:6).

This statement can only be made (if it is not to be a mere matter of insight into the *idea* of God, by which God's reality is left undecided), when I know that in my reality I am given definition by God.

Likewise, the *idea of creation* as cosmological theory is not an idea that belongs to faith. It would be such only if it were a faith that through God's deed for me the reality in which I live and on my own can only view as godless has become God's world. The idea of creation is not a presupposition but the crowning of faith. Luther writes:

> Without doubt, this is the greatest article of faith, in which we say: "I believe in God the Father Almighty, Maker of heaven and earth." And whoever rightly believes this, is truly helped and again put right and has arrived at the place from which Adam fell. But few come so far that they perfectly believe he is the God who creates and makes all things. For such a person must have died to everything, to good and evil, death and life, hell and heaven, and from the heart confess he can do nothing by his own powers.[38]

Particularly characteristic of rationalism is its *belief in providence*. But in rationalism as in the Stoa, providence merely expresses the idea of the purposefulness of world events, under the assumption that I control the purpose (am the purpose!) and thus have at my disposal a criterion by which I can judge whether the world is in harmony with the divine. The pessimism matching this optimism rests on the same assumptions and as such is just as far removed from faith. As an idea of faith, belief in providence can only mean that within the enigmatic world-events into which I am woven and do not understand God leads me to himself.

For such rationalism the problem of God and the world arises in the theoretical question of the relation between *nature* as scientifically comprehensible and reality, the activity of God. And insofar as in the most primitive deism God's activity is not limited to that of the *prima causa*, and thus his invisibility in nature is conceded, nature and God are identified. Nature in its regularity is perceived as a form of the divine activity and contemplated in its purposefulness or beauty; it is in fact perceived as a revelation of God. The truth is that nature as regularity veils God,[39] and we have no right at all to describe the workings of nature thus perceived as the activity of God."Again, if God's word and sign is not there or not seen, it is of no use, even if God himself were there" (Luther).[40] In fact, in nature as such we see nothing but an occurrence conforming to law. Over against such an objective nature faith can only appeal to miracle, that is, must forego identifying the reality of God with that of nature. But in my historical existence, nature does not at all encounter me as an objective reality conforming to law, but as a myriad of possibilities for my acting and suffering, for my decisions. Only when I look away from my existence do I view nature objectively, and insofar as I set myself in relation to it, I see myself as one natural thing among others, as one object among others, living together with them in a reciprocal action conformable to law. And on that basis I never arrive at speaking of God and God's activity, if that speaking is ever to give definition to my historical existence.

The result is the same when *history* is viewed after the analogy of nature as a nexus, to be objectively viewed, made sense of on the basis of principles, and conformable to law. Within this nexus I would be one particular member, an instance of the universal, no matter whether history is viewed materialistically or biologically or even idealistically. I would not have understood history from the perspective of my own historical existence, and I would not see God in it as the power that determines my existence. I would come to a vague historical pantheism.[41]

There is an *ancient rationalism* in total control here, a rationalism that sees past human historicity and perceives human nature in the universal, in the timeless, in the *logoi*, in what I can perceive in myself through abstraction, in what can be grasped under the notion of regularity, something toward which my thought can turn me.[42] Human existence is seen to be secure when it is understood as part of the cosmos in which the law identical to the law of the cosmos is at work, a law recognized in philosophical self-reflection.

*Romanticism* refuses to assign to religion a worldview that lapses into universal truths, into timeless propositions, and polemicizes against a rationalism that attempts to do so. In the religious act, romanticism intuits the universe as a unity, but will not cling to this intuition as something objective, and foregoes the claim to truth.[43]

Religion "stops with the immediate experiences of the existence and action of the universe, with the individual intuitions and feelings; each of these is a self-contained work, without connection with others or dependence upon them; it knows nothing about derivation and connection, for among all things religion can encounter, that is what its nature most opposes."[44] In religion

> only the particular is true and necessary; nothing can or may be proved anything else. Everything universal under which the particular is supposed to be treated, each collection and combination of this sort, either exists in a different territory, if it is to be referred to the inner and essential realm, or is only the work of playful imagination and the freest caprice.[45]

Faith here is thus construed as a universal religious feeling. Nothing at all is believed—experience as such, experience as psychic event, is faith.[46]

Modern theology often comprises a turgid *mixture* of the insight that what is essential in religion should not run out into universal propositions, together with the assertion of faith that it contains specific propositions concerning man, the world, and God. As a result, the tenets of faith are construed as universal truths, though one refuses to establish those truths in clear principles and sees their origin in experiences or attitudes of irrational personal life. This is the case when the tenets of faith are conceived as resting upon *judgments of value*. For example, it is stated that humans have not only a yearning for God but also an intuition of God as highest power and moral will, an intuition, that is, from out of human consciousness of value, a consciousness aware of precisely this intuition as a "value."[47] In order for the feeling of value to become a conviction of its reality, it naturally needs encounter with a reality in which the value appears in truly objective fashion—encounter with a personality, which then preserves a role for Jesus.[48] Thus from value judgments and experiences a Christian worldview is developed that still runs out into universal truths, into propositions taken to be universal and timeless, distinguished from scientific propositions only by the fact that they do not originate in thought, but in the subject, and thus are only subjectivities.

The cult of experience as such is, of course, more recent than a worldview based on judgments of value. For this cult, faith has become a *universal religious feeling*.[49] Its object is *the ineffable*, the irrational. The word is seen to be inadequate, though it is precisely in the word that we are aware of our historical existence, and through the word alone our activity takes on meaning and differs from a natural event or mechanical process. The word is excluded from worship and "sacred silence" is introduced—which still makes sense only when there is speaking. Where one does not go to such lengths, *piety* at least is regarded as an authentic component of faith, and the substitution of a history of Christian piety for a New Testament theology and history of dogma appears as a goal worthy of pursuit.[50] Not even reflection on Jesus' piety is avoided, as if the piety of one man (when really taken seriously) could in any way apply to another. Most often, of course, it is not taken seriously. Rather, piety (the life of prayer, etc.!) is understood as something perceptible in me and others and accessible to psychological analysis.

The error appears in its crassest form in *Ernst Troeltsch*.[51] Troeltsch defines faith as "a total religious attitude of soul, a willing surrender to God and an allowing oneself to be filled by God." "Here, then, faith is identical to religion itself,"[52] it is simply "*piety*."[53] Piety, of course, is the broader concept, and faith in the real

sense is the cognitive element which co-(!)determines piety. Thus
throughout the history of religions, the *myth* or speculative knowledge, *gnosis*, belongs to piety.[54]

According to Troeltsch, what is specific in Christianity is that

> its myth and its gnosis have religious value only as producing a prac-
> tical-religious and ethical intention; that its devotion is not oriented to
> cult or rites, but to a knowledge of God that determines the will, or
> rather to the inner union of essence and will with God that takes place
> in this knowledge. Entirely of its own accord, this knowledge is
> directed to what has significance in practical-religious terms. Its piety
> is faith, and its faith is piety.[55]

The following quotations indicate how on Troeltsch's view faith
pulls itself up by its own bootstraps, when on one hand it gives rise
to the practical-religious and ethical intention, and on the other is the
product of that intention itself.

Troeltsch writes that the peculiarity of Christianity within religious history is its reflection of "the breakthrough of *purely ethical
religiosity*":

> It recognizes only a knowledge that has practical, religious-ethical
> value, is authenticated by this value, and is aware only of a praxis that
> emerges from a pure knowledge of God. . . . The simplest idea possi-
> ble, expressing the practical experience of being lifted to God and
> attributable to an inner self-certainty, is shown to be its all pervasive
> core.[56]

The narrower meaning of faith is of "trust and surrender," "but
precisely *to a reality comprehended in ideas*. It is simply a living and
acting on the basis of an idea."[57]

How is faith related to this idea? All religions trace their faith, as
worked by God, to *revelation*. Faith, therefore (in good Catholic
fashion!), is first of all faith in the foundational revelation and should
of course not be mere assent to the tradition. That is, revelation itself
is nothing but a "heightened belief ranging above the ordinary and
radiating its power." It is "the productive and original appearance of
a new religious force or elevation of life represented as a practical

totality of life and intention, transmitting its powers from its bearers."[58] Faith, thus, is faith in the faith of others!

For the bearer of revelation that totality is represented in a fullness of visions, ideas about God, the world and humanity, that is, in a *myth* shaped by naive fantasy:[59]

> Production of the myth belongs to every religion, which, in such a purely personal-spiritual-ethical religion, presents itself as an embodiment of the idea of God and his aims with the world and man, as well as an image of the peculiar mission of the revelation-bearer. . . . [60] One might also use the term "*symbol*" for it, but may not forget that for the creative genius, myth is in the main reality naively viewed.[61]

> Confident and submissive attachment to the religious totality as it appeared in the hero is then faith in the hero himself and in the religious idea given to him.[62]

In further development the world of ideas is changed. Above all, the hero is glorified. The new totality of life is expressed in dogma and cult, so that faith can now be defined as "a mythical-symbolic-practical, peculiarly religious type of thought and knowledge, a type that begins with an historical-personal impression, that believes in the myth for the sake of the practical-religious powers it mediates, and that knows how to express, objectify and mediate these powers through the myth."[63]

In this development *the dialectic of faith* consists in its tendency to unify the divine, and in its opposition to the world,

> by which humanity, once more related to God as religious, is nonetheless distinguished from God and the world. The restoration to inner unity of these three disparate entities and the achieving of an elevation of life to the absolute through this union comprises the dialectic of the religious idea (ideas of redemption; the chief types: pantheistic-antipersonalistic and theistic-personalistic redemption).[64]

By this means, the knowledge of faith is continually influenced by the current scientific view of the world, to which it adapts the myth and from which it appropriates new religious motifs and mythical personifications. Both occur only up to a certain limit: If the myth is dissolved in a picture of the world, religious substance is also dissolved and new religious formations must appear. If faith is overgrown by new belief-motifs and myths, then it suffocates, and new formations must also appear.[65] If the myth originates in the naive and naive social classes, then *theology* has the task of uniting the naive religious myth with the universal concepts of science. "In doing so theology first of all construes faith as it had become in the previous medium, an authoritative, supernaturally attested and mediated knowledge, and to an extent possible, unites this supernatural knowledge with the prevailing natural or scientific knowledge.[66] Finally, theology arrives at a "psychological analysis of faith," in which "the . . . mythical-symbolic-practical character of faith" is "recognized as its peculiar psychological nature."[67] "By this means also one arrives at a schematizing of the historical-psychological cultivation and development of faith" as Troeltsch offers it.[68]

On this view, *theology* by its very nature would remain a union of science and myth, though not always in the old fashion of juxtaposing supernatural and natural knowledge. It would be such

> in the new way of securing the practical-symbolic type of knowledge that moves toward ultimate religious truth, alongside exact-scientific types that move toward experience. . . . But this occurs by way of psychology and cognitive theory, the latter always containing an element of the metaphysical. The basis for assigning independent cognitive value to faith is an epistemology of faith that does not aim at universal concepts contained in religion, but at a relation to reality that is mediated in it, and that ranks the various types of faith according to the results achieved and according to the embrace of the total values of life ventured.[69]

Now, Troeltsch carries on a kind of *apologetic* by referring to the psychological indestructability of religion, forcing one to concede its value as an a priori. That is, an element of truth belongs even to fantasy.

According to Troeltsch, every conviction of ultimate truths and values is religious in nature, is a faith, so that faith thus extends to the presuppositions of the empirical sciences (an alternation of hypothesis and faith). "Such faith is a total attitude (!) of soul, directed toward truth and value, and thus toward the absolute (!), which, as soon as it speaks of itself, cannot totally avoid mythical form."[70] And insofar as science strives for a total picture, it is always influenced by myth (traditional or spontaneous), by faith. Faith and knowledge are neither identical nor purely to be distinguished. Mythical-religious and scientific-conceptual knowledge interpenetrate, engage in struggle, and seek a balance never to be achieved.

Troeltsch writes that in a formal way religion shares an inner feeling of necessity with logic, ethics, and art. The knowledge of faith has its own certainty, based on its practical indispensability and inner sense of duty, a certainty that of course is only weak in the masses but radiates from strong religious personalities. It furnishes science with the idea of absolute realities, truths, and values. Faith's cognitive value thus rests in a practical conquest of the enigmas of life through a seizing hold of a redemptive power of fellowship with God authenticated in practice.[71]

> The more pure the reflection on the concept of faith in psychological and epistemological fashion, the easier the union with what is "*purely religious*," where all ideas of faith merely express or mediate a religious relation to God, the world and humanity; where, of course, the myth has not died out and cannot do so, but has become the means and expression of the fundamental religious position of the total person.[72] [A]

## §13. Mysticism and Faith

In face of this pseudo-theology, *mysticism* appears to be the only avenue of escape.[73] By mysticism we do not mean *a psychic attitude*—ecstasy, for example—since there is a prophetic as well as a mystical ecstasy. The prophetic variety is a psychic condition in which the prophet hears the word of God he is to proclaim. The mystical variety is an end in itself, an enjoyment in which the mystic is able to hear *arrēta rhēmata (arrēta rhēmata, ha ouch exon anthrōpō lalēsai*—things that are not to be told, that no mortal is permitted to repeat; 2 Cor. 12:4). Meditation in worship, with its thrill in song, silence, or reception of the sacrament, is no more mysticism as a psychic condition than are speculations on the unity of being.

Of course, it is understandable that psychic conditions, ecstasy, and cultic transports should play a great role in mysticism, since the individual thinks he is loosed from himself in them, feels overtaken and overwhelmed by an alien force, thus supposes that he possesses God as the Wholly Other, and in this way has escaped all duality in space and time, and is freed from everything and everyone over against him.[74] This is in fact the decisive perception of mysticism, that *God is the Wholly Other*, beyond the world and humanity, the *epekeina* at once annihilating and filling up the unity of all being.[75] The question is merely where this idea is critically embraced, for only there is there genuine mysticism. Thus mysticism is present neither in ecstasy as such, nor in cultic rapture, nor in a speculative transcending of tangible existence and in a seizing hold of the ground of being through thought. It is present neither in inspiration nor in the intoxication of love, nor in the forgetfulness that comes with the enjoyment of art, when one is "lifted beyond oneself." Where then is the difference from narcotic or alcoholic intoxication, which also has its role in religious history?

Mysticism sees that the idea of God signifies that God is the Wholly Other beyond what is human,[76] that for this reason the human being can produce nothing in himself to bring him to God or procure God for him: neither his action (it is either harmful, in which case the result is quietism; or it is indifferent, in which case the result is libertinism; or it is preparatory, in which case the result is asceticism,[77] but never an action that as such could have positive worth), nor his thought[78] (God lies beyond the *ratio*: thus silence[79]).

Thus, to see God, one must *be free of, be void of self*, must die the threefold death to arrive "whither created sense has never penetrated."[80] The mystics who really "wanted to be mystics, that is, who sought God's revelation, knew right well that one must travel a road on which all of this, the inmost personal experiences, the right and dignity of the personality, all lie soon behind; that for all that meets it and still seeks it the revelation of God spells death; that life is only what is given birth from it."[81] Mysticism is thus strictly dissociated from every religion construed as a tangible, situational human attitude or self-discovery.[82]

This means, then, that the knowledge of mysticism is formally correct, that its idea of God is correct. But it has the idea of God without God, *it believes it has God in the idea of God.* [A]

Mysticism imagines it possesses God in the idea of God, and, what amounts to the same thing, *confuses being with an existent.*[83] Since it aims to conceive God as beyond all that exists, in its abstraction it arrives at a concept of being to which it in turn assigns a being conceived as the highest and all-encompassing existent.[84]

God is beyond all nonexistence and existence. The mystic must step out of self and everything else into the brilliance of the divine darkness.[85] Darkness and light are one. Through not-seeing and not-knowing the mystic arrives at "what is beyond all seeing and knowing."[86]

"*Deus igitur et esse idem*"—Therefore God and being are the same (Eckhart); it is the "*esse purum et simplex,*" not an "*esse hoc et hoc.*"[87] "Therefore God is much more a 'naught' that is yet an incomprehensible 'aught.'"[88] Thus Nicholas of Cusa writes: "The best answer to the question whether God exists is that he neither *is* nor is *not*, and that he is *not*-is and is not."[89]

Only in this way can the statements of Meister Eckhart be understood, to the effect that all creatures per se are a mere nothing,[90] that is, as existent things they are nonbeing.

Since for mysticism being is always the being of an existent thing, being is hypostatized and viewed as a single (or total) existent thing. One imagines that one possesses the reality of God in the idea of being. What applies to the *idea* of the soul the mystic assigns to his *I*.[91]

In mysticism, *being* as the highest conceivable thought is *identified with God*, and for this reason is described as salvation, as the truly valuable. Since being is opposed to becoming which is of no value, the motive is clearly anxiety in face of death: One desires to be rid of becoming.[92]

"If I am not thereby free from death, what are these to me!"[93] Mysticism leads to nothing; it is merely the explication of this anxiety.[94] [B]

"This is the fate of mysticism: it does not stay with the negative character of its knowledge of God and with the knowledge of its meaning.[95] It does not realize that in this negative knowledge of God humanity is truly known."[96]

So also the "*ground of the soul*" is nothing. Of it can only be said that it is everything the particular person is not.[97] It is neither the inner spiritual life, nor what makes a person an I. It is something that from the perspective of the I can only be expressed in negations. And in this not-I the person's real reality is supposed to lie!

Actually, something is correctly seen in mysticism, that is, that everything tangible about the person, the describable I, is not[98] the actual person. But it assumes there is something back of this describable I, instead of seeing that human being is historical, that he genuinely exists in the ongoing historical life of his relation to a Thou.

As a matter of fact, since God is described as the Wholly Other, as the *epekeina*—what is said here is merely what God is not.[99]

In mysticism

> this knowledge of the nothing is related to God, without asking whether one can and may do so. . . . instead of allowing it to be directed toward the only one to whom it could ever refer—the human. Thus mysticism, as strictly and sublimely as it separates the human from the divine, is at the same time entangled in the most unsalutary confusion of the two.—If this knowledge of the nothing is directed toward the human, and conceived as a knowledge of human nature, of sin, then only is it a knowledge of God. It is not an immediate— mysticism regards it as such—but a mediate knowledge of God.[100]

> This is the profound error of mysticism, that it imagines it has seized hold of God when acknowledging him to be the indefinable one. This is and remains a human knowledge of God, and a human knowledge for all that, thus a knowledge of the human, and in the last analysis only a human knowledge of the human—to be sure, the most profound ever conceived by the human mind.[101]

Since mysticism regards negative, formal knowledge as positive and material, it intends to actualize it in the person. That is, such knowledge is not to remain a knowing, but must become an attitude through summoning everything in the self to be silent.[102] It takes this path methodologically, by neutralizing all activity, spiritual activity above all, so that the spiritual person as it were commits suicide. Mysticism intends to conduct a person toward pure passivity. It overlooks the fact that it is just by being passive that a person is most active. Even the method of silence is an activity. Mysticism does not see that abolition of the self by the self is an impossibility—that it is a silence that I construct, an abstracting or ignoring or closing of my eyes.[103] There is no flight for humans from what is given, since one cannot flee from himself, but takes himself along wherever he is.[104] "Where we ourselves are, there is the world. The one who seeks to lay hold of God beyond this world seeks what is impossible. When he thinks he has found God, he has seized nothing more than part of the world, or the world divested of its tangibleness, at best conceived in the abstract."[105] [A]

Mysticism does not take seriously the contrary idea, that as God's creature a human is in God and does not discover God in himself.[106] Ultimately, for mysticism, only being-in-God has actual reality. Separation from God is a seeming existence that relates to actual existence in God as the mirror to its object. Mysticism thus has no need of the fall. It does not see that I do not at all seize hold of *my* reality when I speak of that existence in God, for there is no way in which I can observe how I am in God. Rather, my separation from God *is my* reality. My reality is just where mysticism sees only an image in a mirror. Mysticism makes the standpoint of God its own and intends to see with God's eyes. In fact, the contrast between the I to be annihilated and the souls' ground, which is really real[107] is set *within* the person, within the I and its extinguishing.[108]

But if this is true, then the I-Thou relation between God and the human is abolished and embraced in a third:[109] Beyond *deus* and *homo* there is *Deitas*, over against which, finally, God and humanity are unreal. [B]

Wherever there is the notion of being freed from self in the stillness of silence and of experiencing God's revelation, the result is first the idea of the union of the believer with God, and second the interpretation of psychic experiences as such a union.

Naturally, if the human being must be negated in revelation, and if on the other hand he thinks he actually experiences such a revelation, then in that experience in which he has disappeared, he can only understand himself as filled with the divine being.[110] Thus the mystic, longing to be rid of the human, yearns for *union with the deity*.[111] This union is depicted in various figures: The deity inhabits the believer; the believer is swallowed up in the deity,[112] is united in love with the deity,[113] is singed by the deity as the moth by the light,[114] is changed into the deity, deified (Hellenism)[115]—an identification with deity occurs.[116]

And since this union is regarded as something actually experienced, it is observed in *psychic conditions* that overcome a person, and in which he appears to behave in purely passive fashion. Every sort of awe and rapture that issues in ecstasy can fill him. He waits for it, since everyday life is passed in drought, and once he has it, he sinks from his condition of transport into drought again. How little psychic conditions as such constitute mysticism, but only within a specific life-context, is also evident in the fact that the mystic seldom or perhaps never really experiences union with the deity. Still, he believes in it.

*The first stage of emptying* is a sinking into the works of God, or an exaltation above all creatures.[117] At this stage exists an I-Thou-relation between God and man, for which John Tauler acknowledges the teaching of the church.

At the *second stage* even sinking into the works of God must disappear.[118] "Images" are a hindrance since they clothe the I with its "ownness." The second stage is loss of the I.[119] One is freed from whatever he is that is more than creature.[120] The I-Thou relation to God is broken through; one has entered the divine ground; birth of the divine in the human has occurred. But there must be a *third stage*, for the second does not suffice.[121] It must come to this, that "I am God" becomes "God is." One must also be emptied of the birth of God within, must know nothing of God. One must experience the entire bitterness and misery of this condition,[122] must experience "inner poverty and forsakenness." Thus godlessness arrives at I-lessness, and finally at "unity." By grace the human becomes what God is by nature.[123] This unity is the nothing in which everything that is something vanishes.[124] It is both humiliation and exaltation.[125]

In the last analysis, redemption is an act within the divine which does not concern me.

And since such experiences are made the goal of life, and the emptying of self is taken into the bargain, *the method* of mysticism is developed in which, "contrary to its own assertions," it nonetheless builds "bridges that lead from time to eternity. By developing transitions from the human to the divine, it fills its perceptions—amazingly correct in a formal respect—with human content."[126] It thus becomes *a religion* again:

> Here mysticism raises the requirement to increase emptying. Here the soul is to be rid of all things and activities, in order then to enter the Nothing. Here the soul is to separate itself "from the body that thus it will have nothing more to do with the body or such things for its own profit."[127] Here the soul is set before an infinite task, a task without end, thus a task ever new, ever another. Here the soul turns to the world of the infinitely many, in order through an infinity to attain to eternity. And where it would seize hold of the Nothing, it assumes the infinity of the mystical-moral task of self-emptying, and again stands in midst of the realm of created things and created powers, in order by means of these powers to free itself from created things. It is thus astonishingly clear that the Nothing which should be the withdrawal of all created things to their origin and at that point their divine fullness, has become a moral abstraction, a pious asceticism. And if this moral abstraction were ever achieved or regarded as such, nothing would be gained but the mere state of being void, which, however, would not be such, since it would still always have itself as its possession. There would still be the empty soul in possession of itself, bare of content or relation. Then the psychic state of transport would follow in physical reaction, and after that a readying oneself again for the souls' being void once more.[128]

What characterizes the mystical attitude of life is thus *asceticism*, a despising of the body. According to Porphyry, "Plotinus was like one who was ashamed to be in the body. "One takes flight to the beauty of soul *ouch anaschomenos tou en sōmati kallous, all' enthen anaphygōn*.[129] The concept was developed in thoroughgoing fashion in India:

> Yes, these worlds are joyless, covered with blind darkness. Into them enter all who are asleep and unknowing after death. But whoever sensed the Atman and is conscious that "I am he," what does he want, to please whom would he still wish to imitate the body's sickness?[130]

So it is with Hellenistic as well as medieval mysticism. To the extent this asceticism is still an action and not as in Indian Yoga a total inaction, a mere crouching in self-hypnosis, it is a preparatory action with purely negative significance.

*The action of mysticism* is

> as empty as its knowledge. A deed never has specific meaning, specific content, specific value. All want the same thing, to rid themselves of what they do. They want only to be undisturbed by the content of their action. They always want to forget the why of it. The mystic does not love in order to love, does not help the other because he wishes to do him good, but only because he wants to be rid of himself. The mystic does not seek to conquer suffering in order to turn it into good fortune, but in order to escape from himself and from every experience of suffering or good fortune. He does not seek to maintain his ideas of God in his daily work in order to give his work eternal meaning, but in order to be free and quit even of those absolutely necessary ideas in his inmost soul. Hence, for mysticism, this world is devoid of history, for without the realization and appearance of subjects of value, history is inconceivable. Precisely this does not exist for mysticism. For mysticism, everything belongs to this or that, and it is just from such that it needs to be free and undisturbed.[131]

In fact, *mysticism sees past man's historicity*.[132] It does not realize that life in this and that, in the here and now, characterizes human existence, and that he cannot avoid it at all. It does not realize that everything a person undertakes to do is the undertaking of someone who emerges as qualified by a history and can never escape it. It does not realize that a person's present moment is set within decision, because he is temporal. Fleeing temporality is precisely what mysticism is after. Mysticism does not realize that man's historicity consists in its link to the Thou; it fails to recognize community as qualified by guilt and demand, hate and love.

"For this reason *mysticism is also ignorant of fellowship*. For no fellowship can be conceived without a material value (that is, without the concrete elements that belong to action in the here and now). For mysticism there is only one single value: To be untouched by every value."[133] It does not see that the I only becomes an I through the Thou, and since it fails to recognize the historical character of the I in this way, it errs by conceiving the I after the fashion of the deity as a substance, as a kind of nature. It matters not whether it conceives the deity as existent, as existing beyond or as nonexistent. As long as it does not understand the deity as a Thou, as the how of human-historical existence, it construes it as substance, whether describing it as light or darkness, aroma or brilliance, cold or heat. From this too derives the significance of the "vision," in which the deity is conceived as standing still.

Naturally, these angelic choirs of which mysticism can speak on occasion are not a fellowship, for there is no I and Thou, only a being swallowed up by tones into a harmony. In this way too mysticism can conceive *church fellowship*, for it knows nothing of genuine church fellowship. Fundamentally, it is hostile to the church, though the shrewd politics of the Catholic church has given it room within its walls. Mysticism by nature may have a need to lean on traditional forms, and acquires them easily enough in churchly cult and dogma. Precisely because they are traditional and not self-generated, the forms of cult and dogma, functioning as symbols, can mediate or facilitate a kind of vision of the godhead.[134] But mysticism cannot have a real relation to the church of the Word, since the Word is directed to the concrete historical person, and intends to teach him to understand his concrete historical situation. But it is just the Word that mysticism rejects, and where necessary alters it to a symbol.

The absence of the historical appears just as sharply in the forms of mysticism, forms that by other means than asceticism prepare for a vision of God so as to evoke *ecstatic states*.[135] In India, asceticism is often found connected with hypnotic exercise, in a becoming heated through yoga. Elsewhere, other means are used, such as wine in Persia (where, incidentally, asceticism also plays a role).[136] Erotic states of ecstasy and rapture, playing their role in medieval mysticism, are evoked through immersion in church symbolism, especially in the images of Canticles. A sort of revenge occurs, so that where concrete corporeality is despised, it gets its due again in the most primitive, uncontrollable impulses. Man flees historicality by becoming a beast.

Since one in fact does not so easily avoid his historical character but for the most part is still actively concerned with something and somehow still gives shape to his world, we can understand that mysticism is easily linked to *artistic creation*, because it most often dispenses with a rational setting of goals and reflection and seems to reflect an experience in which the person is passive. The significance of symbols in mysticism indicates that link. The vision's capacity for assuming artistic shape is actualized in the adoption of traditional forms as symbols for the deity or as symbols for the path toward deity and the mystical experience. Where music becomes the symbol, the artistic capacity is "receptively" engaged (thus also active!). In actual fact, however, the mystics as individuals have almost never repudiated the word, not even the Indian mystics. Just as Meister Eckhart is a mighty shaper of words, so Plotinus, and so the Indians. Lyrical poetry above all is characteristic of mysticism, in Persian Sufism as well as in modern lyrical poetry, for example, in Rilke. But even in the plastic arts, in painting and architecture mystical piety has been creatively at work, particularly in the Gothic style of the Middle Ages.

*Speculation* is also linked to mysticism, in India as well as in Plotinus and the Middle Ages, since it can play a role in the methodology of emptying. Through the mystic's very insight into the nature of things, the mystic is freed from those things, and since vision rich in symbol is linked to speculation, complex world systems can be drafted. Indeed, when the "inner light" is opposed to authoritative doctrine, to scripture, etc., and it appears that the inner light must still transmit content, then that "inner light" can simply become an unhistorical and timeless *ratio*.[137]

The worldview of mysticism has its impress in two seemingly opposite types:

(1) In *dualism* this feature of the idea of God is retained, that God is the Wholly Other. Dualism naturally matches the ascetic manner of life, though inconsistently. Hostility toward the body allows the soul to appear as something of value. And when the soul must also be freed from every shape, must be purified from this or that, then the "ground of the soul" is by nature something akin to God. The degree to which the soul (and God) is conceived as substance here, and thus as nonhistorical, is clear. This dualistic anthropology of mysticism, in Hellenism developed from primitive animistic ideas and oriental motifs, pits the body against the soul, and ignores human historicality, because in opposing the soul to the body as something tangible, as a thing, the soul too can only be conceived as a tangible thing. The historical person is body *and* soul, and by the body the person is identified as historical, as bound to a here and now. For Christian faith, the body is not something *attached to* the person, nor is the "soul" the actual person. To regard the soul as something higher, as something related to God that prescribes to the lower its law or checks the sensual drives, is *either* to conceive it in Greek fashion as a contrast between form and matter (the two merely alongside and related to each other—a conception that has nothing to do with the Christian view of man, since it regards him as a work of art) *or* to conceive it in thoroughgoing dualistic fashion. In that case, the soul, the divine spark, is viewed as captive in the body, needing purification and redemption, a purification that may occur in sacrament or devotion, asceticism or ecstasy. By itself, none of this need be mystical, but it can be appropriated by mysticism. It is not at all Christian, since faith knows of nothing in the human pleasing to God. Rather, the human is entirely good or entirely bad. Faith sees no mysterious divine substance *behind* historical existence. It sees humanity *in its* historical existence. And in that existence humanity lives under God's claim, under God's wrath or grace.

(2) In *pantheism or monism* the idea of omnipotence crops up in the idea of God or its mystical formulation, that is, in the idea that if God alone is true being, then the being of the world, though incontestable, must also be God's being. This idea appears in Platonic, Neoplatonic form in Eckhart, when God as "unnatured nature" is revealed as "natured nature." In the Neoplatonic doctrine of the world's *exaplōsis* or *proodos* from God (emanation instead of creation!), as well as in the doctrine of the *epistrophē* borne by *erōs*, pantheistic and dualistic motifs mingle. This is especially evident in the fact that the *hylē* is really a *not*, and all of reality from God up to and including it is diminished. But pantheistic speculations are characteristic even of India and Persia, just as of lyricists such as Angelus Silesius[138] and Rilke.

We read in Eckhart how all this may be spelled:

> All "creatures" hurry to be like God. If God were not in everything, then nature would have neither activity nor desire. . . . If a man were ever so thirsty, if something of God were not in the drink, he would not desire it.

Angelus Silesius writes:

> I know, without me God cannot live for a second:
>    if I be nothing—he must needs give up the ghost.
> There is nothing but I and Thou—and if we two are not,
>    then God is no longer God and heaven collapses.
> I myself must be the sun, must paint the pale sea
>    of the whole Godhead with my beams.
> The rose that your outer eye sees here,
>    has bloomed in God from eternity.
> To God works are all alike: when the saint drinks,
>    it pleases Him as much as when he prays and sings.[139]

This pantheism too is unhistorical. It alters the idea of omnipotence to a speculation or principle of an artistic worldview. *The result* is that none has available to him the idea of omnipotence, in order actually to comprehend the world beneath. In this attempt one views the world as a work of art, not as it encounters him in his historical reality. He views himself as an organic part of a whole, instead of realizing that his existence is at stake here and now.

For the rest, it would be important to analyze more precisely the connection between dualistic and pantheistic motifs in mysticism. [A]

Mysticism is thus the link between the idea of God and the notion that one can possess God in a certain state, or can be aware of having God so.[140] Its error is the failure to recognize human existence as historical, thus, ultimately, an error in the conception of God itself. It is correct only with respect to form. The idea of a formal *epekeina* is, however, false.[141] For as "humanity" is not a formal entity, but always a specific person within a concrete historical situation, so also what transcends him only points him to the here and now.[142] What transcends is always possessed in concreteness. What transcends the human is always his within concreteness. It is not something indefinable but something that cannot be disposed of. On the contrary, it is something that disposes of him, is given to him.[143] Human passivity can never be self-made. It can only be a passivity of reception. From his perspective it can only be a deed.[144] In the very deed God's transcendence is affirmed.

It therefore makes no sense *for Protestantism to adopt mystical elements*. What makes mysticism what it is cannot be adopted without surrendering faith. But if one adopts the mystical view that God is possessed in psychic states, then not mysticism but pagan elements are adopted.[145] [B]

## §14. Faith as Historical Deed

Christian faith is *faith in the revelation of God* in the sense referred to in §11.[146] That is, it is faith in *an historical fact*.[147] But it is such that this fact as objectively verifiable is not revelation. Otherwise faith would be historical knowledge or the uncritical acceptance of historical information, in short, a *fides historica*.[148] To be obliged to believe ideas and reports presented from the outside is a violation. Neither rational arguments nor a resolve of will can safeguard such a faith.[149]

The less faith is such a *fides historica*, the more it is the certainty that through the historical fact of Jesus Christ history is marked as a history of salvation.[150] It is marked by the fact that through Jesus Christ, the one proclaimed, forgiveness of sins is preached, and I as justified enter upon my present moment, in order as a lover who is loved to understand the question of the moment and discover the what, the content of my action.[151]

*Notitia* thus belongs to faith, a *notitia* that is not mediated through historical research but through proclamation of the Word.[152] In the Word forgiveness is proferred, to the effect that Jesus Christ has come into the world and has made of the history of sin a history of grace. For this reason also faith is not a knowledge of universal truths, ideas, etc., but the obedient acceptance of the message of the forgiveness of sins and new life in Christ. For this reason it is primarily *obedience*.

Rom. 1:5: (*Iesou Christou tou kyriou hymōn*), *di hou elabomen charin kai apostolēn eis hypakoēn pisteōs en pasin tois ethnesin hyper tou onomatos autou* ("Jesus Christ our Lord, through whom we have received grace and apostleship to bring about the obedience of faith among all the Gentiles for the sake of his name"). Cf. Rom. 16:19: *he gar hemōn hypakoē eis pantas aphiketo* ("for while your obedience is known to all"), with 1:8: *hē pistis hymōn katangelletai en holō tō kosmō* ("your faith is proclaimed throughout the world"), and 1 Thess 1:8: *en panti topō hē pistis hymōn hē pros ton theon exelēluthen* ("in every place your faith in God has become known"). Rom. 10:3: *agnoountes gar tēn tou theou dikaiosynēn kai tēn idian zētountes stēsai, tē dikaiosynē tou theou ouch hypetagēsan* ("for being ignorant of the righteousness that comes from God, and seeking to establish their own, they have not submitted to God's righteousness"), as the unbelievers in 15:31 are called the *apeithountes*, and believing the gospel in Gal. 5:7 is identified as *tē alētheia peithesthai* (obeying the truth).

Faith, therefore, is not a giving of credence to some remarkable occurrence I will not refute but the recognition that together with this message something is said about *me*, because it is said about my history.

(1) Faith is *obedience*, which means that by it I recognize *myself as a sinner*. Naturally, not that I exhibit greater or lesser weaknesses, errors, or immoral acts, but that I emerge from my history as a sinner, live in a historical context marked as sinful, and from which only God's deed saves me. I renounce the *idia dikaiosynē* and accept the *dikaiosynē theou*. I know that of myself I can do nothing, that by my own power I can perform nothing to free me from sin. I rely entirely upon God's *grace*. [A]

I know that I do not become master of the moment by setting it under my own outline of the future, but that all my own plans and resolves derive from a sinful past; that my action can only be justified by grace. [B]

(2) In this grace I recognize the *judgment* upon me, that is, not lenience toward a few foibles and weaknesses, thus a relaxing of the demand, but rather its carrying out.[153] Since I am forgiven, I am *held fast beneath the demand* and made new for its fulfillment. I thus do not receive some quality of *dikaiosynē* over which I have control. Rather, because I am *dikaios* always and only by God's grace, I live under the imperative of the divine requirement of love. To this extent the Christian's entire life is under judgment, since it is *an entire life in repentance*. "Through repentance there grows in the Christian's inner life a trust in the mercy of God who awakened the pain of it. Clearly, then, Christian faith, when rightly understood, must continually arouse true repentance, and continually overcomes the inner life crisis it brings about."[154]

The obedience of faith recognizes *judgment in grace*, because in grace it first learns to understand what sin is, and *in judgment* it learns *grace*, because it knows it is free from sin only as judged. The sinner is the justified one. And it is senseless to say, for example, that alongside the message of judgment one must also allow the good news to come into its own. The message of judgment on sin *is* the good news.

Naturally faith, which is chiefly obedience, is also *trust*, and is such *simultaneously*, since it is trust in forgiveness, not something in addition to it. It is trust because it is *justifying faith, not a general trust in God*.[155] It is the recognition that such general trust in God cannot at all be at a person's disposal. No more than we can speak of love in general and refer to it as something tangible, needing only to be grasped, but can speak of it only where we are loved and where we love, thus in the concrete historical event—no more is there a trust in God in general. Christian trust in God is thus not general confidence in some purpose behind world order (by which I conceive myself to be the purpose), or a general conviction that God reigns and does all things well ("well" defined according to my goals, desires, and ideals).[156] Rather, just as there is trust between persons only where the one speaks to the other in word or deed, so also between God and humanity. That one can decide on a general trust in God is sheer illusion. Trust in God would then be confused with optimism.[157] It is also presumptuous, for of ourselves we see nothing in our reality to justify trust in God. Further, belief in miracles as well as petitionary prayer are an admission that the idea of omnipotence is not at man's disposal; they cancel out that idea.

As a concept and nothing else, the *idea of omnipotence* is, of course, formally appropriate, but cannot actually say anything. It can do so only when we can say that "it is for our sake God effects the entire reality in which we live,"[158] but that means only when we can speak of God on the basis of what God does toward us. In that general sense even the heathen believe in omnipotence. "All who are outside the Christian church . . . even though they believe in and worship only the *one*, true God, nevertheless do not know what his attitude is toward them. They cannot be confident of his love and blessing. Therefore they remain in eternal wrath and damnation."[159] But if we

> would not shut our eyes to what his revelation creates and overcomes in us, then he stands before us as Lord of all. Out of this grows the confidence that his will is alive in all that belongs to our existence in an infinite world.[160]

> Whatever we may otherwise experience is outshone by this one, and in surrender to the God who reveals himself all else that would claim us must receive the measure of his power and worth.[161]

This also means that just as faith in omnipotence is justifying faith, faith that God determines our historical existence, so also it is always a task, an obedience that affirms this power of God and yields to no other.[162] I cannot believe in God the Almighty if I will not allow him to rule in me. But if I am prepared for obedience, then the Christian form of belief in omnipotence is prayer and belief in miracles.[163]

*Faith* is thus obedience. That is true, of course, but does this not make it a work?[164] It does not, but faith is nevertheless *a deed*. The distinction between work and deed becomes clear when the historical character of human existence is kept firmly in mind. Work, of course, results from a person's doing something; he is concerned with something at hand, something tangible. But the deed is there only in the doing, is never "at hand." When viewed as external event, as something at hand, the deed is not seen as a deed. The deed is taken for a producing of *works* when viewed from its results, from the object of concern that is "at hand" (also, as a state of mind or character trait). In that case, a person is understood on the basis of the object of his concern, of himself as a tangible something, and to which qualities are assigned on the basis of that object. He can then, as it were, present his work instead of himself, and in fact stand alongside it. Thus those Jews who seek to earn a *dikaiosynē ex ergōn nomou*, and imagine they are righteous according to the number of their good works.

A person's *deed* is seen to be his when seen in its execution, that is, in its historicity, when seen as his conduct in decision, as the concrete possibility of his ability to be, a possibility he himself chooses. He *is* in the deed, he does not stand alongside it. Faith, however, is such a decision on behalf of the word of proclamation. It is a deed. And precisely for this reason it is not something one happens upon, something possessed, but is actual only as seized anew. It is not a work to be presented, not an attribute of mine, but a how, the manner-in-which of my historical existence—just as a human I-Thou relationship is actual only in the deed, and not something one happens upon or is possessed. I do not have the attribute of "friend," but I *am* or am not a friend. Faith is therefore not optimism, nor a feeling or mood, but a deed of obedience. Thus in John *ergazetai* can be expressed in paradox when used of faith: *ti poiōmen hina ergazōmetha ta erga tou theou; apekrithē Iēsous kai eipen autois, touto estin to ergon tou theou, hina pisteuēte eis hon apesteilen ekeinos* ("What must we do to perform the works of God?" Jesus answered them, "This is the work of God, that you believe in him whom he has sent"; John 6:28f.).

And precisely when it is seen that faith is *trust*, then it is also seen that it is *deed*, just as is all trust between an I and a Thou:

> In faith, of course, we see also our own free work, when we learn how it is created in us through our experiences of a personal power. If faith is sheer trust, then for us it is free surrender, the exact opposite of arbitrary acceptance. Then it is, in its profoundest sense, our own work. But in just this sense it is felt to be the work of one who is stronger, who compels us from within. In this experience of the unity of dependence and freedom lies the nature of true religion, in which an inwardly *independent* nature is *created*, and for which reason it is an absolutely incomprehensible event.[165]

Still, *safeguarding* faith as deed *against the misunderstanding* of construing it as a work is an urgent theological task. "Here, the Reformers in their theory stood firm on the weightiest concerns of their faith. In Dogmatics till Schleiermacher, treatment of the existential question in Protestantism, as to how a redeeming faith is to be distinguished from a work that a man knows is his own, does not lead beyond this point." The concern is thus to show that "faith" denotes "trust," that it is "the new life of the liberated man created by God."[166]

Hence,[167] through Jesus Christ history is divided into two parts. He is the turning point of the aeons, the *krisis*. The new aeon has broken in. That is, by faith in him the possibility is given of getting free, not of something past but of the past as such; of beginning anew in each present moment; of hearing and fulfilling the claim of the summons to love. Forgiveness thus does not divide life into two tangible halves, so that sin could emerge as a problem after forgiveness. Since faith in revelation liberates from the past as such, forgiveness is always new. It is not new, of course, in such fashion that one could reckon on it; for in that case it would not be understood as forgiveness.

*The new aeon of love and* (insofar as it is rid of the past) *of life* is naturally not an epoch to be objectively documented. It is visible only on the basis of the love seized. Love is thus not to be registered as a being here or there, in various places or everywhere, but can only be seen as a power that determines me, the one who comes from out of a history, and when that power is seized in loving. In this sense, since Jesus Christ the past is visible as a new aeon of life, that is, when I view it and what is brought from it into the present within a forgiveness marked by understanding. Thus, even those political, economic, and social conditions marked by hate are viewed in such fashion, since I am summoned to act in them.[168]

But, in addition, I am aware of the present grown out of the past as the aeon of love only insofar as I am a lover, that is, insofar as I am directed toward the future. The new aeon is a present reality only *as always coming, as present in coming*, and, of course, in a twofold sense: First, it is present as coming in the activity of love, and second, it is present always as coming by faith.

(1) On the first point: *In the activity of love the new aeon is always present as coming*. This means that the activity of love is genuine love only when in the power of the coming aeon. Genuine love, therefore, does not love the Thou for the sake of what the Thou has carried out of the past into the present, as something at hand, but as one forgiven by God in Christ just as I am, thus as the one he will be in light of the coming aeon.[169]

We know that we are in the same situation as our neighbors, that we are sinners and have received grace just as they. In Christ forgiveness is already there for them also, and we must see them as those who are forgiven. In them the love of Christ meets us. We love them because we believe in their love, though we do not see it, even though they themselves do not yet believe in it, because they do not yet understand that they are loved. But by our very faith in them we are to free them for love. This faith in them is not an optimistic conviction regarding the goodness of humanity but is grounded solely in the forgiveness we have received. Otherwise our "love" remains grounded in our own resolve and remains a performance. But love as performance is not love, it is a noisy gong and a clanging cymbal

(1 Cor. 13:1). "Whatever does not proceed from faith is sin" (Rom. 14:23).[170]

Thus love for the neighbor is genuine only when it is also love for God.[171] Only as God's love is love genuinely experienced as a reversing of the natural direction of life, as liberation from the past, as a gift of the future. And only in affirming this love of God can love for the neighbor be genuine love, a love that is not preference based on feelings of sympathy, and for this reason is eternal and never fails (1 Cor. 13:8). Abiding in the love of God alone gives permanence to our love for the neighbor, since in this way hate and mistrust (which sees the neighbor as he is on the basis of the past) are overcome.[172] If true love is only to be seized as God's manifest love, then to love a person means at the same time "to help him to love God," and to be loved means "to be helped by another in loving God." All other love is self-love.

Faith, therefore, is always the presupposition for this love. As our own deed, loosed from the *agapē* of God, our love becomes continually uncertain and doubtful. True love exists only on the basis of faith:

(Rom. 14:23). Love as performance is valueless (1 Cor. 13:1-3). And as our *ginōskein ton theon* is always based on the *gnōsthēnai hypo tou theou* (Gal. 4:9; 1 Cor. 8:2f.; 13:12), so our love is always based on the love of God.

> *eite gar exestēmen, theō; eite sōphronoumen, hymin.*
> *hē gar agapē tou Christou synechei hēmas,*
> *krinantas touto, hoti eis hyper pantōn apethanen.*
> > *ara hoi pantes apethanon.*
> > *kai hyper pantōn apethanen,*
> > > *hina hoi zōntes mēketi heautois zōsin*
> > > *alla tō hyper autōn apothanonti kai egerthenti.*

("For if we are beside ourselves, it is for God; if we are in our right mind, it is for you. For the love of Christ urges us on, because we are convinced that one has died for all; therefore all have died. And he died for all, so that those who live might live no longer for themselves, but for him who died and was raised for them"; 2 Cor. 5:13f.)

*entolēn kainēn didōmi hymin, hina agapate allēlous,*
    *kathōs ēgapēsa hymas, hina kai hymeis agapate allēlous.*

("I give you a new commandment, that you love one another.
Just as I have loved you, you also should love one another";
John 13:34.)

*hautē estin hē entolē hē emē, hina agapate allēlous,*
    *kathōs ēgapēsa hymas.*

("This is my commandment, that you love one another as I
have loved you"; John 15:12.)[173]

The *menein en tē agapē* (in love) corresponds to the *menein en tē
agapē tē emē* (in being loved). The latter is possible only where the
former is actual. That is, the past is present in the here and now only
where the here and now can be determined by the *entolē* from the
future.

This eschatological character of *agapē* is expressly accented by
the eschatological modifier *kainē*. What is *kainē* does not denote a
relative novelty but the eschatological reality that is always "new"
over against the *kosmos: . . . palin entolēn kainēn graphō hymin, ho
estin alēthes en autō kai en hymin, hoti hē skotia paragetai kai to
phōs to alēthinon ēdē phainei* ("Yet I am writing you a new commandment that is true in him and in you, because the darkness is
passing away and the true light is already shining"; 1 John 2:8).

Our love for God is true only when it is also love for the neighbor.
And since this love rests on forgiveness received, it has its purest
expression in the readiness to forgive. In forgiveness the radical
inversion of self-love becomes clearest. In fact, since the will to forgive is aware that it really has nothing at all to forgive, and that the
other *is* already forgiven by God in Christ, this will becomes faith in
the neighbor that frees us both for love.

Conversely, true *pistis* exists only when active in love: *en gar
Christō Iesou oute peritomē ti ischyei oute akrobystia* [carried along
from the past as a tangible something!], *alla pistis di agapēs ener-
goumenē* ("For in Christ neither circumcision nor uncircumcision
counts for anything; the only thing that counts is faith working
through love"; Gal. 5:6).

*hemeis agapōmen, hoti autos prōtos ēgapēsen hēmas.*
*ean tis eipē hoti agapō ton theon*
    *kai ton adelphon autou misē,*
    *pseustēs estin.*
*ho gar mē agapōn ton adelphon autou hon heōraken,*
    *ton theon hon ouch heōraken ou dynatai agapan.*
*kai tautēn tēn entolēn echomen ap' autou,*
*hina ho agapōn ton theon agapa kai ton adelphon autou.*

("We love because he first loved us. Those who say, 'I
love God,' and hate their brothers or sisters, are liars; for
those who do not love a brother or sister whom they have
seen, cannot love God whom they have not seen. The
commandment we have from him is this: those who love
God must love their brothers and sisters"; 1 John 4:19-21.)

This means that the Christian's existence is historical, always present in the here and now, defined by future and past. Neither by the
future alone, for in a real sense the future's claim can only be heard
by one who has received forgiveness, whose history is qualified by
the revelation. Nor by the past alone, for the past becomes tangible,
dead, when not wakened to life through the claim of the future. Only
in the activity of love is the new aeon present as coming.

(2) On the second point: *In faith the new aeon is always present as
coming.* It is such not only insofar as in love it is always present as
coming, and insofar as love actually presupposes faith, but also insofar as this presupposition of faith is made ever anew.[174]

I do not have faith as a possession, as a mental state, as a spiritual
quality such as peace of soul or strength of character. I do not have it
as a conviction but only as the how of my historical existence. I thus
do not have it at my disposal. Otherwise, as something on hand, it
would be prey to the past. It is faith only as ever new, as an ever-new
laying hold of the forgiveness proffered in revelation, as an ever-new
decision. The authority remains authority; the word that is heard
retains its character as address, and faith its character as resolve.
Thus the proclamation is always disturbing, always terrifying, and
destroys security ever anew.

But for this reason the proclamation also establishes a new security. Forgiveness too, of course, is not a something on hand, at some time or other at one's disposal.[175] It is no more always something on hand, so that one must sin "with grace in view," than it is something on hand once for all or a once-for-all historical act available to historical investigation, such as the crossing of the Rubicon. Forgiveness does not divide life into two halves, so that the baptized and "converted" could demonstrate some new trait and live in view of it.

This idea[176] that the believer does not enjoy a new quality, and is righteous only insofar as he is *en Christō*, Protestant dogmatics expresses in the statement that the *justificatio* is *forensis*, consisting of God's judgment. Baier says: "Justification does not mean a real and internal change of man." Hollaz says: "Justification is a judicial, and that, too, a gracious act, by which God, reconciled by the satisfaction of Christ, acquits the sinner who believes in Christ of the offenses with which he is charged, and accounts and pronounces him righteous. *Since this action takes place apart from man, in God, it cannot intrinsically change man.*"[177] It further expresses this idea in the statement that *justificatio* is the *imputatio justitiae Christi*. Quenstedt says: "The form of imputation consists in the gracious reckoning of God, by which the penitent sinner, on account of the most perfect obedience of another, i.e., of Christ, apprehended by faith according to gospel mercy, is pronounced righteous before the divine tribunal, *'just as if this obedience had been rendered by the man himself.'*"[178] The *Apology of the Augsburg Confession* IV, 305–307, reads:

> In this passage "justify" is used in a judicial way to mean "to absolve a guilty man and pronounce him righteous," and to do so on account of someone else's righteousness, namely, Christ's, which is communicated to us through faith. . . . Because the righteousness of Christ is given to us through faith, therefore faith is righteousness in us by imputation. That is, by it we are made acceptable to God because of God's imputation and ordinances.[179]

For this very reason forgiveness is not something that could ever have the character of the available past, in which case the problem of sin could arise after forgiveness. When a person looks to himself, he is of course always a sinner. His existence is always historical, so that he never has time for tarrying, can never appear alongside himself and prove that he is a believer, that he is righteous. As historical, one never has righteousness as a timeless quality, but only as a given, as *God's* righteousness. As a human work his deed is always "world," never part of the coming aeon. His deed is such only when it occurs *en Christō*, that is, in the new aeon, the new *ktisis* that has appeared in history through Christ, and in which he has a share only by grace, on the basis of forgiveness. As soon as he steps outside forgiveness, he acts as sinner. When he looks to himself, to his work to be accomplished, he must always see himself as sinning, never as hallowing anything, for no works are holy. It is thus a matter of *"pecca fortiter, sed crede fortius."*

But he is always tempted to relinquish faith and step outside forgiveness. But as long as forgiveness is preached, it is also preached to him, and he may set himself under it again as part of the new *ktisis*. Of course, forgiveness has not freed him from *something* that is past, that is, from his past up to some specific point in time. It has freed him from the past as such—to begin with, from all the past that will be past in the future.[180] Because it is never possessed, the new aeon is also never lost, but always coming, indeed, coming only for faith.[181]

But as coming, the new aeon is *present*. This means that since Christ the world (history!) is other than it was. Wherever there is preaching, there is no longer heathenism in the true sense, and the world is no longer as before the world of creation, but a new heaven and a new earth, or a hell.

> *amēn amēn legō hymin hoti ho ton logon mou akouōn kai pisteuōn*
> *tō pempsati me echei zoēn aiōnion kai eis krisin ouk erchetai, alla*
> *metabebēken ek tou thanatou eis tēn zōen.*
> *amēn amēn legō hymin hoti erchetai hōra kai nyn estin hote hoi*
> *nekroi akouousin tēs phonēs tou hyiou tou theou kai hoi akousantes*
> *zēsousin.*

("Very truly, I tell you, anyone who hears my word and believes in him who sent me has eternal life, and does not come under judgment, but has passed from death to life. Very truly, I tell you, the hour is coming, and is now here, when the dead will hear the voice of the Son of God, and those who hear will live"; John 5:24f.)

*ho pisteuōn eis auton ou krinetai ho de mē pisteuōn ēdē kekritai, hoti mē pepisteuken eis to onoma tou monogenous hyiou tou theou. hautē de estin hē krisis hoti to phōs elēluthen eis ton kosmon kai ēgapēsan hoi anthrōpoi mallon to skotos ē to phōs.*

("Those who believe in him are not condemned; but those who do not believe are condemned already, because they have not believed in the name of the only Son of God. And this is the judgment, that the light has come into the world, and people loved darkness rather than light"; John 3:18f., cf. 11:25f.; 8:51.)

*nyn krisis estin tou kosmou toutou, nyn ho archōn tou kosmou toutou ekblēthēsetai exō; kagō ean hypsōthō ek tēs gēs, pantas helkysō pros emauton.*

("Now is the judgment of this world; now the ruler of this world will be driven out. And I, when I am lifted up from the earth, will draw all people to myself"; John 12:31f.)

*nyn edoxasthē ho hyios tou anthrōpou kai ho theos edoxasthē en autō.*

("Now the Son of Man has been glorified, and God has been glorified in him"; John 13:31.)

Thus, with the coming of the Revealer *the krisis* has occurred. In a certain sense, the *krisis* spells *separation*. It is not based on an act singled out as *krisis*; nothing occurs outside revelation. The *krisis* takes place in reaction to revelation, and, of course, in the here and now. The hour *erchetai kai nyn estin* (John 5:25), precisely by its being preached. The *krisis* thus unveils what was; it makes evident the two possibilities in the *en tō kosmō einai* (that is, to be or *not* to be *ek tou kosmou*), and qualifies clinging to the world as sin in the true sense, as unbelief and thus as death. By this separation—since the *logos* makes *hamartia* actual—the *krisis* is also *judgment* in terms of condemnation by God's wrath: *ho pisteuōn eis ton hyion echei zoēn aiōnion, ho de apethōn to hyiō ouch opsetai zoēn, all' hē orgē tou theou menei ep' auton* ("Whoever believes in the Son has eternal life; whoever disobeys the Son will not see life, but must endure God's wrath"; John 3:36).

Here too, the character of revelation is manifest as an act of God who qualifies man's existence as historical in a particular how.[182] Just as history is altered by every historical fact, so by the fact of Jesus Christ, though, of course, in the reverse sense.[183]

If faith is a deed, then is it not the case that we intend to be saved through our own doing?[184] If faith is a resolve in decision, does not our salvation rest upon our resolve?

The old Protestant dogmatics replies that the deed of faith is *worked in us by the Holy Spirit.*[185] But what does this mean? It means nothing if the Spirit is conceived as a mysteriously magical power at work behind our doing, so that our doing is no longer *ours*, and our faith is no longer *ours*. The Spirit is neither a tangible "something," having causal effects as things of the world, nor descriptive of a psychic state. Rather, the Spirit denotes a how of our historical existence, makes clear that since Christ it is possible for our existence to be determined by God's grace, possible to belong to the new aeon. For just as *sarx* denotes the how of the unredeemed, so *pneuma* denotes the how of the redeemed—*en pneumati einai* is equal to *en Christō einai,* equal to belonging to the *kainē ktisis.* [A]

New Testament (and ecclesiastical) usage of *"spirit" and "flesh"* is unclarified and unintelligible in its conceptual setting.[186] Its intent becomes clear by the fact that *in one and the same breath* one is referred to the *pneuma* as to his own deed, just as his sin is traced to the *sarx*, though he is also assigned responsibility for it. This indicates that a human is understood in his historical character, and that means that he is neither determined by causes, as are tangible things of nature, nor is he master of himself. He always lives from another; his freedom consists in seizing the possibilities available to him from history and his present life in community, and in this way laying hold of his own possibility. In his deed, then, he is both determined and free (just as is everyone in relation to a friend or spouse;

since a friend or spouse discloses new possibilities of being to him, that friend is not a *causa* inevitably at work, for possibility is seized in freedom. It is as if the one who seizes is in debt to the other for the deed, and the other is answerable for what he means to him).

That one is determined by the *flesh* means that his free choice is never a laying hold of his real possibiilty; that despite all his freedom he is always determined by the possibilities arising from out of his past; that he thus always remains the old, is never the new man, for which reason he never arrives at authentic life. The reason, of course, is that in his unconscious search for authenticity, he misses it, precisely because he wants to achieve it on his own, and can do so only when he understands himself on the basis of something that he owns or produces. He would discover his authenticity if he would let himself go, and this he can do only through the love that surrenders self. Only then does he get free of the past, live from the future, the invisible, the *Spirit*. For talk of the Spirit means that through the forgiveness in Christ it is possible for us to love, to lay hold of authentic life in a free act, to live out of the future. Faith is worked by the Spirit (something, by the way, Paul never says!), insofar as faith has not arisen out of our past, but is offered through the word. Just as I am indebted to my friend for my act of love for which he is the occasion (that is, through him it has become a possibility for me), so the believer is indebted to God for his Spirit who was at work not behind, but precisely *within* the free act of faith. The tracing of faith to the Spirit can only be a confession of the believer, not explanatory proof. Nothing but the deed is visible, not the Spirit.

There is a deeper reason for misunderstanding faith's character as deed. It occurs *when the act of faith is isolated from the deed of the moment*. Faith is one-sidedly defined when understood as the obedient hearing of the word of forgiveness in Christ addressed to me. This cannot be believed *in abstracto*, only *in its relation to the moments* of my actual life.

Only the *word addressed to the moment* may be construed as revelation, and of course, because it teaches one to recognize the claim of the moment. This claim would have to be understood as God's word, and becomes such only through the word of forgiveness addressed to the moment. *Hearing the word of revelation and understanding the moment must thus comprise a unity.* If the one is faith and the other is love, then the two must become one. In the decision of faith the decision of love is made; the one is not without the other.

Practically, *"hearing" the word as an event in time* (in the preaching) does not coincide with the deed required in the encounter with fate and[187] with the neighbor. As the "word" by itself is not the word (the claim) of the moment, of *this* moment, but qualifies the moment when spoken into it (just as the history of salvation is not an event within history, but the handing on of the word in church tradition), so in the true sense preaching and sacrament are removed from historical occurrence. This is clearest in the case of baptism, an event that is prior to every responsible moment of life. Thus the church as church is not a sociological entity. It is "invisible," that is, its meaning as a community of proclamation and faith is not visible as an historical phenomenon. The preacher does not encounter the hearer as a Thou with his claim determining the moment (the person of the preacher is a matter of total indifference to the hearer). *The moment of hearing (as of preaching) is therefore distinguished* from all other moments.[188] But its distinctive character may not be what is produced by liturgical solemnity or a mood of devotion, etc. Such can only be a *sign* that this moment has preeminence through its *meaning*. *Its distinctive character* consists in the fact that the claim to the obedience of faith becoming audible in it does not derive from the historical moment as such, but from the word of revelation spoken into it; that this claim applies equally to all future moments; that it intends to be heard in them, and for the very reason that the particular claim of these moments be heard, truly heard.

Thus, on the one hand we may state that *in the decision to hear and believe, all future decisions to act, the understanding of fate as God's gift (of the world as creation) as well as*[189] love are *anticipated*. In faith forgiveness is affirmed, and with it the will to love at work in forgiveness. On the other hand, *only in deciding to act and to love is the decision to hear and believe actually made.* This indicates once more that the human is understood historically. His temporality is not a succession of moments in time but the extension of his temporal being. In the here and now of the decision of faith he is at the same time the one he will be; he lays hold of his future, and in the deed of love preserves his faithfulness. Without faithfulness his decision was not genuine, but an illusion.

For this very reason the decision of faith is not disposed of once for all, but a decision made for all of life. But this means as a *decision* held to and to be made ever anew, come what may. A person does not have faith as ownership of a considered conviction. He has it only in carrying out the decision of the moment; and he does not have it *alongside* but *within* other decisions. The believer is thus never a finished product, but always becoming—not in terms of the idealistic notion of development ("become what you are," that is, what you are ideally; rather, become what you are through your decision of faith). The believer always lives in uncertainty. [C]

> *ouch hoti ēdē elabon ē ēdē teteleiōmai, diōkō de ei kai katalabō,*
> *eph' hō katelēmphthēn hypo Christou Iesou. adelphoi, egō hemauton*
> *ou logizomai kateilēphenai; hen de, ta men opisō epilanthanomenos*
> *tois de emprosthen epekteinomenos, kata skopon diōkō eis to*
> *brabeion tēs anō klēseos tou theou en Christō Iesou.*

("Not that I have already obtained this or have already reached the goal, but I press on to make it my own, because Christ Jesus has made me his own. Beloved, I do not consider that I have made it my own; but this one thing I do: forgetting what lies behind and straining forward to what lies ahead, I press on toward the goal for the prize of the heavenly call of God in Christ Jesus"; Phil. 3:12-14) [E (perhaps also D)]

With this reference to the *pneuma* we are directed to the new possibility of our historical existence. But we are reminded again that faith in the sense named above[190] is our deed. The mode of being of our historical existence is that it is a capacity for being, thus in the given instance a capacity, my own possibility laid hold of in the deed. The deed is not done by the existent person (as though he were behind it), as though it were something produced by a machine. Rather, the person *is* in the doing. The point is to make obedience under the proclamation intelligible as deed.

In this sense *Wilhelm Hermann* insisted that dogmatics must demonstrate *the origin of faith*.[191] This, of course, does not mean that the psychic process of becoming a believer should be described. Rather, since "faith" is "engendered precisely through what forms its content,"[192] that is, since faith is not a holding to propositions but an act of historical life, it should be described as such. As such it never *is* unless it is *about to be*. It is never without a continual vital relation to its cause. It can never appeal to itself, but only to its cause, a cause it can never have as something stored in knowledge, but from which it can only emerge anew. The question of the origin of faith thus involves a more exact definition of that deed of obedience.

The deed is not something precipitated into a work, something undertaken, but is rather created in us. "In reality the Christian needs an unshakable ground that inwardly compels him, since his faith does *not* involve something he himself could create by his good will. It is rather a certainty created in him, though his natural life is opposed to the horrors of what it unveils to him."[193] Herrmann calls this historical event with its dual sense of being our deed and yet of being worked in us *experience*. Naturally, this does not denote a psychic condition, a tangible something or other in us, and to which we look back or enjoy.[194] What is meant is an experience as a genuine historical event, an experience of trust that is both deed and something brought about, a gift.[195] The experience of trust always has intentional character: "Our trust always lives from the power of what created trust in us."[196] Thus no cult of experience is exacted, but a "truthfulness toward our own experiences,"[197] an openness to the claim made upon us at any given moment, an existential knowledge of the uncertainty of our present life, an historical vitality. It is meant in this sense: "Nothing in history can belong to us other than what we ourselves experience."[198]

But what is *the experience of trust*?[199] It occurs

> when a personal life touches us to which we can relate totally in trust and reverence. Such experiences become revelations for us, of which only we can know we have been totally overwhelmed in free surrender. In a peculiar way, each experience discloses to us something of the one we can appropriately call God. But in fact we find our God in

this spiritual power only when we intend to behave toward it as we experienced it. If it stands clearly before us, as it moved us to total surrender and by that means created true life in us, then we would be untruthful and faithless if we were not to obey it alone and seek to overcome our distresses by it alone. . . . The genuine content of all historical life is the experience of righteousness and goodness, of that spiritual power experienced in the creating of trust. To the upright person this power becomes the living God.[200]

We are thus referred to a genuine, historical I-Thou relationship. And it is clear that in this relationship the unity of deed and gift, of necessity and freedom, of independence and obedience is actual, and precisely in the experience of trust. It is also clear that it is not a matter of seeing a revelation in the other's individuality, a revelation as something ready to hand, but only in the historical event of creating trust:

> Whoever bows before the moral goodness of a person not only has to do with this person when stirred to reverence. By the impression he has received, the idea of a higher power is produced in his own thought, a power acting on him through this single figure. In that simple moral experience we know that we are seized by this higher power in the depths of our being, and that we are totally dependent on it. Reverence for persons, therefore, that inner bowing before the appearance of moral power and goodness is the root of all religion.[201]

Clearly, however, such trust and reverence toward moral power and goodness is *not Christian faith*. To some extent all of this inheres in every human life, and is without value or power when such experiences of trust and reverence alternate with disappointment and mistrust—without which trust does not exist. But trust *alone* does not have the power to transform us from sinners to righteous. Our mistrust always rests on hate, and our hate rests on the fact that even in trust we always bind ourselves to the individual, trust in him instead of in God, cling to the visible, to what is ready to hand instead of to the invisible.

For this reason, we become more and more uncertain of those we trust, and, to the extent we wish to cling to what once was given us in the experience of trust, despite our disappointments in the other, we hold either to an *idea* of goodness as the force of history, or to a *requirement*, which means that we are still under the law.

Ultimately, Herrmann assigns to humanity what is essential. For it is in fact correct that we find God in this spiritual power encountering us in the experience of trust only when we behave toward it as we experienced it. But we fail regularly at this. For this reason we become uncertain of every such "revelation." In the last analysis, such a revelation shows us what is required of us and that we live in hate.

Herrmann himself is aware of this. He continues: "This, of course, does not yet complete the faith that supports a Christian. But Christian faith, if it is genuine, is certainly nothing else than the completion of this beginning."[202] That is correct. The question is only how the completion is conceived. In harmony with traditional church theology Herrmann refers to Jesus at this point, but in what way? Herrmann writes that *the impression of the person of Jesus* redeems us.[203] He is "the appearance of personal goodness" which seizes a man as a revelation," and effects a "reverent lifting of the eye to the power of the good beyond that which is real."[204] He continues:

> Within a rich tradition, the personal life of this man has had the power to create for itself an incomparable organ. From this tradition the receptive person can trace the stirrings of Jesus' soul, what he thought and experienced, what he intended and did, with a marvelous freshness, and from it experience its elevating power. Only he who can find Jesus in this way receives God's perfect revelation, and by it is raised above the world's anxiety, above the distress into which the law unmasked by Jesus sets him. When the personal life of Jesus is thus revealed to us, then by this unhindered power of good will we are not only made certain of God, but by the way in which Jesus acted toward sinful humanity we are reconciled with God.[205]

Our involvement with the person of Jesus is not as with others, to the effect that the moral requirement experienced through them also yields a critical eye for what is perverse in them, to the effect that the ideal we thought to find in them extends beyond them. He rather becomes the interpreter of our conscience, becomes a conscience for us, a judge. "Since he makes the sinner insecure by the simple force of his personal life, he also supports him through his kindness."[206] As he once forgave the sinners who drew near to him, so now retrospection upon his person frees all people from their inner unrest, from the burden of their guilt:

> When this combines in Jesus' impression on us, then our faith is awakened. The person who undergoes it, immediately understands that experience of Jesus' person as a being touched by a supraworldly power full of love and faithfulness. . . . In what he experiences in the person of Jesus the Christian is certain that the power of the good not only judges but redeems him. This is how Christian faith is created. It is simply the trust which Jesus wins from us through his personal life, and then the joyful surrender to the God who appears to us in him and acts on us through him.[207]

*What is stated here is impossible.* In essence, the argument is that the relation of trust toward others, a relation that is possible to us only as broken and uncertain, is nonetheless possible toward Jesus as unbroken, victorious, and to which we can always return.

But *an analogous relation of trust toward Jesus is simply not possible.*[208] It was such only long ago for his disciples. As a Thou (in the sense of a contemporary), he is gone for us now (as every Thou disappears from us when the other dies). We can neither trust him nor let ourselves be judged by him. He cannot at all forgive us. And when we see how he once forgave sinners, this does not forgive us, for one cannot observe forgiveness.[209] As one who forgives another he is visible only to the one in whose life there is forgiveness.

Now, since it is not at all possible to enter into such an I-Thou relationship with Jesus, Herrmann runs the risk of setting *the inner life of Jesus* within world history as a *palpable fact.*

Herrmann, however, is always after protecting himself by stating that the historic Christ as redeemer may not be proved as an incontrovertible fact for everyone,[210] or by saying that the inner life of Jesus is not a fact historical research can prove with certainty, but can be a fact we experience.[211] Such is the case, Herrmann writes, when through the experience of trust one is drawn to a true desire, to reverence and repentance.

But since Herrmann's train of thought cannot result in an I-Thou relationship with Jesus, it finally ends up representing the "inner life of Jesus" as a palpable fact, though it is an absurdity to want to perceive faith or a man's love.

Herrmann has forgotten first, *Jesus' eschatological position* as one who is the *krisis*, the turning point of the aeons, making it possible for our history to be qualified by love. This is a fact that as such is neither demonstrable nor capable of being experienced, but can only be believed. For this reason he has forgotten, second, that *faith is based only on the word, the proclamation*. Herrmann thus removes the scripture from its privileged position. He wants to "broaden" Luther's reference to scripture as the word that can save everyone from his distresses, when he seeks and finds Christ in it:

> The creator of a new life is near us with his work in all in which confidence toward the one invisible God presses in upon us. We experience this *chiefly*[212] in the faith audible to us from Holy Scripture in a marvelous variety and unity. Here in turn the Christ of the New Testament is raised above all other life filled and borne by God.[213]

Thus scripture is not regarded as the word of proclamation that requires the *hypakoē pisteōs*, but as a document that makes visible the faith of personalities who are strong in faith, Jesus above all. So, in the last analysis, we are on the same level with the personalities of scripture, even with Jesus.

Finally, all this is due to the fact that in his *concept of faith* (resulting from opposition to orthodoxy) Herrmann ignores the element *of obedience to the proclamation*. He correctly wishes to avoid the notion of faith as the obedient and uninformed acceptance of doctrines, and to make clear to what extent there can be talk of true obedience that is not a work performed. But he overlooks the fact that the proclamation speaks of a fact that of course is not historical or ascertainable but historic, a fact to which our own existence is linked, though as such it is also an historical fact. For this reason he is always searching for tangible confirmation of the scriptural word of forgiveness, instead of seeing that when this word tells us our historical existence is decisively qualified, it can only be spoken from beyond our understanding, because the understanding of our existence is beyond our grasp. We can only concede it and obediently believe it. *There must be a radical break with looking outside or within ourselves (in experiences) for proof of the word of forgiveness.* Rom. 10:17 must be taken seriously: *ara hē pistis ex akoēs, hē de akoē dia rhēmatos Christou* (but the *rhēma Christou* is the commission to preach.[214] Verse 15: *pōs de kēruxōsin ean mē apostalōsin*). For the word of proclamation, therefore, no other legitimation is to be required, and no other basis to be created than itself. In encountering us it asks whether or not we will hear. Compare to Luther:

> For this reason we must be on our guard against wanting to preserve the gospel by our own powers, not by its own strength. Then it is really lost, and then, however many there are who most want to defend it, it falls. Let's not worry about it at all. The gospel doesn't need our help; it is powerful enough by itself; leave it to God alone whose it is. So I do too, though there may be much and great offence at it. All this doesn't bother me at all, and I don't worry about how I will defend it. I and we all are too weak to produce such an argument for it. I have commended it to the dear God. It is indeed his word, he is man enough to fight it and protect it. . . . In all this there is no better advice than from now on to preach the gospel simply and purely, and pray God to lead and guide us.[215]

How then do we counter the *objection* that the proclamation recites a myth that does not speak of me at all? Should I acknowledge a fact that has nothing to do with the reality of my life? Does faith become the accidental choice of an accidental possibility left to my discretion, and thus only a sham obedience? How does this take seriously (Herrmann) the fact that I can only obey an authority that I recognize as an authority within the reality of my life, that does not become an authority for me only by my resolving to obey it?[216]

The objection overlooks the fact that I am historical.[217] It overlooks the fact that *the word of proclamation* is not an accidental something or other that *encounters me* in a free-floating situation but a word that encounters me *as one who lives within a particular history*. It points me to nothing else but to my history. That is, it actually assumes all that Herrmann quite correctly has to say of my historical existence. It assumes I have those experiences of trust, reverence, and of being judged, and educate myself in truthfulness toward my experiences. In other words, the gospel assumes the law, which as such is given with my historical existence. [A]

The objection is raised by one who has lost his Thou, with reference to which the word is preached to him. In history he sees infinite possibilities; but "there is no bridge from possibility to reality."[218] [B]

But all *these experiences*—trust and reverence, mistrust and indignation, love and thankfulness, hate and ungratefulness, faithfulness and pride, unfaithfulness and remorse—*are disclosed to us only in the proclamation* that teaches us to see who we are in these experiences, who we are in them before God. With the obedience it requires or the grace it gives the proclamation does not produce a magical change in our life. It does not bring into our life a new something or other but opens our eyes as it were to ourselves—naturally, not for observation. Since this perception is an event of our historical life, it is actual only as our deed, and as such it makes our life new.[219] *In our experiences we are always questioned, put to the test*. We cannot *have* them as a possession. We have them only in doing. But the more genuinely we understand our experiences, the more uncertain and doubtful of ourselves we are: We believe our experiences, we do *not* obey them. The proclamation asks whether we intend to believe in them (the experiences) as the possibility set by God within our history. It summons us to believe in them on the basis of forgiveness. The proclamation thus encounters us as historical persons, not outside it, and it proclaims *forgiveness*, that is, does not rapture us from our character as historical but points us toward it. It does not bring a new something or other, neither knowledge, *gnōsis*, nor moods, transports, and mystical experiences. It proclaims justification of the sinner; it points a man to his humanity. It is for *this* that grace applies. And the grace of forgiveness consists in nothing else but this, that this history in which we live is qualified by the *krisis* in

Jesus Christ. We are asked whether we will belong to the new aeon of life or remain in death.

So the question certainly does not come to us by happenstance, from the outside, and the answer to it is certainly not at our discretion. *The question is put to us as we ought to put it to ourselves*, and after all, whether loudly or softly, should always put to ourselves where we ourselves are involved. And it is different from our own questions, not only because it is a radical question, but also because it gives the answer. Ultimately, it asks whether we intend to hear the answer that we are sinners and intend to accept grace.[220] The question is the more urgent the more our history is not only generally aware of those experiences of trust in the I-Thou relationship. Rather, the more our history is aware of encounter with the Thou, an encounter marked by Christian faith and love, the more we stand *within the history of the Christian church.*[221] "The more"—for is it not possible nowadays to say more and simply to confirm that we do so stand? For where is the Christian church? If it had really disappeared, it would still be possible—since the law cannot disappear—to believe the proclamation. This would also make possible the reemergence of the Christian church. But then it is also clear that there is a *twofold proclamation of the word* in the church: There is *preaching* and there is *change*. More than historical existence under the law, historical existence under grace and love can make sense of the requirement of faith to the one who is to believe. "We can help them (the others) in only one way. Through what we see there (in the New Testament) we must be changed and must have discovered a benefit that can delight those who come in contact with us, without our saying much about it."[222] Hermann again:

> The social democrat maintains there is nothing but selfishness in the world. Now we shall prove to him that there is love. Our faith knows that with love there is power over all things. Whether love will save or harden our adversary, we do not know; but it is at work. It has a comrade in his own thoughts. . . . [223]

Naturally, in the proclamation of the change we do not refer to ourselves. This proclamation is in fact not direct but indirect, that is, it occurs only in our *action* in its strictly historical sense. We do not advertise our personality or display our experiences. We *act* in faith and love. We create no basis for the Word of God or point to something on the basis of which there might be faith. All our doing can, of course, be only a *question* to the other, and the result can also be his hardening. But we are aware of the responsibility inherent in the fact that faith is not a universal but an historical possibility, that faith may thus be easier or harder, and that it lies in our power to ease it or make it more difficult for others. By so doing we do not produce anything special, a social politics, say, or an inner mission. There are no special works of faith or love. What is meant is simply the everyday need to do our duty, an action involving ourselves and others.[224]

Nothing of this is to be imported into the proclamation of the word. That is, we must preach the *fides quae creditur*, not elicit faith or speak of people strong in faith and love. We must speak no more of others than of ourselves, least of all, certainly, of ourselves. The rule applies: "Do not preach yourself, but all the more to yourself."[225]

Faith, of course, is not directed toward something outside the reality of life, outside human existence, something to be disclosed by a supernatural authority (the church) or through speculation. It is directed toward something *that encounters me, that* is *not within the possibilities of life available to me*. Faith thus simply recognizes that in fact a person's existence is not at his disposal. It belongs to his very existence that it is not at his disposal but is subject to alien powers, that we are always put to the test as to whether and how we see them. Put in a formal way, this simply means that we are historical; expressed in Christian fashion, it is the test of whether we will belong to God or the devil.

Only from this perspective can the question of the *assurance of salvation* be answered. Faith is certain of salvation only when it is not related to itself, but to what it believes, to the "objectivity" of the revelation.[226] "For it would be a miserable deception if we ever wished to rely on the power of our faith instead of on what faith holds to be true."[227]

In its own way, the old Protestant dogmatics expressed this thought as follows: A faith that is not taken in isolation, not construed as a work, is assured of salvation. Cf. the *Apology of the Augs-burg Confession*, Article IV, line 56: "Faith does not justify or save because it is a good work in itself, but only because it accepts the promised mercy."[228] Luther writes of faith as *insensibilitas*:[229] "Faith sees nothing; it is rather the dark way."[230] Faith can thus be linked to nothing but the *nudum verbum*:[231]

> Faith holds to what it does not see, feel or experience, whether in body or soul. But since it expects good from God, it surrenders to it and ventures upon it, does not doubt that what it expects will happen to it, then surely does. And if feeling and experience come to it unsought and undesired, in and through such an expectation or faith . . . then what have we here? A free surrender and joyful venture upon its unfelt, unsought, unacknowledged blessing.[232]

Luther writes on Matt. 15:21-28:

> This is written to comfort and teach us all to know how deeply God hides his grace from us, how we should not cling to our own feeling and thinking about him, but cling directly to his word. . . . This (Jesus' apparent dismissal of the Syro-Phoenician) shows how it is with our heart in inner conflict. As the heart feels, so Christ is presented here. It imagines only that there is nothing but a no there, that after all he is not true. Now it must turn from such feeling and with firm faith in God's word seize and cling to the yes hidden deep beneath and above the no, just as this little woman does, must concede God's judgment on us. Then we have won and caught him in his own words.[233]

If the question of faith's assurance is something else than the question about the Word of God, then it is a question of *doubt*. Doubt is without certainty and can only be overcome by faith. Just as in an I-Thou relationship of trust I am simply asked whether I trust the Thou, or will not prove to myself through feeling the trust I place in him, so also with regard to God. A faith preoccupied with itself is no more a faith than a love preoccupied with itself is love. Faith is deed and certain of itself only in the doing. To make it a problem afterward is to miss its historical nature, to see faith in what is ready to hand rather than in the deed. But whoever seeks it in what is ready to hand is punished with doubt. [A]

*Faith finds certainty in obedience*, an obedience that of course is actual only as deed, not as a performance that can be documented:

> There is no visible sanctification of a man, no hallowing that one could perceive, establish or measure, that one would not have to *believe*. It is a deed of the divine mercy. It is not and does not become a man's possession or boast. Those who are sanctified are and remain sinners. . . . There is no sanctification that would not be *totally* obscured by what is profane. But there *is* an obedience in sanctification, thus an obedience of *sinners*. . . .[234]

On the other hand, *obedience* must be *understanding* obedience, that is, must not be blind, otherwise it would be a work. This means that the character of the word encountering me must be such that it discloses or offers to me self-understanding, that it teaches me to understand myself, my moment. A word that I cannot understand by understanding myself beneath it I cannot believe. Preaching must proclaim the word in such a way that the hearer can understand sin and grace, faith and love, Christ and Spirit as possibilities of his existence, and the task of theology is to see to it that preaching does so. [C]

## §15. What Is Theology?

What is theology as a science? Its object is God as seen in the only possible mode of access to him, in faith. God is manifest in revelation and is seen in faith. *Revelation and faith* together are the object of theology—the former as can be known in faith, not as a universally visible world phenomenon; the latter as knowledge of the revelation, not as a phenomenon of human spiritual life as such. The theme of theology can thus also be described as *human existence determined by God*. For the revelation is not a worldly phenomenon but an event in existence, an event in a believing existence bounded by the revelation.[235]

Theology is thus not a universal human possibility, as if there were other theologies apart from Christian theology. Theology as discourse concerning revelation and faith exists *only as Christian theology*, while all other alleged theology can only be discourse concerning what is human—if in fact God is accessible only in the revelation through Christ. However profoundly this other discourse may comprehend human reality, it still does not attain to the reality of God. This does not mean it would be senseless. It may have a positive relation to theology. Naturally, it does not speak of God, but of the idea of God. But this does not mean that its topic is an arbitrary structure of ideas. Its topic is human reality as it can be seen apart from God. As such it puts a question to theology.[236]

But what is *the specifically scientific discourse that belongs to theology*? It is a fact that preaching in the church also speaks of revelation and faith! Faith itself speaks! How does specifically theological discourse relate to this? As scientific discourse it does not speak *as* proclamation or *from* faith, but speaks *about* proclamation and faith—not as address or answer, but objectively, in discourse.

*Is this at all possible*? If revelation can be seen only in faith, how is scientific discourse about it possible, discourse that makes faith itself its object? Does it not sheer off from faith? If proclamation is what it is only as address, how can it be explicated in scientific discourse? Is not such discourse set outside the sphere of proclamation?

Construed in purely formal fashion there is not a great deal to this objection. For the *problem* as posed here is *first of all that of every science*. If science is not deduced from an idea of spirit, but always emerges from a *life-relation to its object*, then any science may be asked if in its objectivizing research it does not cut off life-relation to its object. This in fact *can* be the case, but need not be. From the outset a life-relation to the object contains *understanding*, which very thing involves a specifically human relation to the object.[237] The task of science is the very cultivation of this understanding, in which other relations to the object are naturally still in view but are not realized in fact. Every science is capable of losing its object, but also of seizing it in genuine fashion.

This applies not only to the positive sciences that always have in view a sphere of objects to which human *Dasein* is related, but also to *philosophy*, insofar as it makes *Dasein* as a whole its theme. Existence is to be understood only in the act of existing. How can it be made an object of objective science? But existing contains an understanding of self (since it is characteristic of human *Dasein* to relate itself to itself). The task of philosophy is to cultivate this understanding. Philosophy, of course, can go astray in speculation,[238] but by cultivating this understanding it can also reflect on existence and make *existing* self-understanding keen and vital.

The situation in *theology* is analogous. Faith involves a specific understanding of revelation and believing existence. Just this is developed in theology. And the scientific cultivation of this self-understanding of faith can turn back upon believing existence in the shape of constant self-examination. The believer is always in danger of confusing God with the world, of making God an object of speculation, construing God as a world-all, an idea or limiting concept. He is always in danger of confusing revelation with general truths or psychic experiences. The believer is always in danger of confusing the faith with a human attitude, whether with an orthodoxy or an optimism, with a life of feeling or a worldview. He is always in danger of confusing love with an ethical principle or feelings of sympathy. He is always in danger of confusing the scripture as a law book or historical document of a "Christian worldview," of confusing the church with a society or organism based on an idea or on *humanitas*. Clearly theology, merely by scientifically cultivating the understanding of believing existence given in faith, calls faith, and calls the church back to itself. Thus theology, like the other sciences, does not first establish its relation to the object but assumes it, brings it to mind, cultivates it.

This still does not dispose of *the problem of theology as science*. For the relation of believing *Dasein* to God is different from the relation of *Dasein* as such to its objects or to itself.[239] In theology, then, "bringing to mind" a life-relation has another character than in the other sciences. The object of the other sciences is *Dasein* itself and its world. *Dasein* is continually related to itself and its world, and within this sphere each science has the task of continually uncovering the given possibilities. In this sense each science has control of its object; its object is always accessible to *Dasein* on its own. If *the object of theology* is God's revelation, then its object is not accessible to *Dasein* on its own; it is not under theology's control. Because revelation is present in the word of proclamation, accessibility and capacity for being controlled clearly cannot be assumed. And the reason is that in its empirical state it is not yet visible as revelation but merely as the teaching of one religion alongside others, as a "Christian worldview." It is accessible in faith, and faith is not a human attitude, not an exercise *Dasein* may perform on its own. It is the answer to an actual encounter with revelation.

Science assumes that *Dasein* is always linked to its object beforehand and can discover that object on its own. It assumes that for this reason the object's capacity for discovery lodged in scientific discourse can be preserved in propositions, that thus everyone who hears those propositions understands them by virtue of a prior relation to the object or under their guidance can discover or better understand the object. In this sense science has universal validation at its disposal. If the object of theology is transcendent to the *Dasein*, then its propositions cannot claim universal validity in this sense but only in the formal sense that whoever enjoys a relation to the object understands and affirms it.[240] Is it enough, then, to say that theology as science is distanced from other sciences, since its object and the relation to it are of a special kind, but that within this restricted area theology is a science as any other?

If theology develops a general understanding of revelation and believing existence, does it not then distract from the understanding of the moment that faith discovers in light of revelation? In fact, understanding of the moment holds itself aloof from cultivating a scientific understanding. The act of faith, not what is understood in faith, can be understood scientifically. But is not faith obliged to oppose a reflective understanding of itself? In fact, must it not declare that such understanding is absolutely impossible, since it can only see faith as a world phenomenon?[241]

How is it possible that the transcendent events of revelation and

faith can be made the object of scientific research, a research that
like theology can only be a human undertaking?

*The character of faith as marked off* from other *Dasein* is not at
all external. The believer is not removed from unbelieving *Dasein*
once for all and definitively linked to his object, so that theological
science needed only to "remind" him of it.[242] Rather, the believer
*exists*, and just as the revelation is an historical event, so believing
existence is a mode of historical existence.

This fact spells *the possibility and impossibility of theology.*[243] It
spells possibility, insofar as historically existing *Dasein* understands
itself and can consciously cultivate this understanding. In such work
*Dasein* diverts attention from the moment and reflects upon itself. It
spells the impossibility of theology, insofar as such work does not
control its object. In that case[244] then, does it still exist in faith? Is not
theology a human undertaking like every other? And if so, has its
object not become an object within the world? Has it not lost transcendence?

Now, precisely because faith is a mode of historical existence, it
can be actual in no other way than in human investigation. Faith's
transcendence does not consist in its being removed from *Dasein* but
in its hearing and obeying God within *Dasein*.

Just as every human undertaking can be a movement of faith and
be justified as such, so also theology to the extent it is understood
and seized as the requirement of the moment.[245] [D]

Theological work as the conceptualizing of believing existence
would then be possible *if assigned to faith from faith and for faith*,
not deduced from an idea of science.[246] It can have sufficient motive
only within faith itself.

The more a theologically scientific discourse in this sense must be
a believing discourse, *the less is it a "sacred" discourse*, directly
proclaiming or confessing. It is distanced discourse. In it the proclamation is not directly responded to or handed on but as it were
arrested, halted, in order to be examined. By way of analogy, aesthetic observation is impossible without the scientists's being "with
his object" in terms of an artistic view, and yet a specifically scientific understanding differs from direct enjoyment of a work of art. Or

again by way of analogy, an art that has *Dasein* for its object (say, in the passion of love, hate, jealousy, envy) must be with that object in terms of the artist's living this *Dasein* himself, in his passions, and yet is distanced from that object (in terms of a specifically artistic view). Art does not cry, but shapes the cry.

Just as there is no sacred art (or religious art in a sense other than that its object is religious), so there is no sacred science,[247] no sacred theology. This means one cannot *make* it "sacred." But of course, the person who does theology can be a believer, in fact can do so only as a believer.

So it could happen that objectifying research could itself be an act of faith. Only then could there be talk of theology. [C (perhaps also B)]

To dispute *the necessity of theology* is really idle. We simply want to know what is proclaimed to us and what we must proclaim.[248] We are addressed and we are to hand on the address. This handing on *can* of course occur in a simple act such as in the imitative (symbolic) act of worship, but only if it has its meaning from the word, only if *understood*.[249] The sacrament is the *verbum visibile*! Magical powers are neither imparted, nor is anything of the ineffable mediated. The more revelation occurs in the proclamation that is received by faith because it announces that Jesus Christ is the turning point of the aeons, announces that our history is qualified by an historical fact— the more, therefore, the proclamation *tells* us something—the more problematic is the substitution of symbol for the word.

But if it is a matter of understanding the proclamation in hearing and speaking, then theology makes its entrance where understanding is problematic. That is, the task of theology is to care for *the pure doctrine*.[250] Theology is not this doctrine itself, so as to replace the doctrine, but finds and secures it. The necessity for this derives from the fact that the proclamation in scripture comes to us in an alien language and conceptuality, and must thus always be translated into a new conceptuality. It further derives from the fact that the pure doctrine is always threatened by false doctrines, without and within, and where all are concerned.[251] Insofar, therefore, as theology is a discourse on faith, it inquires into faith's right to exist. Naturally, not as though it had to create a basis for the Word of God, but because the Christian knows that in his inquiry after truth he is inquiring after an authority he can unconditionally obey. But obedience is never something settled once and for all. It is ever new, that is, is continually being carried out in decision. This means it must continually make clear to itself the significance of the proclamation, and the task of theology is to state concepts clearly. Hence, it is not required to demonstrate in general that "one" has the right to believe, that faith is "still" in vogue and compatible with modern scientific knowledge. For its own sake it must state clearly of what sort the claims of scientific knowledge and of proclamation are, precisely because faith must always come to a decision. [A]

But *can faith be assumed*? It cannot, if faith is not a move made by *Dasein* on its own, but rather the answer to God's summons. The possibility of theology can thus in fact be recognized. Its necessity is only to be understood by faith (that is, it is to be grasped only as a task assigned to faith for faith), but its genuine realization is not demonstrable, not to be guaranteed. But if it truly is a task for the sake of faith, it must be risked. This means that *it is dialectical*. Its propositions are not "true" in the sense that they can be demonstrated on some available object to be such, or that everyone can supervise or critique their truth. They are true only when it pleases God to make them so.[252] This is the difference between theology and other sciences. Every other science assumes that access to its object is under *Dasein*'s control. Theology cannot assume this. For theology, access is given only in a believing hearing of the proclamation. But it would be sheer unbelief to contest the possibility of theology as a science, since it would deny all access to the object. [C]

Theology therefore does its work *under the assumption of faith*, under the assumption that it is itself an act of faith. But it does not have the reality of what it assumes at its disposal. From this it follows that:

(1) Theology can only be done where it *must* be done, not as an occupation for which one may decide out of "interest" as with other pursuits.[253] It is necessary *within the church* as the fellowship of believers. As such the church is of course invisible. It is visible only

as the church of the ordered proclamation of the word. But faith in the word also entails the belief that wherever the visible church is present, the invisible church is present also.

(2) Theology is aware that the assumption under which its propositions are true is not at its disposal but can be confirmed only by God. Since it is not the reproduction of a given proclamation as of something ready to hand, but rather its critical testing as to whether it actually is pure doctrine, theology must in fact speak of God and his activity. [A]

But if the task of theology, laid hold of in faith, is itself an act of faith, then it participates in shaping faith, since it is itself part of the historical event faith signifies. Naturally, it can do so only when it keeps strictly to the fact that its object is believing existence—to which it also belongs. It can do so, provided it does not take for its object a universally available world-phenomenon, accessible, say, through so-called apperception, thus as a phenomenon of intellectual or religious history, and thus "Christianity" as historical event, or even the human spirit as a timeless spirituality, whose formal structures would require researching, so that theology would be part of a systematic humane science. And it can do so only when it is strictly aware of the dialectical character of its propositions and does not suppose it can infer its object directly from them—as if that object were already at hand with *Dasein*, and thus suppose that by knowing its object it can guarantee access and a relation to it. It can no more do this than the scientific knowledge of what love is can disclose or guarantee love.

Theology has its critical office in conceptualizing the self-understanding of faith, that is, in developing the basic concepts of the understanding of believing existence, as long as persons converse with each other about faith from faith. Theology as science is the critical court of inquiry that asks whether the conversation is appropriate; whether the concepts used in the discussion are appropriate, that is, whether they correspond to the true self-understanding of faith. Thus, for the sake of disclosure, theology discloses the believer's existence in its totality, that is, in its internal structure. The why of theology is given in faith, insofar as it is motivated by the belief that there is such a disclosure of believing existence made for disclosure's sake. Theology is linked to the church by means of its why as well as by its whence, its origin, insofar as faith derives from proclamation in the church. But for this reason, the link is only indirect, not direct. That is, theology is neither proclamation in the church, nor is it obliged to inquire into its practical utility in the church; otherwise it would not be a critical court of inquiry. [c]

Theology sees that the proclamation as such can be uttered only as address, and speaks of it as if it were something tangible, as if one could understand that address in a state of not being addressed. It sees that revelation is what it is only in contemporaneity, and in speaking of it regards it as something tangible, over and done with. Theology can speak in this way only when it is aware that "speaking about" makes sense only when God allows it to become a "speaking from," when it occurs as a sinful undertaking under the grace of justification.[254] This state of affairs finds clearest expression in "*dialectical theology*."[255] It can take this upon itself when it must, that is, when its speaking occurs in service, namely, of the church. Theology knows that it does not guarantee its object in such fashion that its speaking gives the hearer access to its object. For its part, it does not intend to disclose the object but leaves that to the proclamation. It is thus legitimated only in service of the church and of proclamation. What distinguishes it from this is that it is not direct address.

If, though derived from the proclamation, theology assumes a critical stance toward it, from where does it derive its *criterion for criticism*? It derives it from the proclamation heard as proclamation. Naturally, it does not critique the proclamation as proclamation but assumes it to be such, so as to regulate whatever conceptual shape it takes on, and to indicate to the proclamation of its time what it must say, functioning, so to speak, as the vital internal organ of explanation. Or, it performs this service in order to differentiate false from true proclamation.

In a manner of speaking, the material available to theology for critical testing is scripture, dogma, and the historical development of theology. To the extent the proclamation is present in these entities, *they* are *authority for theology*. But to what extent this is true only theology itself can decide, and for this decision it cannot appeal to the authority *of the church*. Insofar as the church is an authority, it is the invisible church, the church that itself is believed, just as is the Holy Spirit, and is thus not an arbiter at one's disposal. It is an authority, but only as laid hold of in faith itself. The empirical church, to the extent the word is proclaimed in it, has within it the invisible church, but it is not itself an authority.[256] The same is true of *dogma and theology* (theological tradition).[257] Nor can theology settle on *scripture* because of a previously established dogma about it. It can do so only for the simple reason that in scripture the proclamation encounters it for the first time. It does so with the claim that this scriptural proclamation itself is the revelation, while all other proclamation harks back to it. Not as if in scripture certain truths are first uttered in a relatively new way, truths needing purifying by recourse to scripture, or needing examination as to their basis in fact. Rather, all other proclamation points to scripture not as its (accidentally) first stage, but as that of which it speaks, as the revelation. This first proclamation *is* in fact the revelation, not something behind it, a history to be reconstructed, personalities, or the like. Scripture, therefore, is the authority, and of course the only authority for theology. The task of proclamation in the church is the further handing on of this word. Consequently, the task of theology is to regulate the church's proclamation according to the scriptural norm.

But this assumes *that the first and genuine task of theology is the understanding of scripture*.[258] It is so, since it must interpret scripture not as a phenomenon of world history, of cultural or intellectual history, but as a genuinely historical fact.[259] The understanding of scripture in theology can only be one in which its own way of being qualified by scripture is expressed. Thus it can never be a neutral, objective understanding or an attitude of wait and see, but only of faith or unbelief. As theological interpretation only the interpretation of faith must apply, that is, an interpretation which by faith as relation to the object, to revelation, makes clear what the scripture says. In a certain way, therefore, theology is historical science, or theology is genuinely and always *historical theology*. Theology's historical retrospection is thus not basically different from that of any historical research. It is critical retrospection on its own history, resulting from the claim of the future heard in the present. Such retrospection becomes faith when it acknowledges the claim of this historical fact (the fact of my history), of the scripture, a recognition that cannot be dispatched as an assumption prior to interpretation but only occurs within it. There is thus no theological exegesis of scripture as a methodological undertaking. It can only be ventured by faith within the church, just as theology in general.

Thus, on the one hand, *theology* was defined as a conceptualizing of human existence as determined by God, and on the other as exposition of scripture. Both are the same, for since theology speaks of existence (not of existentiality) as historical, as marked by a specific historical fact, it speaks of scripture as this fact, and of it as historical, that is, as marking existence. On the other hand, by interpreting scripture, by showing what it has to say of sin and grace, revelation and faith, it speaks of human existence as determined by God, for sin and grace, revelation and faith are construed as the how of existence. Thus, then, there is no longer a particular systematic theology that could describe a system of Christian doctrine according to its own principles. What could be called systematic theology, this "Introduction,"[260] for example, can only be an understanding of self by way of the historical work of exegesis itself, an exegesis motivated by concrete questions of the moment, in this case by the burning question: What is theology? Theology is therefore rational work, work of the *logos* on the assumption of faith, of the *pneuma*. God gives the *pneuma*, the *logos* is our affair.[261] The *logos* does not accomplish it *alone*, and it certainly does not make a *Christian*, but it does make the *theologian*. No matter who the person, absence of the *logos* is not proof of the presence of the *pneuma*. [A]

# Appendix

## Truth and Certainty

*Regarding Bultmann's lecture on "Truth and Certainty," refer to the Editor's Foreword of this volume. The lecture manuscript includes twenty-six pages, written on one side in ink. Four pages are added, which Bultmann seems to have written down immediately after learning of Gogarten's presentation, and just before he was to lecture. The excurses that Bultmann inserted into his manuscript on separate pages are not printed here.*

Whoever has read *von Soden's statements* in "What Is Truth?"[1] knows that *the concept of "truth"* is *ambiguous*. In what follows, the concept is used in the sense common to us, and with regard to the truth of faith, that is, in the sense in which we ask: Is what I believe, or should believe, true? This concept of truth is familiar to us *from Greek tradition*, a tradition which in essence determines our scientific education. In this instance, truth (*alētheia*) first of all quite simply means: *A being unveiled, uncovered*, the true state of affairs, the actual facts of the case. A situation is described as true when seen to be what it really is, unobscured by false opinions and fantasies. Derivatively, *an utterance, a sentence* is described *as true* when it unveils a fact, reveals it in its truth, describes it as it really is. We are accustomed to saying that an utterance is true when it corresponds with the facts.

In this double sense (though a sense with a single origin) truth is referred to as the truth of a fact and as the truth of an utterance, a statement. But since the question about the truth of faith leads beyond this concept of truth—as will become especially clear in Gogarten's lecture—we need to familiarize ourselves at the outset with another use of the concept, a use related to the one referred to above.

As early as in Greek thought, the question, What is truth? was raised, that is, the question about *the* truth.[2] The idea of *the* truth, the *one* truth, cannot be understood on the basis of a purely formal understanding of the concept of "truth." There are as many truths as there are things or imaginable situations. The question about *the* truth makes sense only when truth in a special sense belongs to, is essential to *Dasein*.

Why does *Dasein* inquire into truth? Quite simply because it wants to understand itself, must understand itself in order to be with itself, arrive at its authenticity. The enigmas of the world oppress it because they are the enigmas of *Dasein* itself.[3]

Now it makes sense that to understand itself *Dasein* should turn primarily to the world in order to understand it. From the very beginning, it lives in a world and must understand it so as not to live blindly in it. Greek science is thus motivated by the *kosmos*. This science discovers an infinite number of truths, corresponding to the infinite phenomena and possibilities of the *kosmos*. And it appears as though truth is arrived at when all these possible truths are seen in their totality. This roots in the naive assumption that to know *all* possible truths also means to know their relation to each other and their unity, thus to understand the *kosmos* as a closed entity, as a *systēma*. This is the goal of Greek science. The result is that it conceives the *Dasein*, whose truth is at issue, as a phenomenon of the *kosmos*, which is understood when seen in this *systēma* as a thing among others within its ordering.[4] Greek science supposes that when it *knows about* the world it also *understands* it, that is, as a totality. It assumes the intelligibility of the world, its being guided by the Logos. Truth, as we are used to saying, is also meaning. *Dasein* supposes that it understands itself when it understands the totality of what exists and is on hand in the world as a meaningful whole. But, according to this idea, meaning denotes nothing but unity, *systēma*. Understanding takes place in observing the arrangement of the all, the totality, in *theōria*, and in such activity the *Dasein*, as per the Greek conception, is with itself, in its authenticity, because in understanding the all it understands itself.[5]

Another result is that this understanding eliminates the temporal and historical nature of *Dasein*. Where it is taken into account, the notion cannot arise that *Dasein* is understood when it is understood on the basis of the world at hand and its eternal, that is, timeless ordering. It cannot, because in time every moment is new and has its own, new enigma. If *Dasein* is temporally and historically and ever essentially new, then the question about *the alētheia* has meaning only as a question about the *alētheia* of the moment, my moment.[6]

What finally results from the Greek understanding of *Dasein*, and this is the chief thing in the context of our discussion, is that the truth about which *Dasein* asks is *its* truth; in this instance, the timeless, observable reality of the world-at-hand.

We should note that the modern question as to the truth of history has the very same sense as the Greek inquiry after truth. What is meant by the truth of history is not an unveiling of everything in history, of everything appearing in time, but rather the meaning, unity, and ordering of everything occurring in time. Whoever inquires after the truth of history is asking about some timeless arrangement, and does so because he thinks that when he can perceive it, he is calm and secure.

With regard to our theme, it is important to distinguish:

(1) The truth of Christian faith as an objective genitive: What the Christian faith asserts is true. I will try to show the significance of this question for theology.

(2) The truth of the Christian faith as a subjective genitive: The truth of which the Christian faith speaks. Gogarten will deal with this subject. But then it is necessary to ask, When Christian truth is spoken of, is the discussion in terms of the Greek inquiry after truth? Is the Christian truth an observable unity of world and history, perceptible in *theōria*? And though Christian truth is finally the question

of my own truth, of a genuine understanding of myself, does Christian self-understanding occur in *theōria*, or in what other way?

That our theme can read "Truth and Certainty," that *truth and certainty* can be distinguished, clearly derives from the fact that in
Christian faith or theology the certainty of faith is stated apart from
the assertion of its truth, as truth is usually spoken of. For *truth*, in
normal usage, has the quality of being *universally valid*, universally
observable, of demanding universal recognition. In this sense we
think we can speak only of the truth of scientific knowledge, not of
the truth of faith. But we do speak of the *certainty* of faith. If faith is
nothing but a condition, an attitude of the subject (a *diathesis*), then
in fact there is no sense to speaking of its truth, and hardly of its certainty (or, only in terms of the Stoic *asphaleia*). In that case, to be
certain of my faith can only mean that I am certain of being in a
believing, religious state, just as I can be certain that I am happy or
sad.

Clearly, however, to be *certain of faith* (or also, to be certain in
faith) originally means something else. It means *to be certain of
what I believe in*, certain that my faith is not an illusion. But this only
means that from the outset faith does not understand itself as a condition of the subject, but (put formally) as the subject's relation to an
object; that it has certainty only when it knows this object really
*exists*, and that faith really sees it *as* it is. But then, *certainty and
truth of faith* cannot be separated. Faith has certainty only when it
has truth, that is, when what it believes in is true; when the object of
faith lies unveiled before it; when it sees it in its reality, just as it is.

Truth and certainty are thus inseparable, and *in the formal sense
truth here as everywhere means the same thing*, to the extent we
speak of truth as an object of knowledge, of its being unveiled, of its
reality, and to the extent we speak of the truth of propositions, of
their capacity for unveiling, or of their correspondence to the object.
But for this reason truth here as everywhere has the *character of universal validity*. That is, everyone who sees the object concerned
must see it *in just this way*. Everyone who speaks of it must speak of
it *in just this way*, if the object is to be seen and spoken of. If we see

and speak of it otherwise, then we are seeing and speaking of something else, and not at all of the object in view.

This is not the place to object that of course we can *see the object from different aspects*, then accent what is different about it. Of course we can! But if this difference should apply to the same object, then, what is decisive, what is essential about it, what it is, must be seen, and all that is different must hold true of it, must be understood in relation to this object. It must therefore cohere. Just any statements at all cannot apply equally to God, the statement, for example, that God is a person and not a person; that God is in the world or outside it. Only one of the two statements can apply, or else we are not speaking of the same subject, of God.

The statement often made that I can speak of the truth of an article of faith only as it has become truth *for me*, that I can only believe in God as I *see* Him, spells either rejection of the truth of faith as such—whoever speaks in this way is actually speaking only of his subjective condition and no longer of God—or it means that I *can only speak* of the object of faith *when I really have seen it*, that every article of faith must be independently appropriated and not blindly accepted. Quite right, but *this does not dispose of the concept of truth*. In fact, the statement implies that faith's seeing occurs in a different way than through sense perception or, say, mathematical knowledge. It implies that faith has its own source of knowledge, its own way of seeing. So as Ritschl said, for example, religion does not operate with judgments of being but with judgments of value. But this does not spell the rejection of universal validity. Universal validity does not denote the empirical fact that all see the object but the basic reality that all who see it must see it in this way. It is not determined by knowing subjects but by the object.

As simple as all of this really is, just as ominous have been the consequences of the insight that the truth of faith, because it involves a particular object and correspondingly a particular way of seeing, is a particular kind of truth. In contrast to the seeing and knowing of natural science, the seeing and knowledge of faith appeared to be "subjective." In addition, the object of faith, because it lacks universal validity, seemed removed from the access of scientific thought.

There is talk of a "*double truth*," the truth of faith and the truth of science.[7] And since one held on to theology as a science (despite the "*double truth*") and the unity of science, the truth involved in theology had to become scientific truth as one understood science, while the truth of faith was held to be inaccessible to science.

It appeared to be characteristic *of theology as science* to work untroubled by the truth with which faith is involved. Theology as science may be guided only by scientific truth; it may not be bound to articles of faith, or else it would no longer be free as science. The assumption, of course, is that science does not arrive at results which shake faith, when it is recalled that the certainty of faith has a quite different basis than do the tenets of science and that the object of faith is quite different from that of science.

But how different is it? Theology as science may not be bound to articles of faith; it must be free! Yet the articles of faith express the believer's relation to the object of faith, to God. Now, *either* faith is the sole relation to God, in which case it follows that a theology as science *cannot speak of the object of faith, of God*; that the truth of faith does not fall within its competence. *Or*, there is another relation to God apart from faith, another way of seeing God, so that God can be made an object of science. This notion is contradicted both by faith and by theology, which roundly states that the object of faith can be grasped only in the way peculiar to it, supposedly in a subjective way. So it is that such a theology cannot speak of the object of faith, of God, nor of the truth of faith.

*As theology, however, it does intend to speak of faith.* If so, but without speaking of its object and its truth, then it cannot construe faith as the relation between God and humanity, but *only as a human attitude*. Piety, religion becomes its object, a phenomenon of the human spirit, of human history, of the "world." And it helps nothing continually to emphasize that faith or piety speaks of Someone over against it. For as long as theology supposes it can make faith apart from its object into the object of scientific research and understand it, then it in fact denies the truth of faith and ends with understanding what faith says of its object as the objectivizing of pious feeling, as piety's mythical interpretation of the world.[8] Theology intends to speak of faith without seeing what faith believes in. But if faith is what it is by its relation to its object, this means that theology cannot see it at all. It construes faith as a phenomenon of the world, while faith itself maintains that it is wrought by God. Precisely by supposing that it leaves faith unexplained, not trusting itself to say anything about its object, theology in fact most sharply attacks it.

*The problematic of such a theology* is immediately apparent in the *historical and psychological work* done within theology. Since this work does not take note of faith's object, it obviously does not differ from secular history or psychology. One day, the question will be put as to the significance of such work in theology! Meanwhile, only *systematic theology* is to be carried on. If systematic theology is not simply to be a collection and arrangement of articles of faith, without going into their bases, if it actually intends to be a science, then it encounters difficulty. It prides itself in the fact that it renders faith independent of itself but can no longer say for what purpose it actually exists. This is clearly the case in, for example, Wendland's article on "Theology."[9] "Theology takes root in the life of faith"—but "taking root" here merely means that there can be theology only because there is faith; for in theology, it is said, the life of faith is made the object of reflection. But how theology actually *takes root* in the life of faith remains obscure, and thus, why there should be faith and for whose sake faith exists is made the object of reflection.

At this point, practical motives are sought: Theology satisfies Christians' understanding of one another—for which there is little evidence till now. Theology is supposed to do *apologetics*! But how can it, how can it determine the right- or wrongness of faith when the question of its object, which alone furnishes its basis, does not lie within its competence? What help is there in an apologetics established in terms of the *science of religion*, such that it, of course, does not establish faith but shows why religious faith as such is essential, necessary, and normal; shows by proving a gradual development, by comparing religions and ways of believing, that the Christian faith is the loftiest and highest conceivable form of appearance of the religious life (Wendland); that a height of religious consciousness towering above the basic religious position of Christian faith is not conceivable (Wobbermin)? I say, no thank you to such an apologetic. I do not want to know whether or not my faith is the highest and unsurpassable form of religious life. I simply want to know whether or not what I believe in is true!

Theology was once a science *about* faith as the *fides quae creditur*, a science *for* faith as the *fides qua creditur*. Now it is a science *about* faith as the *fides qua creditur*, and the *fides quae creditur* is lost, as well as the purpose for this science. But in fact theology has lost the *fides qua* along with the *fides quae creditur*, because the *fides qua creditur* is visible only where its object first is seen. But when the *fides qua creditur* is seen without its object, there is no analysis that can subsequently retrieve that object from it, even though (sensitive to the embarrassment of their attempt) Schaeder, Wobbermin, and Bruhn struggle to do so.[10]

A theology whose object is religion and which conceives faith as an instance of religious life has lost faith together with its object once and for all. It does not speak of faith and its truth. Its object is still only *the believing subject*, whose faith is construed as a human attitude.

*Ernst Troeltsch* is an illustration of a theology which consistently functions in this fashion. He unabashedly identifies *faith with piety*, defining faith as a religious attitude of soul. When he gives it more precise definition as a willing surrender to God and an allowing oneself to be filled by God, he seems to validate the relational character of faith. On further examination this is really not the case. Troeltsch distinguishes the *fides quae creditur* from the *fides qua creditur* as *myth* or *gnosis*, as notions about reality which faith automatically produces. According to Troeltsch, all religions trace this knowledge of faith as wrought by God to *revelation*. Mythology speaks of this revelation as having occurred in the past but further founding faith. For actually revelation is nothing but "a heightened credibility, towering above the average and radiating its power." It is "the productive and original phenomenon of a new religious power or exaltation of life, presenting itself as a practical wholeness of life and intention, and communicating its powers through its bearer." For the bearer of the revelation himself, this wholeness is expressed in an abundance of visions, in ideas about God, the world and humanity, that is, in a myth created by naive fantasy. We could describe it as a symbol, "but then may not forget that even where the creative genius is concerned, his myth is primarily a naively perceived reality."[11]

According to Troeltsch, the religious community accepts this myth and enriches it by incorporating the religious hero into it, deifying him and making him the object of faith. So then, faith is a "mythical, symbolic, practical, peculiarly religious way of thinking and knowing, commencing with an historical, personal impression which believes in the myth because of the practical, religious powers it mediates, and which can only express, objectify and communicate these powers through the myth."[12]

On this view, *theology* emerges because the knowledge of faith is always influenced by the prevailing scientific view of the world. This view, however, continually undergoes change and soon comes into conflict with the myth. Theology attempts to suit the old myth to the new worldview, but succeeds only up to a point. If the myth is dissolved by the scientific worldview, then the religious substance is also dissolved and new religious structures must appear.

We should imagine that in such desperate straits Troeltsch would have abandoned theology. How will anyone who has come to realize that dissolution hovers over all myth, including the Christian myth, how will anyone still bother with theological work which medicates itself with some connection between myth and science? Right here, a way of escape, a new possibility for doing theology is opened to Troeltsch—defining theology's task as a *psychological and epistemological analysis of faith*. If the theology of yesterday sought to connect mythology and science by attempting to mediate between natural and supernatural knowledge, the theology of today intends to mediate between science and faith. It does so first by articulating the mythical-symbolic-practical nature of faith, and second by attempting to secure the practical, symbolic way of knowing rooted in ultimate religious truth alongside exact scientific ways of knowing rooted in experience. An *epistemology of faith* must demonstrate the independent value of the knowledge of faith and must secure a relation to reality mediated by religion.

This is strange, very strange! *The reality to which religion relates* is, in this case, of course, not at all visible to it.[13] It is discovered only by means of psychological and epistemological analysis! The reality cannot be God and his revelation, for talk of God and his revelation is, of course, mythology! And the myth cannot hold its own with science! Faith, however, may cling to its mythology! Since it has practical-symbolic character, it harms no one and is of use to someone. But science sees that in fact there lurks in faith a relation to a reality which science alone, by virtue of psychology and epistemology, can see.

What kind of reality might that be? And how must the way in which faith is related to it be conceived?

The reality is nothing but *the so-called Absolute*. And, of course, the Absolute is also conceived as the "creative," producing all life-phenomena as well as a value that gives all values their worth—*all* values, since not only religion, but also science, morals, and art embrace values. In what religious value consists is, of course, not clear. Mythologically speaking, it is God, for Troeltsch maintains that the value of faith's knowledge consists in its practical mastery of the riddles of life through taking hold of a redeeming power of fellowship with God attested to in practice.

This is not very clear. In fact, the result is simply that faith maintains the worth of those values to which science, morals, and art relate.[14] Troeltsch's theory is possible only because in the end, and with a *salto mortale* similar to Heim's, he suddenly allows science, morals, and art to be founded on faith as a *feeling of inner necessity*. Every conviction of ultimate truths and values is of a religious nature, is a faith. Then, of course, it is easy to rescue faith if it is finally nothing but the "purely religious," the feeling of necessity sanctioning all culture, science, morals, and art. To be sure, then finally even myth is vindicated, because ultimate values can only be spoken of in half-mythological fashion and because mythological-religious and scientific-conceptual perceptions interpenetrate.

Here we see how faith's *relation to the Absolute* is actually conceived: Not as an I-Thou relation, a relation of question and answer, sin and forgiveness. Rather, the subject's belief is nothing but the creative activity of the Absolute in the subject, the certainty of the creative or imitatively creative subject regarding itself. *Deus in nobis*! Faith is at bottom the faith of the human spirit, of human culture, in itself. Religion is an indispensable and valuable function of human spiritual life, because this life requires faith in the immanence of the divine within it, needs faith in itself to maintain its security and in order not to fall prey to despair.

If Bruhn quite openly admits that liberalism gave entrée to the Absolute, since, from its study of vital human existence, it was confident that what is from beneath is also from above, then Troeltsch, with a certain stubborn despair, clings to faith in immanence and makes Christian theology into a philosophy of history intent on demonstrating the immanence of the divine, the presence of ultimate truths and values in human spiritual life.[15]

Briefly put, this theology—when faced with the question of truth—refers the human being back to himself and summons him to believe in himself. Such theology is no theology at all because it has lost its object. It speaks neither of faith nor of God. But theology is either what it was, *the teaching concerning God*, or, if it is not such, then it is *not* a theology. If theology is to speak of the truth of faith, it may not speak of the truth of religion, or of a necessary and creative function of spiritual or cultural life. Otherwise, it is not speaking of faith at all. It must speak of the object of faith itself, or else it is no longer of interest to faith, and presumably not even to science apart from faith.

But how shall theology speak of the object of faith? To be able to do so, it must acknowledge *faith as a particular way of viewing its object*, that is, *of viewing God*. It must therefore assign cognitive value to articles of faith, recognizing their truth, acknowledging their character as unveiling divine reality. But here a new detour threatens, one on which theology, to the extent it persists in assigning to faith an independent capacity for knowing, to great extent has lost its way.

Once more, appeal is made to the "*double truth*." If in nominalism reference to that "double truth" meant that two contradictory statements about the same fact can be true (statements based on reason, and statements based on revelation), now, by appeal to Kant's *critique of cognition*, it is asserted that statements based on an a priori of reason—theoretical, practical, or aesthetic—can be equally true, though they express something different and contradictory about an object. For the object, so the argument reads, is first constituted by the faculty of perception, and the statements refer to this object as constituted by reason, not to the object itself. So I can observe a phenomenon of nature in a scientific or in an aesthetic way. I can observe a phenomenon of history, the action of a man, for instance, as the necessary result of a causal train of events, but I can also observe it as an act of freedom.

On this view, faith is made analogous to such types of observation, and one speaks of a *religious a priori* that has its right alongside others. Here, however, two errors are committed:

(1) Never and nowhere does a faculty of perception constitute its object. If talk of perception and truth are still to make sense, *it is the object that determines perception*. If there is to be talk of faith as a capacity for seeing its object, for seeing God, then whatever epistemological reflections are made about faith as a human capacity are totally irrelevant. What faith sees, it does not owe to itself as the capacity that creates its object but owes to God, who reveals himself to it. If the reality that faith sees, if God contradicts the reality I otherwise perceive through sense and reason, it does me no good to tell me that I am looking at quite another object with another capacity. I want to know whether the reality I see is real or an illusion. It appears to be an illusion when I see reality differently with my senses and reason than with faith.[16]

(2) Science, morals, and art involve a world in which the human exists as a creature of nature and history. The phenomena of that world are what science, morals, and art see and shape. If religion is made analogous to science, morals, and art, then *God* is *a phenomenon of the world*. If science, morals, and art observe the world as a totality, then the object of faith is nothing but the world as totality, which means that *faith is understood as a worldview*.

More precisely, a statement can be true that examines man biologically as a creature of nature, as a species of animal, a proposition that knows nothing of man under a moral requirement which he may or may not fulfill, and nothing of his specifically historical connections. Conversely, an ethical proposition or a proposition of the philosophy of history can be true which includes all of this but ignores biological research into what is human. Examination from the perspective of religion supposedly occurs *in parallel*. It is an examination that views humanity and the world as before God and thus ignores the natural-scientific observation of the world and humanity. The latter is directed toward the reality perceptible to the senses, whereas ethical and religious observation is directed toward a suprasensuous reality. Both can exist together unchallenged.

Of course, without fearing contradiction, we can juxtapose individual statements pertaining to various types of observation, such as: A person is powerful because he eats good food, and is worthy of trust because he is truthful. But the problem arises because each method requires consistent carrying out and thus immediately comes into conflict with every other. Each method of observation, whether it be the natural-scientific, the ethical, or the religious, claims *to understand the world and man as a totality*, and to show humans who or what they really are. *Biology* does not at all intend to investigate the individual person merely with respect to bodily function. Rather, it intends to investigate the entire person, to understand his historical life, family and state, nation and culture in biological fashion. It thus levels out the difference between man and the beast and discovers in the beast as well preliminary stages of human-historical life. It pursues animal psychology and sociology; it investigates the intelligence of beasts, etc. *Psychoanalysis* likewise intends to understand all the phenomena of human life, including those of religious life. It makes, for example, faith in God intelligible on the basis of the father complex.

Can faith simply declare its indifference to the closed worldview of natural science, or to the worldview of an historiography that investigates causes, because, due to another capacity, it would regard the world differently? Will not whoever wants to understand the bond of love with another in a seriously psychoanalytic way lose confidence in his love? Will not whoever wants to understand his relation to God in a psychoanalytic way lose trust in God? Does it help to refer to the fact that, for example, I can examine a landscape from a natural-scientific as well as from an aesthetic perspective, neither intruding upon the other? Yes, it does help, provided the natural-scientific examination were not to devour the aesthetic by interpreting it from its own perspective, say, in psychoanalysis, by subjecting my evaluation of what is "beautiful" to its observation, interpreting it quite differently than is meant; or, by drawing my aesthetic observation into its biological orbit and explaining it on the basis of heredity, sexuality, and the like. In such a case, there is nothing to the "reality of the beautiful"!

Nor does speaking of the *double truth* give us any help, since every investigation subjects the entire world, the entire person to itself, and intends to show in what way the world or the person actually exists.[17] Only one type of investigation can be right! To juxtapose different types of research, each derived from a different capacity, each one legitimate, does not help me when I ask, How does the person, how do I then really exist? And the pious hope that the truths of different types of research are only partial, which God will harmonize into one truth, is of no help so long as I see these "partial truths" merely as contradictions and can imagine nothing of their harmony, when in all this talk of the *one* truth, "truth" loses the meaning it otherwise has for us.

*Faith* is taken seriously only when understood as that perspective which treats the[18] world and humanity just as they really are; when it confidently asserts that every other type research making the same claim[19] is false.[20] Faith, of course, cannot do this when it is construed as a worldview that on the basis of an a priori subjects the world and humanity to its observation.[21] Then it unavoidably comes into unresolvable conflict with other types of research.

Help is often proffered by interpreting the scientific observation of the world from the perspective of faith, not the other way around. Strange to say, Rade, Troeltsch, and Heim all agree on this procedure. Heim develops it in the most detailed fashion. In his opinion, it helps to state that *the type of observation belonging to faith rests on a decision, but so does that of science, of morals, and of art,* so that the latter have no advantage over the former. Ultimately, scientific certainty is grounded in faith, since doubt clings even to the certainty of pure experience and the need for thought. Then too, the basis of faith in thought derives from a totally singular, irremovable feeling called the feeling of conviction, or the like.

This is a self-deception. Not even to give validity to one single proposition does science ever lay claim to such a feeling. But in faith this feeling must establish the validity of every article, or better, every article of faith is one that is believed. The doubt that can arise in a science is either Socratic—which only means that it assumes a more basic grounding is possible, and stimulates the search for it— or it is a doubt belonging to an eventual epistemology. Only later is it appended to science and without influence on it whatsoever. Science, in its progress and in the context of furnishing proof, does not bother with it. Such doubt is an artful and absolutely insignificant affair, at which no cock crows. Faith conquers doubt; it is a resolve. But no one has yet decided for a natural-scientific type of observation, in terms of deciding, for example, to believe the proof of a causal connection between two phenomena. In such instances, every proposition rests on proofs and insight. And the entire path of research is not created through decision but is a possibility inherent in observation, a possibility that in fact is always mine.

We may speak of a *decision on behalf of a natural-scientific observation* only when meant as a *worldview*, when I give it unrestricted authority to interpret everything in general and from the very beginning; when I give it authority to see the world and humanity in their authenticity. But for that I must already have a view of it. In that case, it is analogous to faith, that is, if *faith too* is construed *as a worldview*, for which I decide. In that case, I must be aware of faith's way of observing prior to my decision. Hypothetically, then, I could understand the world and humanity in faith without believing—obviously an absurdity, for I cannot examine anything in a believing way before I believe. And the decision for faith would be totally arbitrary. We do not decide for faith, but in faith. Faith is itself decision.

The positive contribution of theology in this situation, that is, in face of natural-scientific or other worldviews, is to make clear the *character of faith*, to mark it off from every other worldview. But before we do so, it should be pointed out that even every scientific observation, if it understands itself as a worldview, that is, if it intends to interpret the world and humanity as a totality, misunderstands itself.

*Philosophical reflection* has tried to settle the conflict between the various types of observation, particularly between natural-scientific and ethical or historical research. It has tried to do so by determining limits, especially the limits of natural and historical science. This involves limiting various spheres of objects to various types of research. It is useless labor, because every investigation intends to understand the world and humanity as a totality. This tendency would have to be repressed, obviously not by reserving certain phenomena for one and certain phenomena for another type research. It can only occur when it is seen that each type of examination intends to understand the phenomena in an unambiguous way, but that *the phenomena* are *more or less ambiguous*; when it is realized that no science can predict how a phenomenon must be interpreted; that interpretation must be prescribed by the object, which to begin with is a puzzle. The argument as to how a phenomenon is to be understood can only be decided through an act of understanding in the individual instance.

So it is that the same phenomenon can be understood in this way or that. But the question is, What interpretation views the phenomenon as it really is; what understanding sees what is true and speaks the truth about it? This, however, cannot be decided at the outset. The error of these types of research is that they a priori intend to interpret every phenomenon and so from the very beginning bar access to the real object through their "principles." Their error is that they are worldviews and not methods of research, worldviews that determine in the lump and from the outset how each phenomenon encountered must be interpreted, instead of preserving freedom. There is no sense to reflecting in general on the limits of natural and historical science. Such limits are not a priori visible in the object. They can only become visible in research. True, limits can be drawn among types of research. But this should not lead us to suppose that such activity would limit their competence in relation to the object. As methods they claim to subordinate every object and, of course, to subordinate it totally.

Phenomenologically, then, genuine science would have to proceed by allowing *the phenomenon itself to enjoy its validity*, allowing the phenomenon to prescribe the type of investigation. Whether or not there are phenomena that are unambiguous is not under discussion here.

Philosophical reflection would further have to explain how one of those types of investigation *can* totally master an object without failing in the first place. It could actually do so on the basis of human *Dasein*. From the very beginning *Dasein* has various possibilities of understanding itself. Stated schematically, *Dasein* has the possibility of authentically understanding itself as historical, or of understanding itself as something ready-to-hand, on the basis of the world at hand around it. The more that *Dasein* in its fallenness understands itself in a practical way on the basis of the world around it, the more in its theoretical reflection it will interpret its existence on the basis of the existence of the world around it, and the more its existence is able to be interpreted in this factual way on the basis of the existence of the world around it.

If *authentic Dasein is possibility*, that is, if human *Dasein*, emerging from its past into the here and now and in face of its future lays hold of its possibility in resolve, then no scientific method that construes it on the basis of things ready-to-hand can understand it in its authenticity. Or, it can do so only to the extent as *Dasein* in its fallenness[22] is itself only something ready-to-hand. Scientific method can do this with regard to a *Dasein* past and gone, a *Dasein* offering itself to view first of all as something that was avilable in the past. It can do so with regard to a *Dasein* of the present when it treats it as something past. If such scientific methods claim to interpret human *Dasein*, they have lost their legitimate scientific significance and lead to false propositions; they are worldviews.

We would describe the philosophical work which must clarify these problems as *the ontology of Dasein*. Its work may not be taken over by theology. But in the present situation we have occasion to be reminded of it when the task is to show what faith is and how *faith* should be *distinguished from science or a worldview*. As long as faith is made analogous to these types of research, it is construed as a worldview which from the outset knows how every phenomenon is to be observed, whether of a natural-scientific nature or as belonging to faith. Then the goal is to search for a religious a priori; then faith is understood neither as faith nor as science. A theology thus engaged abandons its object, that is, it abandons God. Its object is the world and humanity, observed as natural science observes it, from a position available to *Dasein* as such, not from the point of view of God and his revelation.

But, of course, *theology* may not wait for an ontology of *Dasein* to solve its problem as to how faith manages in the conflict with science and a worldview. It must come to terms with the problem without the aid of philosophy, must come to terms with it on its own.

This becomes clear only when it is evident that *faith* is nothing but the answer to God's proclaimed word, which discloses to the human *a specific understanding of himself*, the understanding that he comes out of his past as sinner; is thus headed toward death as the judgment of God, but that God's forgiving grace is available to him in the very proclaimed word of forgiveness; that through this forgiveness he becomes a new man who sees life ahead of him, and along with himself sees the neighbor to whom he is bound in love.[23] The human being is asked whether he will affirm this understanding of himself and thus surrender every other. By contrast, every other self-understanding, whether natural-scientific, Stoic-ethical, romantic, etc., assumes the nature of a temptation, though it may be scientifically, ethically, or aesthetically motivated.

*It is this understanding of faith that theology must explain*, and in so doing it need not inquire into eventual philosophical reflection on the meaning and legitimacy of other expositions of *Dasein*. All other worldviews or expositions of *Dasein* appear in the light of the divine claim. That is, the proclamation puts to everyone the question whether he will venture to understand himself in his authenticity from the perspective of the world,[24] or will be silent as a creature before the Creator, that is, will understand himself as creature. But theology has the task *of explicating the proclamation in such fashion that the understanding of Dasein it offers* becomes *clear* as an exposition in which one can understand himself. This understanding can only be seized in decision. But the decision would be purely arbitrary if the proclamation did not disclose a real self-understanding, in which one can understand himself.

In formal terms, what *truth* means *for faith* can be stated very simply: Articles of faith are true insofar as they unveil or express the true facts of the case. In the same sense, that Christian proclamation is true which differs from faith only as question from answer, as accosting word from acceptance, that is, insofar as it unveils the true facts of the case. The true facts of the case, the truth to which faith is directed, the truth unveiled in the proclamation, or the reality seen in believing,[25] is the reality of God and thus the reality of world and man in their being unveiled.

*The reality of God* made visible in proclamation and in faith in that proclamation is not a datum accessible to neutral, unbelieving observation, no more than the truth of a trust placed in me, a love shown to me, is a fact accessible to the observation of a third person. Just as trust and love are visible only in their being affirmed, thus in mutual trust or in mutual love, so God's truth is visible only *in obedient faith*. This means that by faith I do not understand God as something that exists for itself alone, a supernatural entity with certain attributes, but—as the Reformation and Ritschl quite rightly saw, and as the Erlangen theology at least intended—I understand God by understanding myself anew.

*I understand myself anew*, not by obtaining a new theory about the world and humanity alongside the old ones but by *understanding my here and now anew* as qualified by God's word, by the proclamation. Genuine self-understanding—even apart from faith—always means to understand myself as myself, not as some other person, something ready-to-hand, but always myself, that is, myself in my here and now, in decision. Just this is the self-understanding of faith. And it differs from unbelieving self-understanding only through its hearing the word spoken into the here and now, thus through understanding the moment as qualified anew. *The decision for the word* is the decision of faith. This does not occur as *one* decision alongside others made in the world. Rather, just as I ultimately decide for myself, for my own possibility in all decisions made in the world, so also in the decision of faith. If it is true in purely formal way that in *each* decision I always become someone new, then faith recognizes that only in its decision do I really become someone new, with the result that all other decisions are mere appearance, since in them I never get free of myself, that is, of my past, of my sin. Such decisions are new only in the sense that I decide ever anew on behalf of my sin. Faith sees that only through forgiveness do I become new as a justified person and as one who loves. No decision affecting my life in the world is taken from me by faith, but each decision is qualified by faith, and in such fashion that I can decide as a believer and as one who loves, can suffer and act as a believer and as one who loves.

So it can be quite simply stated that the truth seen in faith is *the truth of the moment*. Now, under the proclamation, in faith, I see the here and now as it really is.[26] The here and now is always mine. Still, this does not mean that what faith sees is subjective. Rather, the here and now which is always only mine is objectively seen, that is, seen in its truth, when it is understood as mine.[27] It would be seen "subjectively" if understood as something I do, something qualified by my willing and feeling, my past. In total contrast to this, faith understands the here and now from out of the future, as a situation advancing toward me, summoning me to decide, calling to me, requiring my obedience, a moment qualified by the divine word, not by a religious condition, a priori or the like, but by the word which I can only hear, to which I can only hearken.

In this basic sense, *the truth of faith is universally valid*. That is, the here and now must be understood in this way and only in this way. There are no varying interpretations with equal rights. My eventual subjectivity is struck down by the very claim of the moment. But the truth of faith is not a universal truth so-called, a truth, say, of the idea of God, of freedom, of divine providence, of the idea of the good, etc. It is absolutely nothing but the truth of God, that is, of the moment. Otherwise, faith would again be made a worldview. But faith does not observe the world and humanity in general and from it draw a conclusion for the here and now as an individual instance. Conversely, for faith every here and now is essentially new, and from out of which faith understands the world and man. Faith understands itself as the justified sinner, the other as the neighbor, and the world as God's creation. Faith, for example, in the creation is thus not a cosmological theory about the origin of the world but the obedient and confident acceptance of the world in which I live as God's creation, in fact, as God's word and revelation, insofar as I understand my here and now as qualified by the proclamation.

Just as faith has disposed of the theory of the double truth, so also of *the question of the one truth*. This is a Greek question. It intends to understand the world as an observable system of existing things that are ready-to-hand, and in which the here and now is absorbed in timelessness. This question draws from the notion of the identity of the World-Logos with the individual Logos in me.

Truth has an unambiguous sense. It always denotes what is true and actual, to the extent it is unveiled and visible in its reality. There are as many truths as there are possible actualities to be unveiled. The question of the one truth in the Greek sense has meaning only when *Dasein* is understood in terms of something that is ready-to-hand, all of which the Logos can survey. If *Dasein* is temporal-historical and always essentially new—and it is addressed as such in the proclamation—then the question of the one truth has meaning only as a question about the one truth of the moment, my moment. Insofar as the believer is not raptured from the world but is addressed in his here and now, he has occasion enough *to be concerned about all possible truths*.[28] Not, however, in order to abstract the one truth from them. He can never arrive at an understanding of the here and now from them. He has reason for concern simply because he must act in the world out of love and because each act must be appropriate. He needs science; he employs natural- or historical-scientific research according to whether he needs it for his task, say, as a physician or an educator, or because in his theoretical work he must furnish the knowledge needed in the practical professions.

Of course, the believer has abandoned the notion of the *cultural value of knowledge*, because ultimately all knowledge should serve only to guide the activity needed in the here and now. The notion that in knowledge man arrives at his highest possibility, whether in the Greek or medieval-catholic *theōria*, appears to him to be an attempt to flee the here and now. As a free lord, subject to none (in faith), he is also *lord of all knowledge and science*. He does not sell himself into slavery to science, as if it could lead him to authenticity. He is aware of the temptation in all knowledge, the *eritis sicut deus* (you will be like God), but he knows that no science can unveil one's existence, my existence, because he sees his existence as before God. Yet he does not close his mind to whatever a science unveils as true. Such a flight would spell the surrender of his lordship.

In awareness of his lordship *the believer takes seriously every scientific statement*. He rejoices that it cannot lead him to faith, though it can facilitate the theological explication of faith. If in an earlier generation he accepted such assistance chiefly from the *critical study of history* which demonstrated to him that, for example, the narratives of the Virgin Birth and the Empty Tomb were legends, and thus aided in destroying a false understanding of faith, in the present—without labeling the assistance of the critical study of history passé—he may learn from *psychoanalysis*. Perhaps no science can so radically destroy the misunderstanding of faith as a religiosity, as a function of the human spirit, as psychoanalysis. What theology as the scientific explication of faith may learn from *philosophy* today, as well as in any time, need not be detailed, nor the fact that theology's attention to philosophy is a most ambiguous affair.

All these reflections are intended merely to illustrate that the truth of faith, that is, the *veritas fidei quae creditur*, does not deal with a datum alongside other data in the world, but that it is the truth of the moment qualified by the divine word.

If, apart from the truth of faith as the truth of the moment, we still wish to inquire into the *truth of theology*, then the answer is that theology is the explication of faith appropriate to faith. In this way its truth is the truth of science. Whoever wants to understand theology as a science on the basis of a scientific system grounded in the nature of the human spirit, misunderstands it. But just as every science does not glean its truth from its a priori, its principles, but rather from its object, that is, when it allows its tenets to be determined by its object, so it is with theology. As the truth of every science is its appropriateness, so it is with the truth of theology.

# Notes

## Translator's Introduction

1. Cf. Hans Hübner, "Rückblick auf das Bultmann-Gedenkjahr 1984," *Theologische Literaturzeitung* 110, 9 (September 1985), 644.

2. Cf. Joseph Cahill, *Religious Studies and Theology* 5, No. 2 (May, 1985).

3. Karl Barth, *The Epistle to the Romans*, trans. Edwyn C. Hoskyns (London: Oxford University Press, 1933), 37.

4. Karl Barth, *The Doctrine of the Word of God: Church Dogmatics*, I/1, trans. G. T. Thomson (Edinburgh: T&T Clark, 1936), 38, 405.

5. *Karl Barth–Rudolf Bultmann Letters: 1922–1966*, trans. Geoffrey W. Bromiley (Grand Rapids, Mich.: Wm. B. Eerdmans, 1981), 161–62; cf. also the helpful essay by Michael Lattke, "Rudolf Bultmann on Rudolf Otto," *Harvard Theological Review* 78 (1985): 353–60.

6. Barth, *The Doctrine of the Word of God,* 153.

7. Rudolf Bultmann, "Theologie als Wissenschaft," *Zeitschrift für Theologie und Kirche* 81 (1984): 453.

8. Rudolf Bultmann, "New Testament and Mythology," in *Kerygma and Myth*, trans. Reginald H. Fuller (London: SPCK, 1953), 44.

9. Cf. Schubert Ogden and Van Harvey, "How New Is the New Quest of the Historical Jesus?" in Carl E. Braaten and Roy A. Harrisville, *The Historical Jesus and the Kerygmatic Christ* (Nashville: Abingdon Press, 1964), 197–242.

10. Bultmann, "Theologie als Wissenschaft," 455.

11. Barth, *The Doctrine of the Word of God*, 339–40.

12. Hans-Georg Gadamer, *Truth and Method*, 2nd ed., trans. Joel Weinsheimer and Donald G. Marshall (New York: Crossroad, 1992), 309.

13. Ibid., 241.

14. Rudolf Bultmann, "Karl Barths 'Römerbrief' in zweiter Auflage," *Anfänge der dialektischen Theologie, Theologische Bücherei* 17 (Münich: Chr. Kaiser, 1967), pt. 1, 124, 136.

15. Ibid., 132–33.

16. Cf. the section entitled "The Structural Inconsistency of Bultmann's Solution," in Ogden's *Christ without Myth* (New York: Harper & Brothers, 1961), 111–26.

17. Hübner, "Rückblick," 644.

18. Barth, *The Doctrine of the Word of God*, 96.

19. Walter Schmithals, *An Introduction to the Theology of Rudolf Bultmann*, trans. John Bowden (Minneapolis: Augsburg, 1968), 299.

20. Karl Hermann Schelkle, "Rudolf Bultmann," *Theologische Enzyklopädie, Theologische Quartalschrift*, l65, 1 (1985), 67.

21. Hübner, "Rückblich," 644.

22. Adolf Schlatter, *Erlebtes* (Berlin: Furche Verlag, n.d.), 19.

23. Adolf Schlatter, "Erfolg und Misserfolg im theologischen Studium," *Zur Theologie des Neuen Testaments und zur Dogmatik, Theologische Bücherei* (Münich: Chr. Kaiser Verlag, 1969), vol. 41, 259.

24. Adolf Schlatter, *Die philosophische Arbeit seit Cartesius: Beiträge zur Förderung christlicher Theologie* (Gütersloh: C. Bertelsmann, 1906), 12.

25. Adolf Schlatter, *Atheistische Methoden in der Theologie: Theologie und Dienst* (Wuppertal: Brockhaus, 1985), Heft 43, 12, 14.

26. Adolf Schlatter, "Noch ein Wort über den christlichen Dienst," *Zur Theologie des Neuen Testaments und Dogmatik*, vol. 41, 131; cf. the comment of Georg Merz in "Adolf Schlatter," *Zwischen den Zeiten* 5 (1927), 525, in which he refers to Schlatter as the "systematician" who leaves Schleiermacher's suggestions "totally aside."

27. Cf. ibid., 527. On this point, Schlatter's attachment to his adopted country had less of the critical component than Bultmann's to the land of his birth. He wrote of the "betrayal" of Germany, of the peace of Versailles as a crime, of Germany's guilt as arising solely from throwing away its weapons, adding that he could not avoid praying the prayer current in Germany during World War I: "*Gott strafe England!*"—"God, punish England!" *Rückblick auf meine Lebensarbeit* (Stuttgart: Calwer Verlag, 1977), 242–51.

28. Ibid., 141–42.

29. Schlatter, *Erlebtes*, 76.

30. Schlatter, "Erfolg und Misserfolg im theologischen Studium," 263.

31. Schlatter, *Atheistische Methoden in der Theologie*, 13.

32. Schlatter, *Rückblick*, 32, 52–53.

33. Ibid., 78–79.

34. Ibid., 83.

35. Schlatter, *Atheistische Methoden in der Theologie*, 5–21.

36. Schlatter, *Erlebtes*, 101.

37. Schlatter, "Karl Barths "Römerbrief," *Anfänge der dialektischen Theologie*, 146.

# Editor's Foreword

1. Bultmann's immediate predecessor in the offering of this lecture by the Marburg faculty was Martin Rade. Rade last announced an "Introduction to the Study of Theology" for the summer semester of 1925. Bultmann himself had heard lectures on theological encyclopedia in his student years at Tübingen, first by Gottschick in the summer semester of 1903, then by Häring in the summer semester of 1904.

2. Till 1933, the lecture was occasionally announced as a two-hour survey. A one-hour lecture was announced just for the 1936 summer semester, and for the first time in the Department of Systematic Theology.

3. For his writing material, besides the fragments from an account book partially written on in another hand—Bultmann used blank pages of seminar examinations, letters, notices, official mail, bills, opened envelopes, and the like.

4. Thus, for example, the inside of a few Deutsche-Industrie-Nummer-5 covers contain statements on "false doctrine" or the understanding of history.

5. For the most part written on 165 leaves of an account book (numbered by Bultmann), and only on the left half of the right-hand side.

6. Enlargements of the 1926 draft appear on the right half of the right- and left-hand sides, and on numerous leaves later inserted. These often replace earlier sections, which Bultmann eliminated.

7. To these indices belong, for example, Bultmann's abbreviations for frequently occurring ideas, altered during the course of the years; the color of ink; the width of pen or ball-point stroke; postmarks or other data on the inserted leaves; publication dates for the literature discussed; and alterations in content.

8. A: 1926; B: 1928; C: 1930; D: 1933; E: 1936.

9. This Table of Contents was drafted when Bultmann set about reworking the 1933 lecture with the 1936 lecture in view. Compared with the 1933 lecture, it indicates clearly recognizable alterations (e.g., regarding the numbering of sections), though it does not match the final draft, which it still closely approximates. This table contains detailed page references on §§10–11.

10. We cannot be sure whether he even read these sections in the one-hour lecture of 1936.

11. Such a concluding chapter would almost serve as counterpart to the first chapter and its development of the theme of a "theological encyclopedia" (cf. the concluding section of chap. 1 below). It would only be a bit shorter than the first chapter.

12. They are referred to by a capital "O," prefixed or added.

13. Translator's note: Where necessary, abridgments and abbreviations were written out in full.

14. In the few instances where the edition Bultmann cited was not available, this principle could not be followed.

15. In most instances, Bultmann quotes from the fifth edition of H. Schmid, *Die Dogmatik der evangelisch-lutherischen Kirche* (5th ed., 1863), but also from J. Kaftan, *Dogmatik* (Tübingen/Leipzig: J.C.B. Mohr, 3rd and 4th eds., 1901) among others. Our translation cites the English version of Schmid, *The Doctrinal Theology of the Evangelical Lutheran Church*, trans. Charles A. Hay and Henry E. Jacobs (Minneapolis: Augsburg, reprint 1961)

16. Translator's note: Texts from the Lutheran Confessions are taken from *The Book of Concord*, trans. Theodore G. Tappert (Philadelphia: Fortress Press, 1959).

17. For example, "*das*" (= "that" or "which") instead of "*dass*" (= "that" or "so that").

18. E. Dinkler, "Die christliche Wahrheitsfrage und die Unabgeschlossenheit der Theologie als Wissenschaft: Bemerkungen zum wissenschaftlichen Werk Rudolf Bultmanns," in: O. Kaiser *et al.*, eds., *Gedenken an Rudolf Bultmann* (Tübingen: J.C.B. Mohr, 1977), 15–40.

19. In a letter to Bultmann, Oskar Siebeck writes: "I wonder whether or not you can still decide to prepare your 'Theological Encyclopedia' for publication, along with work on your John commentary. We may both surely count on its being a book that will have wider readership the longer it is on the market. It seems to me, then, that much depends on the outline's

appearing soon, entirely aside from the fact that the 'Encyclopedia' would be the proper introduction to the 'New Theological Outlines.'"

20. "As for my Enyclopedia, I thoroughly intend to work on it now. Since I will be working on lectures in encyclopedia again next semester, the book will be pushed along." This matches Bultmann's remark in a letter to M. Heidegger on August 24, 1930: "In my lectures on encyclopedia, read again last semester, I believe I have come a bit further still. . . ."

21. O. Siebeck writes to Bultmann on February 18, 1936: "If I have rightly understood you on my visits to Marburg, you would like to postpone the 'Encyclopedia' until the theological situation is cleared up a bit more."

22. As far as we know, this occurred in greater detail in his lecture on "Theology as Science," held in Alpirsbach at the Pentecost retreat of the Gesellschaft für Evangelische Theologie (June 4–6, 1941), at which time Bultmann also delivered his "New Testament and Mythology."

23. The other respondent was Pastor Karl Fischer (Lauenstein/Saxony), who spoke in place of Karl Aé (Dresden), who had taken ill. A report of the retreat by R. Paulus is printed in the *Christliche Welt* 43 (1929): 1018–1026.

24. Gogarten's lecture was published in *Zwischen den Zeiten* 8 (1930): 96–119.

# 1. The Task of Theological Encyclopedia

1. Ed.: Section titles are given according to the final Table of Contents from Bultmann's hand (see Editor's Foreword, n.9).

2. Ed.: The first draft of lecture A was not yet announced under the title "Theological Encyclopedia" but as "Introduction to the Study of Theology" (see Editor's Foreword, n.1).

3. Ed.: *orbis ille doctrinae, quem Graeci enkyklion paideian vocant* ("that sphere of teaching which the Greeks call *engkyklion paideia*.")

4. Ed.: G. Heinrici, "Enzyklopädie, theologische," *Realenzyklopädie für protestantische Theologie und Kirche,* 3rd ed. (Leipzig: J. C. Hinrichs, 1896–1913), 5:351–64. For his discussion of Protestant theology, Bultmann will also cite the first and second editions of *Die Religion in Geschichte und Gegenwart*, the first edited by F. M. Schiele and L. Zscharnack (Tübingen: J.C.B. Mohr, 1909–1913), and the second by H. Gunkel and L. Zscharnack (Tübingen: J.C.B. Mohr, 1927–1932).

5. Of special significance is P. Bayle's (1647–1706) *Dictionnaire historique et critique* (Rotterdam: Reinier Leers, 1697); and M. Diderot's

*Encyclopédie ou dictionnaire raisonné des sciences, des arts et des métiers par une société des gens des lettres, mise en ordre et publiée par M. Diderot, et quant à la partie mathématique par de'Alembert* (Bern/Lausanne, 1782). Cf. the article on "Dieu": "Since the existence of God is one of those primary truths that take forcible possession of the entire thinking and reflecting mind, it seems that the great volumes produced to prove it are useless, and in some way injurious to men; at least should be," vol. 10, 963.

6. Ed.: Cf. Georg Wilhelm Friedrich Hegel, *Werke* 8, *Enzyklopädie der philosophischen Wissenschaften in Grundrisse* (1830), Part 1 (Frankfurt, 1970), 60.

7. This idealism has its origin in René Descartes; cf. Gerhard Krüger, "Die Herkunft des philosophischen Selbstbewusstseins," *Logos* 22 (1933): 225–72, esp. 235.

8. Cf. Karl Barth, "Ludwig Feuerbach," *Zwischen den Zeiten* 5 (1927): 11–33.

9. English translation by Terrence N. Tice (New York: Edwin Mellen Press, 1988).

10. Ed.: The contradiction between the opening sentences in these two paragraphs ("Schleiermacher's undertaking corresponds . . ." or "Schleiermacher's approach appears to be different . . .") is explained by Bultmann's combining pieces of the various drafts of his lecture without harmonizing the links between sentences.

11. Ed.: Emphasis by Bultmann.

12. On this subject cf. §6: "When this same knowledge is acquired and possessed without relation to the 'government' of the Church, it ceases to be theological and devolves to those sciences to which it belongs according to its varied content."

13. Ed.: Cf. n.12!

14. Cf. §48 ("Basic Principles for Apologetics")! and §79 ("Historical Theology").

15. Cf. §37!

16. Ed. Parentheses by Bultmann.

17. Friedrich Schleiermacher, *Grundriss der philosophischen Ethik* (Leipzig: Felix Meiner, 1911), 1; Friedrich Schleiermacher, *The Christian Faith*, ed. H. R. Mackintosh and J. S. Stewart (Edinburgh: T&T Clark, 1948), 2.

18. Ed.: The predicate is missing in Bultmann's manuscript.

19. Schleiermacher, *Brief Outline of Theology as a Field of Study*, trans. Terrence N. Tice (Lewiston: Edwin Mellen Press, 1988), §33: "Philosophi-

cal theology can thus take its point of departure only beyond Christianity in the logical sense of the term, that is, in the universal concept of religious or believing fellowship."

20. Cf. §2.2 of *The Christian Faith*: "The general concept of 'Church,' if there really is to be such a concept, must be derived principally from Ethics, since in every case the 'Church' is a society which originates only through free human action and which can only through such continue to exist" (p. 3). Cf. §2, Postscript 2: "By ethics is here understood that speculative presentation of Reason, in the whole range of its activity, which runs parallel to natural science. By Philosophy of Religion is understood a critical presentation of the different existing forms of religious communion, as constituting, when taken collectively, the complete phenomenon of piety in human nature" (p. 5).

21. Cf. §252: "Knowledge of the historical career of Christianity which must be presupposed for the purposes of philosophical theology need only pertain to chronicle, which is independent of theological study, whereas scientific treatment of this historical career within all the branches of historical theology presupposes the results of philosophical theology." (At this point, §7 of the first edition reads: "Philosophical Theology takes its standpoint above Christianity, Historical Theology within it.")

22. The prevailing confusion is clear, e.g., in view of the question of the relation between body and soul.

23. Or it must be reduced to the principle of "suitability to type." Type cannot at all be defined unequivocally; the defining of it is itself a decision.

24. Thus no objection can be raised when theology is oriented to phenomenological philosophy, insofar as it is not a worldview but simply works out a genuine inquiry into things. Naturally, theology may not surrender its object to philosophy!

25. Sigrid v. d. Schulenburg, ed., *Briefwechsel zwischen Wilhelm Dilthey and dem Grafen Paul Yorck v. Wartenburg, 1877–1897* (Halle: M. Niemeyer, 1923).

26. Jacob Burckhardt, *Force and Freedom: Reflections on History*, ed. James H. Nichols (Leipzig: Kröner; New York: Pantheon Books, 1943).

27. Ibid., 82.

28. Cf. also Hugo v. Hofmannsthal (1874–1929).

29. Ed.: The pen-name of the literary historian Friedrich Gundelfinger, member of the circle around Stefan George.

30. Cf. Herrmann's concern for historicity in contrast to neo-Kantianism.

31. Karl Barth, *Der Römerbrief* (Bern: Bäschlin, 1919).

32. "Die Krisis der Kultur" (lecture of October 1920), in Friedrich Gogarten, *Die religiöse Entscheidung* (Jena: E. Diederichs, 1921), 32–53.

33. Cf. Karl Barth, "Die dogmatische Prinzipienlehre bei Wilhelm Herrmann," *Zwischen den Zeiten* 3 (1925): 246–80, and 246, with reference to his reading of Herrmann's ethics: "From then on I think I was independently involved in theology."

34. In addition to Franz Overbeck (1837–1905).

35. Cf. *Zwischen den Zeiten* 1923–33, in association with K. Barth, Fr. Gogarten, Ed. Thurneysen, ed. by Georg Merz; Emil Brunner also contributed.

36. Ed.: The manuscript gives no clear indication of order in the following sections.

37. Ed.: In the manuscript, the preceding sentence appears in the margin alongside the (not erased) sentence ahead of it here. Whether or not it is intended to replace or supplement this sentence is not clear from the manuscript.

38. How is one to get hold of God, get a grip on him? Through revelation! Indeed, but this obscures the question. For revelation is grasped through faith, not science. Our question is precisely how there can be a *science* of God!

39. In any event we must not commit the error of scientific doctrine and set encyclopedia *ahead of* theology. Encyclopedia can only obtain knowledge of its object from a theology which is in fact vital, and in the doing of which the object becomes known.

40. As does Mulert, p. 2 [D]. Cf. Hermann Mulert, *Religion Kirche Theologie, Einführung in die Theologie* (Giessen: A. Töpelmann, 1931).

41. Cf. Stephan, "Theologie II," *Religion in Geschichte and Gegenwart*, 2nd ed., vol. 5, col. 1116, in which he writes that according to its root meaning, theology is scientific discourse concerning God, the "doctrine of God and divine things." Then was added all the knowledge necessary for the education of pastors, and the entire enterprise was called *sacra doctrina*, theological science. Further, in evangelical theology, the apparent or actual impossibility of speaking scientifically about God led to making faith rather than God the object of theology. With this move, historical and psychological science gains the upper hand in theology. [D]

42. Cf. psychology, philosophy, history, all of which have lost their object!

43. Cf. Karl Barth's skepticism toward my work, as if it were my intention to investigate faith, Christianity, as an historical phenomenon.

44. The question whether theology as a science has an object peculiar to
it, is not chiefly directed to theology from popular anti-Christian polemic,
but from philosophy (Heidegger, Jaspers, Grisebach). It derives from the
fact that philosophy also treats the problem of existence on its own, thus
claims for itself phenomena which seemed or still seem to be the object of
theology. The question is explicit in the works of Gerhardt Kuhlmann
(pupil of Grisebach): "Krisis der Theologie?" *ZThK* 12 (1931): 123–46;
"Entweder-Oder" (in opposition to Hirsch), *ZThK* 15 (1934): 247–55; *Die
Theologie am Scheidewege* (Tübingen: J.C.B. Mohr, 1935); *Theologische
Anthropologie im Abriss* (Tübingen: J.C.B. Mohr, 1935). [E]

45. This would result in theology's treating the question of truth merely
as the question of the historicity of phenomena relating to Christian faith,
not as the question concerning the truth of what is believed. [D]

46. Ed.: D inserts, "or sociology"

# 2. The Object of Theology

1. Ed.: The margin of the manuscript reads: "The question of §3, to what
extent theology, in order to be a science of God, must and can be a science
of faith, must be elaborated in §4. Can faith be the object of theological science when God is 'put in parentheses'?" [D] This marginal note relates to a
draft of §3 omitted in the final draft of the lecture.

2. Ed.: "Since" is an insertion in draft D.

3. Ed.: At this point the manuscript refers to sections later omitted.

4. Otto Piper, *Theologie und reine Lehre* (Tübingen: J.C.B. Mohr, 1926),
29f.

5. And theology would not be a science if it collected, arranged, and
combined into a system traditional tenets of church doctrine or of scripture.
Science is the obtaining of knowledge from a primal relation to the object
*itself.* Traditional tenets—which, insofar as they derive from a primal relation to the object, can and should lead to that object (in this, of course, their
meaning consists), but can also obscure and falsify it—are to be tested by
the object, retrieved as regards their origins, or critically corrected. Science
is not a formal arrangement but a discovery. [E (perhaps also D)]

6. Ed.: D inserts "its product" and "Theology asks" up to "to render it
intelligible."

7. It already *has* the truth in the sense that it is possible only in the
church on the basis of hearing the word. Its peculiar dialectic consists in the

fact that on one hand it is based upon the hearing of Christian teaching and on the other intends first to uncover it. [D]

8. Ed.: D inserts "and it can only say this. . . ."

9. Karl Barth, *Die christliche Dogmatik im Entwurf* (Münich: C. Kaiser, 1927), I, 54, contains an excellent argument against theologians who view faith (the life of the gods, etc.) as the supposed object of theology; cf. ibid., 96–99! [B]

10. So it is, incidentally, with every science; for "faith" in theology denotes the relation to an object peculiar to it. One never has this relation *alongside* or *prior to* research, but *in* it. Any science can lose its object and run idle. Of course, the object of theology is not simply ready-to-hand as with the natural sciences. [O]

11. Ed.: In the original draft the preceding sentence and the beginning of this sentence read: "It is clear that faith as the 'pure doctrine' of theology is conceived as a *fides quae creditur*, as a doctrine that theology does not first discover or beget, but that can only be unequivocally established against confusions with heresies, so that the believer within the church is secure. His faith. . . ." (The corrections and supplements appear in draft D.)

12. Cf. Wendland's article on "Theologie" in *Religion in Geschichte und Gegenwart*, 1st ed., vol. 5 (cols. 1197–1205), col. 1197.

13. Ed.: In Wendland's article printed in spaced type.

14. Wendland, col. 1202: "Theology thus roots in the life of faith. But if there is such a life, then it can subsequently be made the object of reflection." Certainly it *can*! Why? Out of curiosity, from so-called interest!

15. "Agreement"! This is an odd motive. Theology actually disunites!

16. The position of Bruhn (cf. below!) is sturdier; he flatly sets the philosophical above the theological necessity. [D (perhaps also B)]

17. Wendland, *Theologie*, col. 1202. Cf. the apologetics of Wobbermin (*Systematische Theologie nach religionspsychologischer Methode* [Leipzig: J.C. Hinrichs, 1925], III, and in addition: *Theologische Literaturzeitung* 51 [1926]: cols. 529–533, especially col. 532), to the effect that a height of religious consciousness towering above the basic position of Christian faith is not conceivable! [B]

18. There was once a science *about* faith as the *fides quae creditur*, *for* faith as the *fides qua creditur*. Now it is a science *about* faith as the *fides qua creditur*, while the *fides quae creditur* and its purpose have been eliminated. Instead, the *fides quae* has been generalized, with the result that it no longer applies to anyone. The popular formulation reads: It does not matter *what* one believes, only *that* one believes!

19. Wilhelm Bruhn, *Vom Gott im Menschen—Ein Weg in metaphysisches Neuland* (Giessen: A. Töpelmann, 1926). K. Barth opposes Bruhn in "Polemisches Nachwort," *Zwischen den Zeiten* 5 (1927): 33–40.

20. Bruhn, *Vom Gott*, 19: "Today, of course, the thinker must strive not only to weave into a harmony the monstrous split in the life of the world and humans (29: 'the desire for *harmony* is not only present in each person as a basic instinct of self-preservation; it is above all the great problem and distress of contemporary humans, shaken at the roots of their existence'). Every religious person, though certain of this harmony in faith, must and should be required to pursue it in thought, if he intends to be a whole person [a mere believer, then, is not yet a whole person! R.B.]. He should not forget that thought and experience, the two functions with the same sacred (!) claim, inhere in his personhood, and that it is not at all godly to suppress doubt for the sake of godliness." This is of course quite correct. But a faith that doubts is evidently not faith, and if not, how shall theology be able to discover the harmony between faith and science if faith is not yet present, but is only the result of the harmony achieved?

Bruhn, 20: "What we must stress is this: The thinker in man, not faith, must establish the harmony destroyed by thinking. One should not pass off *reflection* as *faith*. Reflection should not aim to penetrate the organism of the experience of faith. Rather, from the outside, for the sake of sheer thought, it should be content with approaching the datum of faith and asking to what extent its certainty is valid also for thought." Can thought—here, of course, conceived apart from faith—understand faith at all?

On p. 21, Bruhn defines the task of theology thus: "In scientific method to communicate, describe, and explain the historical-intellectual datum of the human *experience* of God," and on 23 he writes that the theologian is to investigate "whether and how far he can, say, push through the experience of God to the self of God. . . . Theology is the investigation of the experience of God, aiming at the self of God."

Theology stands alongside the church. The church "mediates" the self of God "in a personal and as it were accidental way," since it seeks to urge the individual to his own experience of God. On 24, Bruhn writes that theological science does this "in a material and objective way by lifting out from the totality of the human experience of God the kernel of what is necessary and human, based on the conviction that what is fundamentally human is directly rooted in the divine." It thus seeks the "nature of religion," in order "where possible to verify the necessity of experience by the necessity of *thought*"! On 30, Bruhn states that such a science is not an inquiry into existence, but is "as it were a need for neatness; and as such, of course, unavoidable"! In the same passage it is openly stated that this task is a philosophical problem to be solved by the theologian as philosopher.

Bruhn's real motive is thus not at all theological, but the philosophical need for a unified worldview. It is simply assumed that where theology is concerned, the basic instinct of self-preservation is legitimate (24: "the immanence of the divine in pure humanity." In fact, it is assumed that what is "fundamentally human is rooted directly in the divine." But how is it rooted in the divine, if, say, theology or faith is to describe the necessary and human as sinful and devilish?) and the self-assertive person can claim to understand his existence scientifically, which for Bruhn means *not* on the basis of faith, thus as unbelieving. As if theology would have to content itself with this forthwith. As if its object were perhaps not inaccessible to unbelieving science. But a believing science would have no need of this game, no need to act as though it were unbelieving, as though it could position itself beyond faith and make it the object of research. [Ed.: Bultmann's pencilled note in the margin reads: "How, if faith were above thought? If it were to have its turn only when thought strove for harmony?"]

Bruhn recognizes no thought born of faith (cf. the sentence cited above): *Though* certain of harmony in faith, one must *nevertheless* pursue it in thought. Faith is referred to experience *next to* thought. Bruhn is opposed to thought born of faith: Reflection is not to be passed off as faith. But if God is actually the object of faith and accessible only through faith, then a science apart from faith cannot understand faith at all, since it does not understand its object—which can only be understood in faith. Then it cannot push through to it by faith.

In any event, theology can have no interest in the work of Bruhn; nor, probably, can science.

21. The lover in doubt does not want to know the power or nature of *love*, but the *beloved*! [E]

22. Barth, *Christliche Dogmatik* I, 437: "Let one guard against [as dogmatician, R.B.] not, say, criticism, doubt, skepticism, the enemy does not stand on this side, but against apologetics, against every desire to sneak up on the subject by roundabout ways, as if God could be known even without God, as if he could be second, when he has not also been and been acknowledged without shame as first." [B]

23. *On Religion: Speeches to Its Cultured Despisers*, trans. Richard Crouter (New York: Cambridge University Press, 1988).

24. "Piety." [O]

25. The "religious communities." [O]

26. *erōs—erōs tinos.* [O]

27. Friedrich Schleiermacher, *The Christian Faith*, ed. H. R. Macintosh and J. S. Stewart (Edinburgh: T&T Clark, 1948), §§3 and 4, pp. 5–18.

28. Ibid., §3, p. 5.

29. Cf. ibid., §3.3, p. 8: Psychology understands life as an alternation between the subject's abiding-in-self (*Insichbleiben*) and passing-beyond-self (*Aussichheraustreten*). Knowing and doing are the latter, feeling the former.

30. Ibid.

31. Ibid., §3.4, p. 10.

32. Contrition and the like, which are also "pious" apart from their relation to knowing or doing, thus not at all understood as a movement of existence. [O]

33. Schleiermacher, *The Christian Faith*, §3.4, p. 11; cf. §3.5.

34. Ibid., §4.1, p. 13.

35. Ibid., §4.3, p. 16.

36. Ibid., §4.4, pp. 16–17.

37. Ibid., §4.3, p. 16.

38. Ibid., §5.1, p. 19.

39. Ibid., §5.3, p. 22.

40. Ibid.

41. Ibid., §4.4, p. 16.

42. Ibid., 17–18.

43. Schleiermacher, *Brief Outline of Theology*, trans. Terrence N. Tice (New York: Edwin Mellen Press, 1988), §22, p. 24.

44. Schleiermacher, *The Christian Faith*, §6.2, p. 27.

45. There is a total misunderstanding of Schleiermacher in Rudolf Otto, *The Idea of the Holy*, trans. John W. Harvey (London: Oxford University Press, 1923), 9ff.

46. Cf. Edv. Lehmann, "Erscheinungswelt der Religion," *Religion in Geschichte and Gegenwart*, 1st ed., vol. 2, cols. 497–577.

47. F. Kattenbusch, "Theologie," *Realenzyklopädie*, 3rd ed., vol. 21, 900–13; the quotation is taken from 912.

48. Cf. Troeltsch's definition of theology below, §12 (according to *Religion in Geschichte and Gegenwart*, 1st ed., vol. 2, cols. 1441, 1442, and the article on "Glaube, III: Dogmatisch," cols. 1437–1447) [B].

49. W. Bruhn, *Vom Gott im Menschen* (supra n. 19), 47: Liberalism gave "access to the absolute since, on the basis of living human being, it

was confident that what is from below is also from above"! [B (perhaps also C)]

50. Kattenbusch, 912. Cf. especially E. Troeltsch, *The Absoluteness of Christianity and the History of Religions,* trans. David Reid (Richmond, Va.: John Knox Press, 1971 [1902]); and "The Significance of the Historical Jesus for Faith," in *Ernst Troeltsch: Writings on Theology and Religion,* trans. Robert Morgan and Michael Pye (Atlanta: John Knox Press, 1977 [1911]), 182–207.

51. Georg Wobbermin, *Systematischer Theologie nach religionspsychologischer Methode,* vol. 1: *Die religionspsychologische Methode in Religionswissenschaft und Theologie* (2nd ed., 1925); vol. 2: *Das Wesen der Religion* (2nd ed., 1925); vol. 3: *Wesen und Wahrheit des Christentums* (2nd ed., 1926); *Schleiermacher und Ritschl in ihrer Bedeutung für die heutige theologische Lage und Aufgabe* (Tübingen: J.C.B. Mohr, 1927), and *Richtlinien evangelischer Theologie zur Überwindung der gegenwärtigen Krisis* (Göttingen: Vandenhoeck and Ruprecht, 1929).

52. Ed.: In the margin Bultmann refers to the manuscript of his lecture on "Truth and Certainty, " appended to this volume.

53. Cf. Wobbermin, *Richtlinien,* 131: For Christian faith, the religious history of the Old and New Testament is the history of salvation, because it offers God's revelation. Ibid., 97: Insight into the significance of the *fides qua creditur* requires "expanding the individual's faith through regard for one's fellow believers in the concrete visible church. For (!) one's own personal faith does not arise except from the proclamation of the word of God (Rom. 10:17)."

54. Thus as when sociology researches the reciprocal action between the individual and the group. [O]

55. On the "pole," cf. *Richtlinien,* 117, and 120: "Faith as the believer's subjective attitude can only be understood from the relation to its objective content or opposite objective pole. This pole, as the *conditio sine qua non,* is the support base for faith" (120).

56. Cf. *Richtlinien,* 115: "At its very beginning [theological reflection] must also take faith into account as one's own personal conviction and experience" (!)

57. Cf. ibid., 138: Scripture is unconditional authority in matters of faith, but not of knowing or perceiving. Indeed, but does not faith perceive or know? In addition, dialectical theology is reproached for rejecting all "concern for one's own experience of faith" in understanding scripture (cf. 139). It certainly does, since according to dialectical theology faith itself experi-

ences scripture, and is not subjectivity. For Wobbermin, scripture is the testimony of faith in terms of the New Testament authors' expression of faith (cf. 140f.). And when Wobbermin can occasionally describe faith as the reciprocal relation between the objective (God) and subjective pole (faith), then faith is a reciprocal relation between two poles, of which he himself is one. [o]

58. Ibid., 24.

59. Ibid., 25.

60. Ibid., 26f. Cf. the definitions on 28: "Science is the sighting, establishing and expanding of human knowledge by way of a method." Cf. 29: "Science is the striving for the most precise and complete knowledge possible of the reality accessible to us."

61. Ibid., 34ff.

62. Ibid., 38. Then, regarding the question of truth, the only recourse is the religious a priori.

63. Ibid., 38 and 45ff.

64. Ibid., 52.

65. Ibid., 61. Cf. Barth's criticism in *Christliche Dogmatik* I, 54f.

66. By way of analogy, in his *Christliche Dogmatik* I, §2.2, 144ff., Barth rejects any prolegomena to dogmatics that would consist in "laying a religious-scientific foundation," and allows only selected and prospective portions of dogmatic work to be regarded as prolegomena, since reflection on the nature of dogmatics is not to be recognized *in abstracto* but only *in concreto*, "only in the act of dogmatic reflection itself." Cf. §9.1, 126ff.: "Dogmatics can only be introduced dogmatically" (p. 127). [B]

67. Cf. Heidegger, *Was ist Metaphysik?* (Bonn: F. Cohen, 1929). The question cannot be answered by speaking *about* metaphysics, but only by discussing a particular metaphysical question, that is, by letting metaphysics itself speak. Cf. Kant's definition of ontology according to Heidegger, *Kant and the Problem of Metaphysics,* trans. Richard Taft (Bloomington: Indiana University Press, 1990 [1929]). [o]

68. Just as for Plato *erōs* can only be understood as *erōs tinos.* Cf. Paul Friedländer, *Platon* (Berlin: De Gruyter, 1928), vol. 1, 60. [B] Ed.: Are the sentences from "insofar as science . . ." up to "in the life-relation to it" a later insertion in B? D adds "or even primarily discloses" following "does not beget its object."

69. Ed.: A pencil note in the margin after "*qua creditur*" reads: "which it understands as religion; and sees its first task in proving that religion is a necessary function of the human spirit. It sees its second task in developing

a religious worldview. It is aware that the religious function is not activated everywhere, not formed everywhere with equal clarity. A person views the world differently, he has a 'worldview,' according to the robustness or clarity of his religious life."

70. Ed.: A pencil note in the margin reads: "Since Christian theology sets forth a view of the world as offered to the Christian religion, it takes the place of doctrine. How must a believer view the world? A host of different doctrines of faith emerge in answer. Church doctrine is not the norm of theology. It is, of course, an exponent of piety. Every believer, every religious person must initially be able to produce a Christian worldview. Thus emerges the problem of nature and truth (nature: the Christian worldview; truth: the character of religion as norm)."

71. Thus the problem of Bruhn! [c (perhaps also b)] and of Wobbermin. [o]

72. Cf. Adolf Schlatter, *Der Glaube im Neuen Testament* (Stuttgart: Calwer Vereinsbuchhandlung, 1905), 5f.

73. Ed.: e (perhaps also d) later inserts "there is danger of confusing" up to "and."

74. Liberalism makes a faith of theology; Orthodoxy makes a theology of faith. [d]

75. *Fides quae creditur = quod deus dixit*! Theology = what humans say. [d]

76. Orthodoxy views the *fides quae creditur* as something *recognized*, instead of proclaimed and confessed; as something a person says, not something that *is* said to him.

77. Analogy: Whether or not my wife loves me, only *one* in the whole world can know, that is, I, myself, and I do not care at all for objective proofs.

78. Barth, *Christliche Dogmatik*, I, 421: Pure doctrine is not a formula or system of formulas; this was the fatal error to which old Protestantism fell prey in that same period of transition and decadence in which also Holy Scripture became for it an inspired letter. [b]

79. If theology no longer knows today what or how much belongs to pure doctrine, and speaks of such frightful things as the mysticism of faith, it only indicates that it is infected with liberalism.

80. Barth is distinctly aware of the critical character of theology. Cf. *Christliche Dogmatik*, I, §1.1ff., and §8.112ff. Cf. 123: *The* dogma is either an eschatological concept or an attempt at approximation, always provisional in character. [b]

81. There is an apparent contradiction between adducing *proof* for

"doctrine" and the demand that reason submit to it. But they cohere, since they treat the *fides quae creditur* at the same level: To the extent it is able, reason gives proof for it, then, to the extent it is able, submits to it. [E (perhaps also D)]

82. Wilhelm Herrmann, *Die mit der Theologie verknüpfte Not der evangelischen Kirche und ihre Überwindung* (Tübingen: J.C.B. Mohr, 1913), 21: In their desire to hold ideas handed down in the apostolic age to be true, "they [the orthodox, R.B.] can somehow defend themselves against attacks from without, but not against the deep uncertainty at the basis of existence. What we cannot be absolutely certain of because we cannot experience it ourselves, is revealed to us in its uncertainty precisely when we want to make it the basis for confidence in life. The more vigorously we insist on it, the more surely it begins to collapse." 40: "Parading about, asserting that we intend to hold as true something we would not hold as true on our own does not make an honorable man, to say nothing of a Christian."

If something else were required to be believed, then something else would be believed. [O]

83. Wilhelm Herrmann, "Die Lage und Aufgabe der evangelischen Dogmatik in der Gegenwart," *Gesammelte Aufsätze* (Tübingen: J.C.B. Mohr, 1923), 95–188. The quotation is from 106.

84. As in every science *notitia* is the admission that we have no "*intuitus originarius.*" (Liberalism would happily get free of even *notitia*). [D]

85. Cf. Herrmann, "Die Lage und Aufgabe," 105f.

86. Cf. ibid., 105f., and "Der geschichtliche Christus der Grund unseres Glaubens," and especially, "Von der dogmatischen Stellung des Kirchenregiments in den deutschen evangelischen Kirchen," *Gesammelte Aufsätze*, 306f., and 376.

87. Naturally, the discussion of liberalism and orthodoxy could not be neutral. It could only be critical, as theological discussion must be. It is critical, of course, only when it is *also* positive; when it appreciates that liberalism intends to correct the error of orthodoxy, which takes the *fides quae* for doctrine, and gives no primary place in theology to the *fides qua*. Liberalism aims to do the latter, and orthodoxy rightly resists it, since it neglects the *fides quae* or eliminates it on the basis of the *fides qua*.

## 3. Theology as the Science about God

1. §7 would not be needed in a dogmatics, though indeed in an encyclopedia. [D]

2. Cf. the words of Goethe with which Nietzsche begins his treatise, "The Use and Abuse of History:" "I hate everything that merely instructs me without increasing or directly quickening my activity." Cf. Nietzsche's own conclusion to the Foreword: "I do not know what meaning classical scholarship may have for our time except in its being 'unseasonable,'— that is, contrary to our time, and yet with an influence on it for the benefit, it may be hoped, of a future time."And cf. Nietzsche's polemic in §4, against the study of history from supposed educational interest: "Our modern culture is for that reason not a living one, because it cannot be understood without that opposition [that is, between inner and outer, thus without pride in the inner life, R.B.]." In other words, it is not a real culture but a kind of knowledge about culture. "In modern times the Greeks were very 'uneducated.' We moderns have become 'wandering encyclopedias,' and so we have the custom of no longer taking real things seriously ('living memories')." [c] Ed.: Cf. *The Complete Works of Friedrich Nietzsche*, ed. Oscar Levy (New York: Russell and Russell, 1964), vols. 2, 3, 5, 32, 33.

3. Cf. the child, primitive peoples, and the origin of science.

4. Ed.: "By the concern, etc." is a later addition (in B or C). So also is the addition in D, from "since one lives in a world" up to "is not reducible to Spirit." In the margin D contains the following note: "Cf. the question of 'objectivity'; modern polemic against it is understandable; in essence it polemicizes against the idea that objectivity is achieved in observation, an impossibility as regards historical phenomena (not a subsequent evaluation!)."

5. Cf. the question of the national-international character of a science. Science in the concrete is national, that is, defined by national spirit. As science, however, it is also international, since its national character is no criterion for truth. The criterion for truth is always the object's capacity for proving its identity. Viewing an object is always an individual matter; but what is seen can be shown to all who enjoy any relation to it.

6. Cf. American positivism, behaviorism.

7. Since the question of purpose is not the criterion for the question of truth.If the question of truth is raised, it can achieve independence, as it were. It is precisely *interest* in the matter that requires disinterested observation (an explanation of the paradox in the matter of education: Parents' interest in the child may not spoil what the child is to learn; yet interested parents are better educators than disinterested teachers, better, for example, than teachers whose interest is psychoanalytic.) Cf. the physician and the student of medicine.

E. Troeltsch, *Der Historismus and seine Probleme, Gesammelte Schriften* (Tübingen: J.C.B. Mohr, 1922), vol. 3, 69, opposes a purely contemplative science, and strives for a philosophy of history, by virtue of which present and future are linked to the historical view. [D]

8. But by this means life too has gone astray! [E]

9. Cf. Cohen: "Can you name a single book written by an animal?"

10. Cf. "Heit" and "Keit" in Carl Spitteler, *Prometheus und Epimetheus* (Jena: E. Diederichs, 1923), 9.

11. The deadening of nature in modern natural science. [D]

12. Mythology dies off.

13. Cf. medicine in particular!

14. Viewed ontically, without regard to whatever ontological structure of *Dasein* is revealed in ontical concern. [O]

15. In a sermon of Moering, the newsboy moved by concern and the worker on the assembly line are referred to their "cultural significance." Ed.: Ernst Moering, since 1915 a pastor in Breslau, friend of Bultmann, and "successful preacher of the educated . . ." (*Religion in Geschichte and Gegenwart*, 2nd ed., vol. 4).

16. Cf. Dostoyevsky's "The Grand Inquisitor" (in *The Brothers Kara-mazov*), and Franz Werfel's comment in "Die christliche Sendung—Ein offener Brief an Kurt Hiller," *Die neue Rundschau* = XXVIIIter Jahrgang der freien Bühne (1917), 92–105.

17. Cf. feeding and housing, traffic, heating and lighting, etc.

18. Unfortunately, socialism with its dream of a cultural ideal does not recognize this.

19. Culture has meaning only to the extent it really brings the person to himself. [D]

20. Ed.: Johann Wolfgang v. Goethe, *Faust*, trans. George Madison Priest (Chicago: Encyclopaedia Britannica, 1952), I (Night, Faust in his Study), 16.

21. With all his knowledge Wagner has forgotten that life itself brings the true possibilities and necessities for knowledge, that I really know nothing if I do not recognize it in its significance. Cf. *Faust* II, 2, 162–63 (A High-Vaulted, Narrow, Gothic Chamber), *Mephistopheles:*

> A great desire comes on me truly
> To show off as a proud professor newly,
> As men think they've a perfect right to do.
> The learned know how to attain that level;

> It is an art long since lost by the devil. . . .
> Also a learned man
> Still studies on since there's naught else he can.
> A moderate house of cards one builds him so;
> The greatest mind does not complete it, though.

But cf. also *Faust* I , 41 (Faust's Study), *Mephistopheles*:

> Reason and knowledge, pray despise!
> Let but the Spirit of all Lies
> With works of dazzling magic blind you;
> Then, absolutely mine, I'll have and bind you [D]

22. Cf. Paul de Lagarde, *Deutsche Schriften*, 37f., in Hermann Mulert, *Religion, Kirche, Theologie* (Giessen: A. Töpelmann, 1931), 9. [D]

23. Cf. K. Barth's attempt to define culture theologically in "Die Kirche and die Kultur," *Zwischen den Zeiten* 4 (1926): 363–84. [B]

24. Originally, observation (*Hinsehen*) denotes an authentic way of seeing, insofar as it is rooted in *Dasein* motivated by authentic concern.

25. Reference to "culture" may hide the awareness that in order to come to himself a person may not stay by himself. But he may also not be directed toward a place in which he does not come to himself.

26. Nationality is an historical entity; it cannot be evaluated as something assumed. Contemporary decisions cooperate in giving it birth.

27. But cf., for example, the Icelandic sagas.

28. German can of course be an index of what is correct, but not a criterion. One can reflect on German custom in a period of decline. But there are also German abuses, cf. Tacitus.

29. As an actual historical entity, science contributes toward establishing national character. It does not simply assume it, for it is itself historical.

30. The reaction in Goethe, Nietzsche, Spitteler, cf. above, nn. 2, 9.

31. Max Scheler, "Liebe and Erkenntnis," in *Krieg und Aufbau* (Leipzig: Verlag der Weissen Bücher, 1916), 393–429.

32. Scheler's error is that he does not understand "love" as a specific I-Thou relationship possible only in Christianity. For him, love is a universal human capacity, and of course the capacity for relating oneself to being as such. Cf. Hannah Arendt, *Der Liebesbegriff bei Augustin* (Berlin: J. Springer, 1929). [C]

33. Ed.: In Scheler "modern" is written in spaced type.

34. Ed.: The quotation is in Scheler, "Liebe und Erkenntnis," 393, 394. Bultmann adds further bibliography in the margin of D: Max Scheler, *Wesen and Formen der Sympathie,* 3rd ed. (Bonn: F. Cohen, 1931).

35. Of course, to what extent Scheler's understanding of the Greeks is correct, is a matter all by itself. Cf. P. Friedländer, *Platon* (Berlin: de Gruyter, 1928), vol. 1: For Plato the "center" is the state, interest in the state.—37: "The *eidos* was spiritual in nature, and was so from the outset. The just, the brave, the religious, the good: these were the names given the ideas Plato first saw when looking at Socrates' soul. 51-67: *Eros* the driving force (p. 59: "Thus *eros* is the guide to philosophy, to the Idea." 61: The unity of the experience of love and the vision of the ideas; 63, of Eros and Polis. "There is no *arete* and *paideia* which would not have significance relating to the state.") [C]

36. More exactly, by some existing thing that has the capacity for becoming an object of knowledge.

37. Ed.: The pronoun inserted by the editor.

38. Goethe (at a visit of the Duke and Duchess of Cumberland): "If yesterday lies clear and open, and today you work mightily free, then you may hope for a morning, that equally happy may be."
Cf. Karl Löwith, *Nietzsches Philosophie der ewigen Wiederkunft des Gleichen* (Berlin: Verlag die Runde, 1935), 139ff.! [E].

39. Ed.: In the manuscript the compound is abbreviated to "mathemat.-mech.," which could conceivably be deciphered "mathematic-mechanistic."

40. Cf. M. Heidegger, *Kant und das Problem der Metaphysik* (Bonn: F. Cohen, 1929), 8. [O]

41. Barth tears apart what is scientific and what is objective, cf. *Christliche Dogmatik*, I, 115f. [B]

42. Cf. Heidegger: What belongs to the positivity of a science is (1) that a certain entity is set forth as a possible theme; (2) that that entity is available in a prescientific access and relation, in which its durability and way of existing is shown; and (3) that this prescientific approach is illumined and led by a non- and preconceptual understanding of being. [B]

43. Cf. Heidegger, *Being and Time*, trans. John Macquarrie and Edward Robinson (New York: Harper and Row, 1962), §4, 32–35: "There is some way in which *Dasein* understands itself in its Being, and that to some degree it does so explicitly. It is peculiar to this entity that with and through its Being, this Being is disclosed to it. *Understanding of Being is itself a definite characteristic of* Dasein*'s Being. Dasein* is ontically distinc-

tive in that it *is* ontological" (32). Cf. §31, "Being-There as Understanding"; §32, "Understanding And Interpretation"; §34, "Being-There and Discourse. Language"; and §44, "*Dasein*, Disclosedness, and Truth." [B]

44. Cf. Lagarde, *Deutsche Schriften.*

45. Cf. Hans v. Soden, *Christentum und Kultur* (Tübingen: J.C.B. Mohr, 1933); and Nietzsche's *Thoughts Out of Season,* in *The Complete Works of Fredrich Nietzsche*, vol. 2, against the time for the time and for the future.

46. Cf. the manuscript "Truth and Certainty." In the Greek worldview, "the" truth as the truth of the moment is the result of knowing all truths or all truth about the *kosmos*, a truth aware of the cosmos in its totality as a unity (there is a deprivation in positivism, where "the" truth is the result of empirical research). In the historical understanding of *Dasein* the relation is reversed: All truths serve responsibility for the moment, serve the question about "the" truth. [E]

47. Cf. Carl Spitteler, *Prometheus und Epimetheus.*

48. M. Heidegger, *Being and Time*, 256–73; Hans v. Soden, *Was ist Wahrheit?* (Marburg: N.G. Elwert, 1927); R. Bultmann, "Untersuchungen zum Johannesevangelium, A. aletheia," *ZNW* 27 (1928): 113–63 (also in *Exegetica* [Tübingen: J.C.B. Mohr, 1967], 124–73).

49. The *formal* meaning of truth = the identical can be discovered! Thus also universal validity. [E (perhaps also D)]

50. Though, of course, to the extent it is assumed that in science objects are accessible to *Dasein*. Thus everyone *can* see the object. [D]

51. So also "*the*" truth as truth of the moment is universally valid. Of course, this does not mean that every "reasonable" person must see it, but it does mean that the moment *requires* this answer, this perception. If faith sees *the* truth, then it is not on this account "subjective." Cf. the manuscript "Truth and Certainty." [O]

52. First of all, *theological* judgments are universally valid for everyone who has a relation to the object. While for the sciences the object is usually accessible to natural life, the object of theology is so only to faith. Faith knows *the* truth and with it theology. [O]

53. Ed.: The second "not" appearing in the manuscript is of course to be omitted.

54. Plato, *Phaedrus* 248b: "Great eagerness to see where the plain of truth is," *Plato, with an English Translation*, Loeb Classical Library (Cambridge: Harvard University Press, 1960), I, 478.

55. Or, this question is meant to stand alone: What is the practical

thing to do, the thing that promises success? while success itself is not subsumed under the question about the truth. When I know everything, I always know what is relevant. [o]

56. Cf. Plato, *Phaidon* 99e: *edoxe dē moi chrēnai eis tous logous kataphygonta en ekeinois skopein tōn ontōn tēn alētheian* ("So I thought I must have recourse to conceptions and examine in them the truth of realities"; *Plato*, I, 342).

57. If the question of the truth is the question about God, then theology cannot answer it. The "truth" of theology is only the truth of science. To what degree, then, can it still be a science about God? [o]

58. Ed.: In the manuscript, instead of "existence" (-philosophy) D originally read: "understood as the ontology of *Dasein*" (philosophy).

59. Cf. Max Reischle, "Erkennen wir die Tiefen Gottes? Eine Untersuchung über Adäquatheit und Inadäquatheit der christlichen Gotteserkenntnis," *ZThK* 1 (1891): 287–366.

60. Acts 17:27f.: *zetein ton theon, ei ara ge pselaphēseian auton kai euroien, kai ge ou makran apo henos hekastou hēmōn hyparchonta. en autō gar zōmen kai kinoumetha kai esmen* ("So that they would search for God and perhaps grope for him and find him—though indeed he is not far from each one of us. For 'in him we live and move and have our being'"; cf. 14:17: *kaitoi ouk hamartyron auton aphēken agathourgōn* ["yet he has not left himself without a witness in doing good"]).

61. Cf. Paul Natorp, *Religion innerhalb der Grenzen der Humanität*, 2nd ed. (Tübingen: J.C.B. Mohr, 1908), 39ff., 99f.

62. The "unconditioned" is either a mere negation, or the essence of everything conditioned in its unity, or, as an Origin yielding unity—in that case the God of Hellenism or of Idealism. [E (perhaps also D)]

63. The "unconditioned" is oriented more to space, the "eternal" more to time. Whether or not one has a right to speak of the Eternal *One* instead of *the* Eternal [neuter], is problematic.

64. To the degree that something *positive* is expressed in the idea of the unconditioned, it is the idea of an unconditioned requirement. [D]

65. Ed.: D inserts: "isolated" and "as that of the here and now in face of the future."

66. "It" added by the editor.

67. On the other hand, the fact that we do not know *the* good on sight, but must come to know it only by way of venture in the here and now, does not express the inadequacy of our knowledge of God, but only the recognition that we are historical. [D]

68. Wilhelm Herrmann, "Warum bedarf unser Glaube geschichtlicher Tatsaschen," *Gesammelte Aufsätze* (Tübingen: J.C.B. Mohr, 1923), 214–38, quotation on p. 236.

69. This is the error of gnosticism. [D]

70. H. E. Eisenhuth, *Philosophische Studien zum Begriff des Irrationalen* (Frankfurt: 1931). [O]

71. Origin of the idea of the irrational in Neoplatonism! [O]

72. Ed.: Bultmann's Heidegger quotation (omitting where it appears) agrees almost literally with the publication of Heidegger's lecture, "Phänomenologie und Theologie," first appearing in 1969, but held March 9, 1927, at Tübingen, and repeated February 14, 1928, at Marburg (instead of "by rational means," the galley proof reads "by purely rational means"). Martin Heidegger, *Gesamtausgabe* (Frankfurt: Wegmarken, 1976), lst section, vol. 9, 47–67; quotation from p. 62.

73. Ed.: Ibid.

74. Karl Barth, *The Christian Life*, trans. J. Strathearn McNab (London: SCM Press, 1962), 61 (on Rom. 12:lf.).

75. God is not an absolute *X*. No one could speak of such, and it would be of no interest. If someone says that *X* enlivens us, then, of course, something has been said of its significance, its function in life, and it is just this that needs proper definition. [D]

76. The unknowability of God denotes *the unknowability of the moment*, when the question of God is a question about the truth, and when the truth is the claim of the moment.

77. We can adopt the observer's viewpoint neither toward God nor toward ourselves.

78. Cf. "Welchen Sinn hat es, von Gott zu reden?" *Glauben and Verstehen* (Tübingen: J.C.B. Mohr, 1933), vol. 1, 26–37.

79. God is not an absolute *X*. Being set in motion by an *X* implies knowledge of its significance and function for life. (Even in nature there can only be an *X* in the impulse toward it.) [O]

80. Of course, he is also subject, since he is object. He is not only ontic, but also ontological. [O]

81. It is the assumption that I am a free lord in my inner life, that I can freely regulate my ideas, impulses, and resolves, and by this means get free of the world. [E]

82. Paul Fleming (1609–1640): "Nach des VI. Psalmens Weise" ("In allen meinen Taten . . ."): "Es kann mir nichts geschehen, /Als was er hat versehen /And was mir selig ist," *Evangelisches Kirchengesangbuch*, Aus-

gabe für die evangelisch-lutherischen Kirchen Niedersachsens (Göttingen: Vandenhoeck & Ruprecht, 1952), pp. 346–47.

83. Hans Jonas, *Augustin and das paulinische Freiheitsproblem* (Göttingen: Vandenhoeck & Ruprecht, 1930); Heinrich Schleier, Art. "Eleutheros etc.," *Theological Dictionary of the New Testament*, ed. Gerhard Kittel, trans. Geoffrey Bromiley (Grand Rapids, Mich.: Wm. B. Eerdmans, 1964), vol. 2, 484–500. [E]

84. God is also unknowable in the second sense that we do not recognize the truth of the moment in only a theoretical but also in a practical way.

85. Conscience *is at ease* only in a "good conscience."

86. Cf. A. Ritschl, "Über das Gewissen," *Gesammelte Aufsätze*, Neue Folge (Freiburg/Leipzig: J.C. Hinrichs, 1896), 177–203; M. Heidegger, *Being and Time*, 319–48; H. G. Stoker, *Das Gewissen* (Bonn: F. Cohen, 1925).

87. The "accompanying" conscience is basically a conscience that exercises judgment, insofar as the person is committed to the act prior to the deed, and anticipates judgment on the deed.

88. Cf. Fr. Gogarten, "Ethik des Gewissens oder Ethik der Gnade," *Zwischen den Zeiten* 1 (1923): 10–29, esp. 16.

89. Ed.: In the manuscript Bultmann writes *charis* instead of *dynamis*.

90. Enabling through the cross. Hope!

Love, call of the moment to action grounded in faith

Hope, call of the moment to receive life [O]

91. To the extent that we referred to God's unknowability in the first sense, that is, to God as the truth of the moment, his knowability was in some sense already assumed. How is this possible? [O]

92. Temporality is not a mere expiration, but a being toward and a being from. [O]

93. We do not have existence in our knowledge of it, but in our existence we also have knowledge of it.

94. Man is not only an ontic, but also an ontological being. [O]

95. Cf. the First Part of the explanation to the First Commandment in Luther's *Large Catechism*, in *The Book of Concord*, 365.

96. Ed.: Ibid.

97. Theodosius Harnack, *Luthers Theologie*, 2nd ed. (Münich: Chr. Kaiser Verlag, 1927), vol. 1, 69f.

98. Ibid., 70f.

99. Ibid., 72b (Ed.: Weimar Ausgabe, vol. 46, 669, ll. 24-26: The exposition of John 1:2 in the sermons of 1537/38), cf. 74f., where this knowl-

edge is clearly described as a knowing in the asking. Karl Jaspers, *Das Wissen der Empörung*; *Prometheus*, in *Philosophie*, III: *Metaphysik* (Berlin: Springer, 1932), 71ff.: Rebellion against the ground of my being. The question as to the justification of Being. Relegating responsibility to the Creator. The desire to get behind the world.) [O]

100. Ed.: The statements written in ink in this section replace the following text (in C, stricken and bracketed): "The question about God is the question about truth, about the claim of the moment. The question is urged by conscience that directs a person to take possession of himself in the here and now. But though he knows about his existence and is able to hear the claim of the moment in his conscience, a person does not yet believe in God, and the science which exhibits these structures of *Dasein* is not theology but a philosophical analysis of *Dasein*."

101. Is always heard by *me* and ever *anew*! [O]

102. Ed.: Draft E adds "or the Lord" up to "and favors us."

103. Ed.: E adds "or favored."

104. The moment as divine utterance has become certain, unambiguous, full of "joy," which no one can take away (John 16:22); full of "peace," such as no one can give (John 14:27). [E]

105. I do not know whether I have unreservedly resolved, either upon a deed or upon seizing hold of my destiny. [E]

106. Thus, for example, the word of forgiveness from sin should open my eyes to an actual neighbor.

107. Ed.: O inserts "in a certain sense" and "(better: heard ever anew)."

108. Ed.: The manuscript first read "National Socialism."

109. Cf. Jacob Burckhardt, *Force and Freedom: Reflections on History*, ed. James H. Nichols (New York: Pantheon, 1943).

110. In the poetry of C. Spitteler, St. George.

111. So it does not sit—as Hirsch supposes—in *chambre séparé*; and if its contribution consisted simply in making us aware of the mysteriousness of God under pressure of the war experience, its service would be minimal.But its concept of God is linked to an understanding of human existence within the context of an intellectual movement that in all areas of life is struggling for a new understanding of that existence.

112. "Is" inserted by the editor.

113. Martin Heidegger, *Die Selbstbehauptung der deutschen Universität* (Breslau: Verlag Wilh. Gottl. Korn, 1933)—the rector's address of May 27, 1933.

114. What genealogy, type, or race mean for such a destiny is an urgent question. To have brought it to mind does us service, but it is an open question that may not be obscured by a biological ideology.

# 4. The Idea of Revelation

1. *apokalypsis, phanerōsis, revelatio.* Cf. R. Bultmann, *Der Begriff der Offenbarung im Neuen Testament: Sammlung Gemeinverständlicher Vorträge* 135 (Tübingen: J.C.B. Mohr, 1929).

2. Ed.: cf. R. Bultmann, *Glauben und Verstehen* (Tübingen: J.C.B. Mohr, 1960), vol. 3, 1–34.

3. Ed.: From "brings to light" up to "veiled from me" is an insertion in D.

4. Cf. Emil Brunner, *The Mediator: A Study of the Central Doctrine of the Christian Faith*, trans. Olive Wyon (Philadelphia: Westminster Press, 1947), 21f.: All religions appeal to a revelation.

5. The analysis is terse and a bit one-sided in J. M. Verweyen, *Philosophie und Theologie im Mittelalter* (Bonn: F. Cohen, 1911).

6. Walter Betzendörfer, *Glauben und Wissen bei den grossen Denkern des Mittelalters* (Gotha: L. Klotz, 1931); Ernst Wolf, "Der Mensch und die Kirche im katholischen Denken," *Zwischen den Zeiten* 11 (1933): 34–57. [O]

7. In D, "[skepticism] toward human being as a whole" replaces "the nature of the revelation as scandal" in A. D inserts the sentence that follows ("The limit. . .").

8. Unfortunately, Karl Barth also proceeds in this fashion (cf. *Die Christliche Dogmatik im Entwurf*, I, 226ff.). He too wishes to establish the revelation's capacity for being conceived "a posteriori," that is, back of faith, and by express appeal to Anselm, to the effect that the essential relevance of theological propositions must be understood even by outsiders (228). [B]

9. Cf. Anselm, *Cur deus homo.*

10. *The Summa Theologica of Saint Thomas Aquinas*, trans. Fathers of the English Dominican Province (Chicago: Encyclopaedia Britannica, Inc., 1952), I, Question 1, Art. 2, 4: There are sciences "which proceed from a principle known by the natural light of the intellect, such as arithmetic and geometry and the like. There are some which proceed from principles known by the light of a higher science." Thus music rests upon arithmetic, etc. "And in this way sacred doctrine is a science, because it proceeds from principles established by the light of a higher science, namely, the science of God and the blessed."

11. Aquinas, *ST* I, Q. 1, Art. 1, 3–4, Whether, besides Philosophy, any further doctrine is required: "because the human is directed to God as to an end that surpasses the grasp of his reason. . . . Hence it was necessary for the salvation of man that certain truths which exceed human reason should be made known to him by divine revelation." Further, revelation would be required even for such knowledge of God as reason could discover, since the path of reason is too long and too greatly mixed with error. Thus, besides the philosophical sciences, which investigate *per rationem*, theology, which investigates *per revelationem,* is also needed. The object, God, may be the same, but the mode of observation is different, as for example, the astronomer and the physicist have the same object, the earth, but observe it differently. According to Q. 1, Art. 5, 5, the certitude of theology is greater than that of other sciences: "because other sciences derive their certitude from the natural light of human reason, which can err, while this derives its certitude from the light of the divine knowledge, which cannot be deceived."

12. Cf. *ST* II-I, Q. 3a, Art. 5c, 622 and 638.

13. Ed.: Bultmann's quotation is from J. Pohle, *Lehrbuch der Dogmatik* (Paderborn: 1908). Translator's note: Cf. the English translation in *Decrees of the Ecumenical Councils*, ed. Norman P. Tanner, S.J. (Kansas City: Sheed and Ward; and Washington, D.C.: Georgetown University Press, 1990), vol. 2, 810.

14. Ibid., vol. 1, 16f.

15. Ibid., 19.

16. Cf. Ernst Troeltsch, *Die wissenschaftliche Lage und ihre Anforderungen an die Theologie*, SGV 20 (Tübingen: J.C.B. Mohr, 1900), 25ff.

17. Cf. Pohle, *Lehrbuch der Dogmatik*, 23.

18. Orthodox development was prepared for by Melanchthon's *Loci* of 1535 (in contrast to the *Loci* of 1521), which aim at conceiving theology within the system of sciences. Cf. Wilhelm Dilthey, *Weltanschauung und Analyse des Menschen seit Renaissance and Reformation*, in *Gesammelte Schriften* (Leipzig/Berlin: De Gruyter, 1914), vol. 2, esp. 179. [B]

19. Schmid, 17. Note the reference to God as a *substantia spiritualis* ["a spiritual substance"]. [D]

20. Ibid. Editor's note: Bultmann cites the old Protestant orthodox theologians according to Julius Kaftan, *Dogmatik*, 3rd ed. (Tubingen: J.C.B. Mohr, 1901), or according to an older edition of Schmid (1st ed., 1843).

21. Schmid, 26.

22. Ibid., 105.

23. Ibid., 26.

24. If a supernatural revelation is affirmed (John Locke 1632–1704), then its pedagogical purpose is to lead to the goal of pure rational knowledge. [D]

25. Friedrich Schliermacher, *The Christian Faith*, ed. H. R. MacKintosh and J. J. Stewart (Edinburgh: T&T Clark), §10.3. Postscript, p. 50.

26. In either instance reason supplies the criterion for the revelatory character of the doctrine. In either instance the appeal is to reason. [D]

27. Pohle, *Lehrbuch der Dogmatik*, 23.

28. Wilhelm Herrmann, "Die Busse des evangelischen Christen," *Gesammelte Aufsätze* (Tübingen: J.C.B. Mohr, 1923), 33–85; the quotation is from p. 46.

29. Erlanger Ausgabe XIV 260 (archive on WA, Operationes in Psalmos 1519–1521, T. II, 1981, 317, 14).

30. Herrmann, "Die Busse des evangelischen Christen," 47, n.1. It is the *person* who believes. [O]

31. W. Herrmann, "Der Streitpunkt in betreff des Glaubens," *Gesammelte Aufsätze*, 254–74; the quotation is from p. 267.

32. Schleiermacher, *The Christian Faith*, §10.3. Postscript, pp. 49–50.

33. When faith in revelation as doctrine has occurred, then it no longer *has* a revelation, but stored knowledge; and it is just this that cannot be from God. [A]

34. Søren Kierkegaard, *Training in Christianity*, trans. Walter Lowrie (London: Oxford University Press, 1941), 198–206.

35. The fact that the person of Jesus also appears as the content of doctrine should not confuse us about this. As revealer he cannot be the content of revelation other than as revealer. [O]

36. Kierkegaard, *Training in Christianity*, 26–34.

37. R. Rothe (*Zur Dogmatik*, 2nd ed., 1869, 67) in Kaftan, *Dogmatik*, 37.

38. The "*actus*" of revelation is thus not an "explanation of the meaning" added to the revelation. In that case, it would obviously be a *ginōskein* and not a *gnōsthenai* and would only make what was revealed a revelation—which it would not be without that explanation. (Ed.: A later marginal note in draft D or E: "There is something true in this! Revelation in the flesh! It can be understood in a twofold way!") Something can only be a revelation when it cannot be perceived beforehand as a worldly fact or event, an event that retains its quality as revelation through interpretation. A revelation can only be something which when perceived is perceived as revelation.

39. Ed.: The editor has omitted the "not" at this point in the ms.

40. Cf. the persiflage of rationalistic belief in providence in C. Spitteler, *Prometheus der Dulder* (Jena: E. Diederichs, 1924), 146ff.

41. E. Troeltsch, *Die wissenschaftliche Lage* (n.16 above), 36.

42. "It [religion: R.B.] wishes to intuit the universe, wishes devoutly to overhear the universe's own manifestations and actions, longs to be grasped and filled by the universe's immediate influences in childlike passivity," Schleiermacher, *On Religion: Speeches to Its Cultured Despisers*, trans. Richard Crouter (New York: Cambridge University Press, 1988), 102.

43. Ibid., 105: "To present all events in the world as the actions of a god is religion; it expresses its connection to an infinite totality." ("Actions" understood here as artistic creation, since they are perceived in intuition).

44. Ibid.

45. Ibid., 102. Cf. also Schleiermacher's marking religion off from a theoretical concept of the world as unity on 58 and 60f.

46. Ibid., 108.

47. Ibid., 109.

48. Ibid., 110.

49. Cf. Goethe, *Ganymede* ("Embracing embraced! / Upwards to thy bosom, All Loving Father!" etc.) *Satyros. Prometheus Fragment* (2. Act, *Prometheus*:) "When from the innermost, deepest ground." [D]

50. Schleiermacher, *On Religion*, 113.

51. Schleiermacher is thus to be evaluated positively from his polemic against rationalism and moralism!

52. There is genuineness where it is intuited in truly artistic fashion. But this "intuition" cannot be preached! [O]

53. "For our faith raises the claim that it alone—and, of course, in a radically different way than a lame science can have any hope of doing—allows us to see a totality in the infinite world," W. Herrmann, *Die mit der Theologie verknüpfte Not der evangelischen Kirche und ihre Überwindung*, (Tübingen: J.C.B. Mohr, 1913), 7.

54. Cf. the criticism of C. Spitteler's *Olympischer Frühling*, especially "Hera und der Tod" (Jena: E. Diederichs, 1922), vol. 2, pt. 5, 4, 329f.; *Prometheus der Dulder*, 142ff.

55. Besides that, it does not genuinely understand human limitation. It assumes that access to God = to the universe, is always open to him. It recognizes neither death nor sin. [B]

56. Ed.: B inserts "since the decisive idea" to the end of the sentence.

57. E. Troeltsch, article on "Glaube, III. Dogmatisch," in *Religion in Geschichte und Gegenwart*, 1st ed., vol. 2, cols. 1437–1447: Revelation is "a heightened faith, exceeding the average and radiating its power"; a "heroic and basic [that is, to an historical development, R.B.] faith." "Revelation is the productive and original appearance of a new religious force or heightening of life, manifest as a practical totality of life and intention, its powers communicated by its bearer" (col. 1439).

58. Cf. Bultmann, "Die liberale Theologie und die jüngste theologische Bewegung," *Theologische Blätter* 3 (1924): 73–86 (*Glauben und Verstehen*, vol. 1, 1–25), esp. 75ff.

59. K. Barth, *Christliche Dogmatik*, I, 345f.: The orthodox doctrine of inspiration and liberal theology are under the same condemnation. "The statement that the Bible is God's Word, just as the statement that Jesus is Lord, has meaning only when it occurs in decision, on the razor's edge between faith and offence." Orthodoxy does not grasp this. "Even the newer theology's absurd 'God in history,' displacing that late-orthodox theologoumenon, was an attempt to set aside the character of that knowledge as decision. Violent elimination of the scandal there was matched with the attempt to reinterpret it into its opposite here." [B]

60. The result is a surfeit of revelation as in rationalism. [B]

61. Cf. Barth, *Christliche Dogmatik*, I, 360, on experiential theology: "The *capacity* for being revealed is not revelation, even if it were a capacity within the most sacred and deepest parts of our inner life. By itself, what is in me is no more God's Word than a sacred book by itself. Subjectivism and objectivism are both alike absurd absurdities. We also said that *two things* belong to the self-evident nature of divine truth, and repeat them now in reverse order: To such belongs not only *the one for whom* something ought to be true, but also *what* ought to be true by itself." [B]

62. However weakly, the concept of "experience" still reflects the tendency to distinguish the objectivity of the revelation from the mere objectivity of a historical fact. But, "one would need to let only a half-year go by and the contradiction noted here would no longer be a contradiction. In that half-year, even the 'innermost' experience would have become nothing but a 'mere objective, historical fact,' and there would no longer be anything one could justly call a revelation. But it was not even there from the beginning" (Friedrich Gogarten, "Mystik and Offenbarung," in *Die religiöse Entscheidung* [Jena: E. Diederichs, 1921], 54–74; the quotation is from p. 57f.).

63. From the definition of revelation as bursting *limits* follows the task of understanding the limited nature of existence. [O]

64. Cf. Rudolf Otto, *The Idea of the Holy*, trans. John W. Harvey (London: Oxford University Press, 1923).

65. Cf. §8 above.

66. Ed.: Here and in the sentence following A originally read "Thou," instead of "the One over against me" (in B or C?)

67. H. Frick, "Der katholisch-protestantische Zwiespalt als religions-geschichtliches Phänomen," *Kairos: Zur Geisteslage and Geisteswendung*, ed. Paul Tillich (Darmstadt: O. Reichl, 1926), 345–84. [D]

68. E. Brunner, *The Mediator*, trans. Olive Wyon (London: Lutterworth Press, 1937).

69. Ibid., 22.

70. Ibid., 24.

71. Ibid., 25.

72. So he does not at all *explain* but merely *defines* the once-for-all as absolutely decisive. But there are many decisions! The problem is how all of them are qualified by a single event.

73. Brunner, *Der Mittler* (Tübingen: J.C.B. Mohr, 1930), 7 (translator's translation).

74. And pp. 303–08 do not explain the concept "once for all," but contain only a confusing definition of the concept "history." And what does fulfillment of history mean? Nor is the concept of the eternal any better explained! Cf. *The Mediator*.

75. In Brunner two clearly related questions are lumped together: (1) the question of the uniqueness of the revelation, which does not exclude its repeatedly becoming event, (2) the question of its relation to the single historical event of Jesus Christ.

76. Brunner, *The Mediator*, 86. Cf. 503: "The Cross, and thus the Atonement and Revelation, are *absolutely unique*." But "the Cross of Christ is not the absolute turning-point simply as an historical event." "The Atonement is *not* history. . . . It is super-history. . . . What matters is that it *did* actually take place. But if it has taken place, then it has happened *once for all*." What does all this mean? Cf. ibid., 290: "Nothing else in the whole world is unique in this sense. For this event alone has no connection with other events. In itself it is absolute. For it is the Incarnation of the Word, the coming of the Son of God, the Atonement."

77. Cf. ibid., 291: "The Incarnation of the Son of God is determined by sin. . . ." What is involved is "the restoration of a fallen Creation."

78. Friedrich Gogarten, *Ich glaube an den dreieinigen Gott* (Jena: E. Diederichs, 1926), 17–39. [O]

79. Ibid., 600–619.

80. *Christliche Dogmatik*, I, 73ff.

81. Ibid., 332.

82. W. Herrmann, *Die mit der Theologie verknüpfte Not*, 21: "Millennia have not sufficed to protect this word [faith, R.B.] from being associated with what people usually call religion."

83. Cf. K. Barth, *Christliche Dogmatik*, I (§18: "Die Gnade und die Religion"): To make theology the science of religion, and dogmatics the philosophy of religion, means to subordinate by way of a method the reality of God to the reality of religion, thus to surrender it irreparably, so that it becomes a non-theology, in fact an anti-theology, as a matter of fact, an a-theology. Then "faith" or theology is irretrievably surrendered to the attack of Feuerbach. Cf. K. Barth, "Ludwig Feuerbach," *Zwischen den Zeiten* 5 (1927): 11–33. [B]

84. Cf. Friedrich Gogarten, "Die Krisis der Religion," *Zeitwende* 7 (1931): 22–38. [D]

85. Cf. Walter Gut, *Der Sinn freier Theologie* (Zürich/Leipzig: 1925). R. Bultmann, "The Problem of 'Natural Theology,'" in *Faith and Understanding*, trans. Louise Pettibone Smith (New York: Harper & Row, 1969), 313–31. [D]

86. Cf. the "division" of religions, e.g., in Julius Kaftan's *Dogmatik* (§2.5): In natural religions mysticism is the highpoint; in religions having to do with ethics the religion of redemption appears in contrast to national religions. Cf. also H. Weinel, *Biblische Theologie des Neuen Testaments— Die Religion Jesu und des Urchristentums*, 3rd ed. (Tübingen: J.C.B. Mohr, 1921).

87. Ed.: The manuscript reads "of whom."

88. Cf. Fr. Gogarten, *Ich glaube an den dreieinigen Gott*, 76f.; K. Barth, *Christliche Dogmatik*, I, 250f. (with reference to the problem of the canon).

89. Ed.: The final Table of Contents (cf. Editor's Foreword) from Bultmann's hand, the table normative for our edition, omits the earlier §10 ("The Historicity of *Dasein*"), though its expositions were apparently still included in the 1933 summer semester lecture. The beginning of §1 alludes to the earlier paragraph. §8, also referred to here, now corresponds to §9.

90. §10a.

91. §8a.

92. §10a.

93. This also applies when in fact the word that encounters a person first makes him aware of the question of the moment. It is also assumed that

where he is concerned the moment contains the question, that openness is a possibility for him, an openness actualizable through the "word" as well as through some other encounter.

94. Ed.: The manuscript reads "holds" (*halte*) instead of "had" (*hatte*).

95. There is death only where there is the desire to live; this desire makes death what it is.

96. Cf. R. Bultmann, "Der Begriff der Offenbarung im Neuen Testament," SGV 135 (1929), in *Glauben und Verstehen*, vol. 3, 1–34. And this too in opposition to all mysticism that construes the reception of revelation as a being snatched from human existence, and devalues the creation. [E]

97. Ed.: E adds from "(1) that the human is a creature" up to "is for him."

98. Ed.: E adds "trusting in the Creator and. . . ."

99. Ed.: E adds all of (1).

100. Ed.: E adds all of (1), and the numeral 2.

101. Ed.: E adds "and also by assigning to the Gentiles a knowledge of the law (Rom. 1:32; 2:14f.; cf. Phil. 4:8)."

102. The definite article supplied by the editor.

103. R. Bultmann, "Das christliche Gebot der Nächstenliebe," *Glauben und Verstehen*, vol. 1, 229–44.

104. In opposition to Max Reischle, "Erkennen wir die Tiefen Gottes?" *ZThK* 1 (1891): 287–366, esp. 316f.

105. R. Bultmann, "Kirche and Lehre im Neuen Testament," *Glauben und Verstehen*, vol. 1, 153–87.

106. Cf. Martin Kähler, *The So-Called Historical Jesus and the Historic, Biblical Christ*, trans. Carl E. Braaten (Philadelphia: Fortress, 1964), 61, 66; R. Bultmann, "Die Christologie des Neuen Testaments"; "Der Begriff des Wortes Gottes im Neuen Testament"; and "Die Bedeutung des geschichtlichen Jesus für die Theologie des Paulus," *Glauben und Verstehen*, vol. 1, 245–67; 268–93; and 188–213.

# 5. The Concept of Faith

1. Adolf Harnack, "Geschichte der Lehre von der Seligkeit allein durch den Glauben in der alten Kirche," *Zeitschrift für Theologie und Kirche* 1 (1891): 82–178. Heinrich S. Denifle, *Die abendländischen Schriftausleger bis Luther über iustitia dei and iustificatio* (Mainz: F. Kirchheim, 1905).

2. J. Pohle, *Lehrbuch der Dogmatik* (Paderhorn: 1908), vol. 2, 432.

3. Cf. the Catholic doctrine of justification according to the Council of Trent, session 6, chap. 7: "Finally, the one formal cause is the justness of

God: not that by which he himself is just, but that by which he makes us just and endowed with which we are renewed in the spirit of our mind, and are not merely considered to be just but we are truly named and are just, each one of us receiving individually his own justness according to the measure which the Holy Spirit apportions to each one as he wills (see 1 Cor. 12:11), and in view of each one's disposition and co-operation." Section 6, Canon 10: "If anyone says that people are justified without the justice of Christ by which he gained merit for us; or that they are formally just by his justness itself: let him be anathema," *Decrees of the Ecumenical Councils*, II: *Trent to Vatican II*, 673, 679. Cf. Hurter, *Theologiae dogmaticae compendium*, Tom. III, Tract. VIII, pars II—de gratia habituali seu de justificatione, 7th ed. (Oeniponte: Libraria Academica Wagneriana, 1891), 125–212; Denifle, *Die abendländischen Schriftausleger* (n.1 above). On the subject, cf. Karl Holl, "Die iustitia dei in der vorlutherischen Bibelauslegung des Abendlandes," *Festgabe A. von Harnack* (Tübingen: J.C.B. Mohr, 1921), 73–92.

4. The reference to Paul (Rom. 10:9f.) is correct, insofar as *pisteuein* here is linked to the *hoti*-clause, and in fact Paul construes faith as faith *in*. Insofar as the Catholic polemic is directed against the view of faith as a universal, subjective trust, it is correct.

5. Pohle, *Lehrbuch*, 432.

6. Georg Hoffmann, *Die Lehre von der fides implicita innerhalb der katholischen Kirche* (Leipzig: A. Pries, 1903).

7. Pohle, *Lehrbuch*, 384, 435.

8. Ibid., 436.

9. And, of course, this is a *cogitare cum assensione* (Augustine), that is, an act of the intellect moved by the intent to consent.

10. Pohle, *Lehrbuch*, 442: "If repentance at the end of the road is at once dictated and fulfilled by *perfect* love (*contritio caritate perfecta*), then justification *immediately* takes place, even before reception of the sacrament [of baptism or penance, R.B.], though not without the desire for it (*votum sacramenti, sacramentum in voto*)." On the other hand, an imperfect repentance (*attritio*) leads to justification only by way of receiving the sacrament.

11. Ibid., 441f.; on No. 4: If true repentance is motivated by *perfect* love, then justification follows immediately without the sacrament; if it is incomplete (*attritio*), then justification is achieved only through receiving the sacrament (cf. n.10). So it would almost appear as if *fides formata* corresponded to the Protestant concept of faith, in which case *fides informis* would correspond to the *notitia* and *assensus* of Protestant dogmatics.

Actually, in Protestantism *assensus* is a dubious affair (cf. below). In their starting-points, however, the Catholic and Protestant doctrines are basically at variance, since what the Catholic calls faith is not at all such for the Protestant. Further, in the Catholic scheme there is no inner connection between the stages (!) in the process of justification.

12. Ibid., 442f.

13. Ibid., 439, and the English translation in *The Summa Theologica of Saint Thomas Aquinas*, translated by the Fathers of the English Dominican Province (Chicago: Encyclopaedia Britannica, 1952), II, 364–65.

14. Ed.: In the margin of D Bultmann notes, "here for the first time a polemic against the *fides informis*. cf. 99 verso." We have not followed this reference. In our edition 99 verso matches n.18 below. Cf. also n.19.

15. Cf. Schmid, and Johannes Gottschick, *Luthers Theologie* (Tübingen: J.C.B. Mohr, 1914).

16. Cf. Luther's explanation of the Third Article of the Apostles' Creed.

17. Ed.: *The Book of Concord*, 541.

18. Cf. Schmid, 420, and the *Augsburg Confession*, Article IV: "It is also taught among us that we cannot obtain forgiveness of sin and righteousness before God by our own merits, works, or satisfactions, but that we receive forgiveness of sin and become righteous before God by grace, for Christ's sake, through faith, when we believe that Christ suffered for us and that for his sake our sin is forgiven and righteousness and eternal life are given to us. For God will regard and reckon this faith as righteousness, as Paul says in Romans 3:21-26 and 4:5." *The Book of Concord*, 30.

Cf. *The Apology of the Augsburg Confession*, Article IV, para. 27: "It is false, too, that by its own strength reason can love God above all things and keep his law, truly fear him, truly believe that ("rely on the fact that") he hears prayer, willingly obey him in death and in his other visitations, and not covet. But reason can produce civil works (though to some extent outwardly capable of an honorable life and good works), *The Book of Concord*, 111. Cf. para. 33: "If the mind that is set on the flesh is hostile to God, then the flesh sins even when it performs outward civil works. If it cannot submit to God's law, it is certainly sinning even when it produces deeds that are excellent and praiseworthy in human eyes." Cf. para. 34: "Our opponents concentrate on the commandments of the second table, which contain the civil righteousness that reason understands. Content with this, they think they satisfy the law of God. Meanwhile they do not see the first table, which commands us to love God, to be sure that God is wrathful at our sin, to fear him truly, and to be sure that he hears us. But without the Holy Spirit, the human heart either despises the judgment of God in its smugness, or in the midst of punishment it flees and hates his judgment," ibid., 111–12. Cf. para. 35: "So it does not obey the first table. . . . Such people despise God when they do these things, as Epicurus did not believe that God cared for him or regarded or heard him. This contempt for God corrupts works that seem virtuous, for God judges the heart," ibid., 112. Cf. para. 37: "It is easy enough for idle men to make up these dreams that a man guilty of mortal sin can love God above all things, since they themselves do not feel the wrath or judgment of God. But in the agony of conscience and in conflict, the conscience experiences how vain these philosophical speculations are." Cf. Luther quoted in Martin Rade, *Luther in Worten aus seinen Werken* (Berlin: Hutten Verlag, 1917), 119ff. (esp. 119, 123, 125).

19. For this reason also the *fides informis* is rejected. Luther, Erlanger Ausgabe [EA] IV 456: "Nor is faith a human work. It is rather the gift of the Spirit of Christ. Unformed faith, however, is the notion or imagining of men. . . . In fact, it is the figment and vainest idol of the heart of those who do not know what they are saying" (Gottschick, 18, n.l = Contra Satanam et Synagogam ipsius, WA 59, 721, lines 9–10, 3, 4).

20. In Schmid, 419.

21. Cf. Chemnitz: "Justifying faith presupposes and includes general faith," Schmid, 4.

22. Chemnitz in Schmid, 420.

23. The meaning of *fiducia* is also clearly held to in polemic against the Catholic understanding of works. It is seen that faith as the how of the historical human being is not something *attached to* him that must be supplemented, but determines his entire existence. Cf. Hollaz: "The epithet, working by love (in Gal. 3:6), is an attribute of a faith which has justified, not of one which will in the future justify, much less the form or essence of justifying faith *so far as* it justifies," in Schmid, 423. Cf. the *Solid Declaration*, Article IV, paras. 10 and 11: "Oh, faith is a living, busy, active, mighty thing, so that it is impossible for it not to be constantly doing what is good. Likewise, faith does not ask if good works are to be done, but before one can ask, faith has already done them and is constantly active," *The Book of Concord*, 552–53. Cf. *The Augsburg Confession*, Article IV, paras. 142–43: "The faith of which we are speaking, moreover, has its existence in penitence; that is, it is conceived in the terrors of a conscience that feels God's wrath against our sins and looks for forgiveness of sins and deliverance from sin. This faith ought to grow and be strengthened in these terrors and in other afflictions. And so it cannot exist in those who live according to the flesh, who

take pleasure in their lusts and obey them," *The Book of Concord*, 126. Cf. *The Augsburg Confession*, Article XX, "Faith and Good Works."

24. W. Herrmann, "Die Lage und Aufgabe der evangelischen Dogmatik in der Gegenwart," *Gesammelte Aufsätze* (Tübingen: J.C.B. Mohr, 1923), 95–188, quotation on 106.

25. WA 25, 337, line 30/31; cf. Gottschick, 19. Cf. WA 7, 215, 1–15 (on the Apostles' Creed, 1520): "We should note here that faith is of two kinds. First of all, it is about God, that is, when I believe that what is said of God is true, just as when I believe that what is said of the Turks, the devil and hell is true. This is more a knowledge or a taking note than a faith. Second, God is believed in, that is, when I not only believe that what is said of God is true, but set my trust in Him, set out or propose to deal with Him, and believe without any doubt that He will be and do to me just as it is said of Him. I would not believe a Turk or a man in this way, however highly one valued his praise. I can easily believe that a man is pious, but do not dare for this reason rely on him. Such faith that ventures on God as it is said of him, whether in life or death, this alone makes a Christian, and obtains from God all he desires, a faith no false heart may own. For this is a living faith, and it is commanded in the first commandment which reads, 'I am thy God, thou shalt have no other gods.'"

Cf. WA 10, III, 285, 3–9, 24–26, 28–30 (A Sermon on the Unrighteous Mammon in Luke 16:1-10, for the Ninth Sunday after Trinity, August 17, 1522): "Some hear and read about the gospel and faith, and quickly hit upon it, and call what they think about it faith. But they do not think further of faith than of something in their power to have or not to have, like another natural, human work. So when they conceive a thought in their heart that says, 'the teaching is really true and I believe it to be so,' then they think faith is present. . . . But the true faith we are talking about cannot be manufactured with our ideas. Rather, it is a pure work of God without any help from us. . . . For this reason it is also a mighty, active, restless, creative thing that just makes a man new, that behaves differently, and goes about in an entirely new way. So, it is impossible that the self should not do good without letup."

26. *The Book of Concord*, 114.

27. Ibid., 118.

28. Cf. Quenstedt in Schmid, 414. Cf. Baier: "This, therefore, is the faith which is said to apprehend Christ or His merit, particularly as it is assent joined with confidence, or confidence joined with assent, consisting of those acts united, and is designated now by the name of the former, and

then by the latter, the other always being implied." Schmid, 414. Cf. Hollaz: "By *general* assent, the universal promises of the grace of God and the merit of Christ are regarded as true. By *special* assent, the converted, regenerate sinner regards these general promises as pertaining to him individually," Schmid, 415.

29. Or *fiducia* is in danger of becoming subjectivity, of becoming the warm heart, etc. This is the error of pietism, cf. below.

30. Johann Gerhard, *De justificatione per fidem*: *Loci theologici*, ed. Fr. Frank (Lipsiae: J.C. Hinrichs, 1885), vol. 3, 354: "*Assensus = judicium approbans ea, quae in verbo credenda proponuntur*" (cf. O. Kirn, "Glaube," *Theologische Realenzyklopädie*, 3rd ed., vol. 6, 678).

31. Cf. above, §6.

32. Cf. above, §6.

33. Cf. Martin Kähler, *The So-Called Historical Jesus and the Historic, Biblical Christ*, trans. Carl E. Braaten (Philadelphia: Fortress Press, 1964), 119–21, which contains a criticism of O. Ritschl's Christian "worldview" as Stoicism.

34. In the manuscript "me and my destiny" (not crossed out!), originally in A, is written above the words "the moment"—from B?

35. Wilhelm Herrmann, *Die mit der Theologie verknüpfte Not der evangelischen Kirche und ihre Überwindung*, (Tübingen: J.C.B. Mohr, 1913), 7f.: "Faith, however, is the power to trace within the world the all-embracing activity of a living One who is the origin of our life. But when Christian faith in this way enables a person who is otherwise lost in the vastness of the world to conceive it as a totality, then it clearly makes no sense when Christian theologians want to establish a worldview by scientific means. By doing so they in fact deprive faith of its honor. The requirement of a Christian theology is that it seek to show what faith means when it reveals to us a totality rich with life in the world. We should not establish this claim of faith, say, in a scientific way, but as faith itself establishes it, this is what we should seek to set in pure light."

36. And "all the 'Christian' drapery over this worldview alters nothing of its bondage to the self, its profoundly un-Christian character, and its quite evident unbelief. . . ." (Fr. Gogarten, *Ich glaube an den dreieinigen Gott* [Jena: E. Diederichs, 1926], 190. Cf. in general p. 190f.).

37. W. Herrmann, "Der evangelische Glaube und die Theologie Albrecht Ritschls," *Gesammelte Aufsätze* (Tübingen: J.C.B. Mohr, 1923), 1–25, and 14: "For example, we do not have the religious idea of God's omnipotence when we think of a power that can do anything at all. We have it by faith

only when we think of a power that now is bringing about the total reality in which we live for our sake." Cf. Herrmann, "Der Glaube an Gott und die Wissenschaft unserer Zeit," in ibid., 189–213, and 208: "But the person who could not yet find the power for faith does not come nearer to it when he allows himself to be convinced that a god may be coming to help him. This can easily conceal from him the fact that he is still far removed from the certainty that God is actually coming to do so. Only such certainty is faith."

38. WA 24, 18, 26–33 (Preface to the Sermons of 1527 on Genesis); cf. WA 12, 439, 16–22 (the Sermon for March 15, 1523: "A Sermon and Introduction to Genesis"). Cf. Luther on the impatience that was unwilling to suffer, in WA 56, 303, 13–15 (exposition of Rom. 5:3 in the 1515/1516 lectures): "Thus for that person no one will be Jesus, that is, Savior, because he does not wish to be damned; *no one will be his Creator, because he does not wish to be nothing, of which he may be Creator.*"

39. Cf. Spitteler.

40. WA 17, II, 132, 21–22 (Sermon on the Epistle for Septuagesima Sunday, 1 Cor. 9:24-27; 10:1-5, the Fastenpostille of 1525).

41. Cf. above, §10.

42. W. Herrmann, *Die mit der Theologie verknüpfte Not*, 32: [What orthodox and liberal] "understand by religion is over and done with for all who experience God's redemption in that power over their inner life wielded by the person of Jesus, who has appeared to them in the New Testament. Such persons will no longer be inclined for salvation's sake to declare with the conservatives that something is true that they would not hold to be true on their own. . . . No more than they will be ready with the liberals to seek salvation in the reality of the universal, and no longer in history. They owe the new life given to them and called faith in Holy Scripture to a truly historical fact, a fact, however, that cannot at all be demonstrated to be true by the cognitive methods of science."

43. On Schleiermacher cf. above, §10. Cf. Barth's criticism of Schleiermacher in *Christliche Dogmatik*, I, 308–11, and 309: "The *homo religiosus* in Schleiermacher has . . . no counterpart." If need be, Schleiermacher can altogether dispense with the idea of God. Feeling does not have God as object; rather, God is "given" in feeling "in an original way." [B]

44. Schleiermacher, *On Religion: Speeches to Its Cultured Despisers*, trans. Richard Crouter (New York: Cambridge University Press, 1988), 105–06.

45. Ibid., 107.

46. So also Schleiermacher's "Doctrine of Faith" intends to show how

the character of spiritual life created in the Christian expresses itself in particular ideas. The result is that faith is treated as a condition of soul given
once for all, and of course as a particular modification of the feeling of
absolute dependence, a natural endowment supposedly within human self-
consciousness. The question is: "What must occur if the Christian condition
of soul already exists?" Nothing is said as to how faith comes about, since
the idea of revelation is lacking. On this subject cf. W. Herrmann, "Die
Lage und Aufgabe der evangelischen Dogmatik in der Gegenwart," *Gesammelte Aufsätze*, 95–188, esp. 112ff. (the quotation is from 113f.). Cf. the
summary of Herrmann's criticism of Schleiermacher in K. Barth, "Die dogmatische Prinzipienlehre bei Wilhelm Herrmann," *Zwischen den Zeiten* 3
(1925): 246–80, 253f.

47. To the extent this means that in the deed of God (in which I truly recognize *myself*) I have a prior understanding of revelation, it is correct. But it
is all ruined by the concept of "value." Value *exists* without anyone's realizing it. It *exists*, that is to say, as something required of me. In such a theology, (1) God is made an ideal, and (2) a tangible character is assigned the
ideal along with its character as requirement. Or, value is "what is valuable
for me," thus an ideal which then is hypostatized.

48. Cf. Rudolf Paulus, *Das Christusproblem der Gegenwart: Untersuchung über das Verhältnis von Idee und Geschichte* (Tübingen: J.C.B.
Mohr, 1922), 67.

49. W. Herrmann, "Der evangelische Glaube und die Theologie Albrecht
Ritschls," 1–25, and 12: "What [the liberal theologians] want to put in place
of this false [Catholic, orthodox, R.B.] faith is not Christian faith, but a religiosity, grounded in their opinion on the nature of the human spirit. They do
not understand that Christian faith is an unconditional surrender to a power
distinct from the Christian's inner life, that is, to the revelation of God. Of
the two propositions, that faith saves and that faith is surrender to the
authority of the revelation, they want to retain only the first. Ritschl maintained them both."

50. In this way, history is "interpreted" from one's own religious experience. And this interpretation can never give to the interpreted historical
fact "basic religious value, but will only be able to say that the same experience underlies this fact as the experience from which its interpretation
derives. . . . And in this case, where the revelation occurs ever anew,
though essentially always the same in the soul, the community will not be
mediatrix and bearer of the revelation. On the contrary, it will be only the
result of the experience of the revelation," Friedrich Gogarten, "Mystik

und Offenbarung," in *Die religiöse Entscheidung* (Jena: E. Diederichs, 1921), 54–74; the quotation is taken from 55f.

51. E. Troeltsch, "Glaube, III: Dogmatisch," *Religion in Geschichte und Gegenwart*, 1st ed., vol. 2, cols. 1437–1447.

52. Ibid., col. 1437.

53. Ed.: In the margin, and in capital (red) letters, Bultmann refers to his lecture, "Truth and Certainty": "cf. the manuscript Truth and Certainty, 8–10 (Troeltsch), 15f. (Heim)." Are the additional bibliographical references below from a later period, from D? or E?: Karl Soll, "Die wissenschaftlichen Aufgaben einer Geschichte der christlichen Religion," *Preussische Jahrbücher* 98 (1899): 12–57, and "Die Entwicklung der wissenschaftlichen Theologie in den letzten 50 Jahren" (Bonner Rektoratsrede), 1912.

54. Troeltsch, "Glaube, III: Dogmatisch," col. 1437.

55. Ibid., col. 1438.

56. Ibid., col. 1438 (emphasis by R.B.).

57. Ibid., col. 1438f. (emphasis by R.B.).

58. Ibid., col. 1439.

59. Cf. K. Barth, *Christliche Dogmatik*, I, 90: "As is well known, *L. Feuerbach* threw out the question whether the so-called objective content of religion, chiefly the idea of God, but with it everything that might in any sense denote an actual divine counterpart of the human, is only a psychologically intelligible, yet superfluous, and indeed harmful product of fantasy; whether the nature of God is anything else than hypostatized human nature, and whether thus theology, rendered sensible, can truthfully and honestly be any thing else than anthropology." [B]

60. Troeltsch, "Glaube," col. 1439f.

61. Ibid., col. 1440.

62. Ibid.

63. Ibid.

64. Ibid., col. 1443.

65. Cf. ibid., col. 1443f.

66. Ibid., col. 1441.

67. Ibid.

68. Ibid.

69. Ibid., col. 1443.

70. Ibid., col. 1445.

71. Ibid., col. 1442f.

72. Ibid., col. 1447.

73. Cf. Friedrich Gogarten, "Mystik und Offenbarung," 54–74. Oriented in incorrectly psychological fashion, but with good material: Edvard Lehmann, *Mystik im Heidentum und Christentum* (Leipzig: B. G. Teubner, 1908). Evelyn Underhill, *Mysticism: A Study in the Nature and Development of Man's Spiritual Consciousness* (New York: The Noonday Press, 1955); Rudolf Otto, *Mysticism East and West*, trans. Bertha L. Bracey and Richenda C. Payne (New York: Meridian Books, 1957). Friedrich Karl Schumann, *Der Gottesgedanke und der Zerfall der Moderne* (Tübingen: J.C.B. Mohr, 1929). [B, C]

74. Ed.: D adds from "and in this way" up to "from everything and everyone over against him."

75. Ed.: D adds from "at once" to the end of the sentence.

76. "Where the creature ends, God begins" (Eckhart).

77. Or, it is achieving and preserving (yielding proof of the new nature).

78. Vedic: "Neither through speech, nor thought, nor sight is he grasped. 'He is!' Through this word he is grasped, and in no other way" (quoted in Lehmann, *Mystik im Heidentum*, 29).

79. Not a *ginōskein* but a *gnōsthēnai*! The *ratio* would have to conceive God as manifold, but God is sheer unity. Not a what, but only the that can be stated. God as *sige*, not as *logos*. Naturally, however, mysticism may not be defined as the "stressing to a very high degree, indeed the overstressing, of the nonrational or suprarational elements in religion" (Rudolf Otto, *The Idea of the Holy*, 22), for (1) the concept of the irrational raises a question, and (2) what does "stressing to a very high degree" mean? At what point does mysticism begin? The criterion that makes mysticism what it is is not even named!

80. Eckhart according to Gogarten, "Mystik und Offenbarung," 57. Plotinus, *Enn.* VI 9, 9–11 (cf. E. Underhill, 335ff.). [D] Surrender of all "attributes," cf. R. Otto, *Vischnu-Narayana*, 2nd ed. (Jena: E. Diederichs, 1923), 76:

> Who, what, however I be found to be
> of body and spirit and qualities;
> and what I may be, I take today to the heap
> and lay it down, Lord, at thy feet.

Tauler: "The soul is just a hindrance between time and eternity." The one thing needful is "that you know how the Nothing is your own, with all that you are, and whoever you are of yourself." "In the Ground, sink into your

Nothing" (J. Tauler, *Predigten*, ed. W. Lehmann [Jena: E. Diederichs, 1913], vol. 1, 22, 207f.).

Cf. Tauler (1300–1361) in Underhill, 330f. [D].

Cf. Otto, *Mysticism East and West*, 78–79: Only what is "inward" in the human being—the Atman in Shankara, ground of soul in Eckhart—is the site of mystical experience. Not only the "lower" powers of sense and impulse and inferior understanding are seen as outward things to be put off, but the higher powers as well: memory, reason, and rational will.

Cf. also Eckhart's description of "quiet" in Underhill, *Mysticism*, 318–20. Cf. Ruysbroeck (1294–1381): "Behold! here all human works and active virtues must cease [in the uniting, R.B.]; for here God works alone at the apex of the soul. Here there is nought else but an eternal seeing and staring at that Light, by the Light and in the Light" (Underhill, *Mysticism*, 345; cf. in general 335.). [B]

Katherine of Genoa (1447–1510) in Underhill, *Mysticism*, 461. [D]

81. Gogarten, "Mystik und Offenbarung," 59. Cf. Plotinus: In union with the deity the soul lays off its shape, even of what is spiritual in it. For as long as it still is or becomes something, it can neither see the Highest nor become a unity with him.

82. What is correct here is the insight into the idea of omnipotence, insofar as the "being" of God does not merely assume a different metaphysical shape than the being of the world (metaphysical dualism as such is not mysticism, cf. below, p. 127). The error is in the view that humanity simply does not exist over against the being of God; that one is not merely absorbed in mystical vision, but is such through God, and that he exists only insofar as he is in God (from this derives the possibility of pantheism, cf. below, pp. 128f.). Thus, outside of God nothing exists by itself or is secure, for which reason also there is no possessing. A person does not live (as he imagines in his anxiety) in a world that he controls, where he is in possession of himself or anything else. Cf. R. M. Rilke, *Das Stunden-Buch*.

83. The mystic believes he has the "essence" of things in concepts. He imagines he has the "one" in the unified concept, which, when dematerialized, embraces plurality in unity. [D]

84. "The more perfect and simple a thing is in essence, the richer in its relations," etc. (Eckhart); cf. Otto, *Mysticism East and West*, 21, and Otto's description of mystical knowledge according to Eckhart, 65.

85. Philo of Alexandria, *On Rewards and Punishments*, paras. 39f.: God has mercy on Jacob and gives him a sight of himself (*thea*), "in so far as it

was possible for mortal and created nature to contain it. Yet the vision only showed that He *is*, not what He is. For this which is better than the good, more venerable than the monad, purer than the unit, cannot be discerned by anyone else; to God alone is it permitted to apprehend God," *Philo*, trans. F. H. Colson (Cambridge: Harvard University Press, 1954), VIII, 335.

86. Dionysius the Areopagite in Underhill, *Mysticism*, 320.

87. Thus Eckhart and Shankara in Otto, *Mysticism East and West*, 9–10.

88. Ibid., 25.

89. Cf. Otto, *West-Östliche Mystik* (Gütersloher Verlagshaus: Gerd Mohn, 1971), 82 (cf. 11f. in the English text).

90. Otto, *Mysticism East and West*, 92.

91. Ibid., 100.

92. Ibid., 18ff.

93. Yajnavalkya in ibid., 19: "To be free from death and the world of death and from the transitory, that is to reach the true, immortal Being."

94. Cf. Otto, *West-Östliche Mystik*, 50f., 116. Otto cites Eckhart's hatred of the time, of the here and now, *Mysticism East and West*, 66f.

95. This is very clear in Eckhart's statements quoted in Otto, *Mysticism East and West*, 29f., 87ff. [B]

96. Gogarten, "Mystik und Offenbarung," 67. This holds true, insofar as mysticism actually negates man's entire existence. But insofar as negative knowledge merely negates plurality and arrives at the concept of Being, Mysticism does not even recognize man. [D]

97. Eckhart I, 90. 182 according to Otto, *West-Östliche Mystik*, 106–09. Underhill, *Mysticism*, 406. [B]

98. Ed.: The negative is inserted by the editor.

99. Only this is said of the human in a positive way, that he is god*less*, a sinner. . ." that in the negativity of this knowledge of God as the Wholly Other human guilt is revealed," Gogarten, "Mystik und Offenbarung," 67.

100. Ibid., 68.

101. Ibid., 72.

102. Cf. Underhill, *Mystik*, 261ff.; chap. 3, "Die Reinigung des Selbst" (e.g., 269, purification as self-simplification). Cf. in general the second part, p. 221ff.; "Der mystische Weg." Heightened to self-annihilation, to "emptiness," Underhill, ibid., 413ff., cf. p. 447. [B]

103. Myein = to close the eyes! Plato, *Soph.* 239e; *Theat.* 164a. H. Leisegang, "Mystik I: Begrifflich," *Religion in Geschichte und Gegenwart*, 2nd ed., vol. 4, col. 334–37. [D]

104. The "world beyond" that he reaches through such methods, is not

such a world at all. Wilhelm Herrmann, "Die Lage und Aufgabe der evangelischen Dogmatik in der Gegenwart," 95–188, and 124: "The idea of the world beyond" is "secured only . . . where one has experienced the inescapability of the judge within his own moral judgment, where he does not arrive at the idea of the beyond on his own (and thus make it an abstraction), but where he knows he is set into what is on this side by what is beyond."

105. Wilhelm Herrmann, "Andacht," *Theologische Realenzyklopädie*, 3rd ed., vol. 1, 497–501, quotation from 498. Cf. the grotesque examples in R. Otto, *Das Heilige*, p. 23f.: "The total stillness of the night shuddered in solemn silence. The darkness enclosed an appearance which was experienced the more strongly it was not seen. I could no more doubt God's presence than my own [!thus God a tangible thing! R.B.]. Indeed, I felt, if that is possible, as the *less real* of the two of us." "I was alone with him. . . . I did not seek him, but I experienced (!) the total *union* of my spirit with his own." "I had the experience (!) as if I had lost my own self."

The mystic will no longer be creature, but creator. Since I share in the "idea," I am this idea, am eternally in God, am the Son, etc., Otto, *Mysticism East and West*, 99f. [B]

106. On this topic cf. J. Tauler, *Predigten*, 209–11.

107. Cf. above, p. 120.

108. And yet one is supposed to effect this absorption himself! Cf. Tauler, *Predigten*, 20: "One should gather himself to himself, turn toward his inner Ground with exalted soul and tensed powers, with an inner sight of God's presence, and, above all, with an inner yearning for the most lovely will of God, with a sinking away from self and all creaturely things, and an ever deeper sinking into the glorified will of God."

109. The I-Thou relation has validity only at a lower stage of the way toward the divine. Cf. *Meister Eckeharts Schriften und Predigten*, ed. H. Büttner (Leipzig: 1903), vol. 1, 172 (we pray "that we be free of God").

110. Likewise from the standpoint of speculation: if I *am*, and if *being* = God, then I am one with God. The soul "enjoys all creatures in God and God in all creatures" (Underhill, *Mystik*, 271, cf. 432f.). In actual fact, the identity of God and I: Otto, *West-Östliche Mystik*, 132f., 134f. [B]

111. On the *unio mystica* cf. Max Scheler, *Wesen und Formen der Sympathie*, 3rd ed. (Bonn: 1931), 36f. [D]

112. The reciprocity formula reads: "thou in me and I in thee."

113. The significance of Canticles for mysticism! The eroticism of Christian monks and nuns, Persian Sufism, etc.

114. The idea is Persian, cf. E. Lehmann, *Mystik im Heidentum* (n.73 above), 39.

115. Reflect the Godhead!

116. In the Godhead, which then only *is*, there can be no duality.

117. Tauler, *Predigten*, vol. 1, 180, cf. 168.

118. Ibid., 22.

119. Cf. Eckhart, *Schriften und Predigten,* vol. 2, 7.

120. Cf. Tauler, *Predigten*, vol. 1, 180; Eckhart, *Schriften und Predigten*, vol. 2, 52.

121. Tauler, *Predigten*, vol. 1, 183.

122. Ibid., 170.

123. Ibid., 171.

124. Ibid., 211.

125. Eckhart, *Schriften und Predigten*, 50f.

126. Gogarten, "Mystik und Offenbarung" (n.73 above), 65.

127. Eckhart, *Schriften und Predigten*, 162.

128. Gogarten, "Mystik und Offenbarung," 66.

129. "Not ashamed of what is beautiful in the body, but fleeing from it," Porphyry on Plato's life and the sequence of his writings, 1, 1. Plotinus, *Enn.* V, 9, 2.

130. Lehmann, *Mystik im Heidentum,* 28.

131. Gogarten, "Mystik und Offenbarung," 67f.

132. Cf. the view of the creation: Humanity and world are not primarily qualified by God's *claim*, but are construed aesthetically as a work of art; cf. Eckhart, *Schriften und Predigten*, vol. 1, 90, 182 ("For it is the nature of everything good to impart itself"). It is in the nature of God to create (now interpreted as "love"); the analogy of the sun which must shine. [o]

133. Gogarten, "Mystik und Offenbarung," 68 (the addition in parentheses by R.B.).

134. Cf. Philo in relation to the Old Testament, Plotinus in relation to Plato, the gnostics and medieval mystics in relation to the Catholic church.

135. William James, *Varieties of Religious Experience* (New York: Longmans, Green, 1917), 387; cf. Underhill, *Mystik,* 96, n.1. [o]

136. Cf. in Lehmann, *Mystik im Heidentum,* 39f.

137. Cf. the move toward rationalism on the part of fanatics of the Reformation period.

138. In the manuscript originally, Tersteegen was also mentioned after Angelus Silesius; his name was later set in parentheses.

139. Eckhart in Lehmann, *Mystik im Heidentum,* 106. In Eckhart, God equals unity, cf. Otto, *Mysticism East and West,* 64f. Cf. also examples for the unity of God and the world (and also the I) in Leisegang, "Mystik I: Begriffich" (n.103 above). (Incidentally, Leisegang confuses the mystical "worldview" with pantheistic speculation!) [D]

Angelus Silesius in Lehmann, *Mystik im Heidentum,* 124. Cf. the Indic; R. Otto, *Vischnu-Narayana,* 76:

> If without thee I have no patron,
> without me Thou wouldst lack a client.

And p. 75:

> Sinking into *Dasein*'s floods, finally
> in Thee I may still gain the shore.
> And Thou wilt gain in me no less:
> a vessel, thoroughly to flow with grace.

Jelaleddin in Otto, *Vischnu-Narayana,* 72. [B]

140. Mysticism a type of exposition of one's own existence. [O]

141. Mysticism rejects this-sided-*ness* and wants that-sided-*ness.* [D]

142. Not to be reached by the *via eminentiae* or *negationis.* [O]

143. His actual world beyond is always his future. [O]

144. Cf. Herrmann's interpretation of "absolute dependence" = free self-surrender. Not the otiose (mysticism), but the passive (faith)! Thus, being the object of the divine activity and being oneself summoned to act coincide. [D]

145. *Is there* really a mystic? The question has the same meaning as the question, *is there* really a believer?

146. In the first draft, §8 was referred to here.

147. Cf. Karl Barth, "Die dogmatische Prinzipienlehre bei Wilhelm Herrmann" (n.46, above), 246–80.

148. Such "faith" is always prey to doubt. [D]

149. Cf. Wilhelm Herrmann, *Die mit der Theologie verknüpfte Not,* 21! "The desperate and so faithful appearing resolve to want 'to believe' everything in the Bible is actually the resolve to veil from oneself the reality that is there. This is just an expression of anxiety toward the Bible and a dismal sign of confusion overtaking our church through men who mean well but labor with want of sense." (Cf. ibid., 35, and also what follows).

150. §11 above: faith is directed to Christ, not as an event available in the past but as it encounters him in the proclamation. [D]

151. "By the fact that" to the end of the sentence is (presumably) a later insertion in B.

152. For its legitimation this word cannot appeal to an ascertainable historical event, but only to the New Testament mediated through the tradition, thus to the "it is written." [B]

153. Barth, *Vom christlichen Leben* (Münich: Chr. Kaiser, 1926): "It is so that everything which we are is against God and there is no stage in our life where we would be otherwise, it does not happen that somewhere in our existence a corner is discovered where we could say: now it is no longer so dangerous, now I am for God. But the proper state of being admonished consists just in this, that we finally let it be said to us: you are against God!" (17). "Our true life in God consists just in this, that we admit to ourselves: We do not live in God, but far from God. Whoever is in God, just he knows that he is far from God, knows that he needs mercy. The situation never occurs that he would have need of something else than pure mercy, where something other than grace could be important for us" (18). [B]

154. Wilhelm Herrmann, "Die Busse des evangelischen Christen," *Gesammelte Aufsätze*, 33–85; the quotation is from 55.

155. In his *Christliche Dogmatik*, I, 88f., Karl Barth correctly emphasizes that *fiducia* is heartfelt trust in God, but that it also has juridical significance besides the emotional. *Fiducia* is a corollary of the *promissio*, and is the relation to what it believes; p. 90: it is answer. [B]

156. Not any one at all can sing "Befiehl du deine Wege." It is sung in the community of the justified.

157. Then trust in God would be prey to all sorts of scorn and skepticism.

158. Wilhelm Herrmann, "Der evangelische Glaube und die Theologie Albrecht Ritschls," 1–25; the quotation is from 14; see also §12 above.

159. M. Luther, *The Large Catechism*, in *The Book of Concord*, 419 (WA 30, I, 192, 10, 11–14).

160. Wilhelm Herrmann, "Die mit der Theologie verknüpte Not," 23, and "Der Glaube an Gott und die Wissenschaft unserer Zeit," 189–213, esp. 208–10.

161. Herrmann, "Die mit der Theologie verknüpfte Not," 42.

162. Ed.: Bultmann includes a marginal note (written in ink and almost illegible): "A note on the investigation of Jesus' preaching by Paul and John."

163. Cf. Wilhelm Herrmann, *Offenbarung und Wunder* (Giessen: 1908).

164. Cf. Bultmann, "Zur Frage der Christologie," *Zwischen den Zeiten* 5 (1927): 41–69. [B] (*Glauben und Verstehen*, vol. 1, 85–113).

165. Wilhelm Herrmann, "Die Lage und Aufgabe der evangelischen Dogmatik in der Gegenwart," 95–188; the quotation is from 111.

166. Ibid., 105, 106.

167. In A, the following pages (88–94 in the manuscript) were originally a part of §8 ("The Idea of Revelation"). This section was dropped after its division into §§9–11 (88–94 are thus part of §11: "Revelation as Historic Deed"). In the final draft these pages were affixed to §14 (behind pages 134/5 in the manuscript).

168. Naturally, not in romantic-sentimental feeling, or since I "interpret" them, but since I love, I can act in them.

169. Whoever is moved by Christ's love knows no one according to the flesh, whether according to his good or bad qualities, 2 Cor. 5:16.

170. Presumably, B adds the entire paragraph.

171. For this reason also the requirement of love is never fulfilled! Rom. 13:8 (*mēdeni mēden opheilete ei mē to allēlous agapān*).

172. Cf. Søren Kierkegaard, "Leben und Walten der Liebe," *Erbauliche Reden* (Jena: E. Diederich, 1924), vol. 3, 97–141, esp. 113 and 118: God is the middle term in the relations between persons.

173. 1 John 4:10: *en toutō estin hē agapē, ouch hoti hēmeis ēgapēkamen ton theon all' hoti autos ēgapēsen hēmas kai apesteilen ton hyion autou hilasmon peri tōn hamartiōn hemōn* ("In this is love, not that we loved God but that he loved us and sent his Son to be the atoning sacrifice for our sins").

174. K. Barth, "Kirche und Theologie," *Zwischen den Zeiten* 4 (1926): 18–40, and 25: "Certainly, the kingdom in which the *peccatores electi*, cleansed and reconciled by the incarnate Word, await redemption in history, is itself history in all its appearances, and with all other historical realities lives in the same dark shadow. But not only this is to be said of it, but also the other joyous word, that this kingdom in midst of the realm of shadows is the kingdom of light, ruled by the heavenly Lord, believed in by the poor, his elect and called, the one holy and catholic *church*."

Karl Barth, "Die Kirche und die Kultur," *Zwischen den Zeiten* 4 (1926): 363–84, and 377: "The Word of God is . . . a word of *redemption*. It has (not finally, but throughout) *eschatological* form. That is, it is related at every point to what is *not* inherent in humans, *not* possible for humans, *not* attainable by humans. At every point it speaks of a keeping simply and exclusively in and through God, of a coming from God, to be shaped by God, to be realized by God. At every point it speaks *sub specie aeternitatis*, that is, with a view to a fulfillment grounded solely in God himself and his faithfulness." [B]

175. WA 6, 215, 13–15, 16–18 ("Von den guten Werken," 1520): "But if you say, how may I know for sure that all my work pleases God, when I still fall at times to much talk, drink, sleep. . . . Answer: This question shows you still think of faith as another work, and do not place it above all works. For this very reason it is the highest work, because it abides and purges the same daily sins."

176. The manuscript reads "brings."

177. Schmid, 428.

178. Schmid, 431.

179. *The Book of Concord*, 154.

180. This can only be stated or heard as *address*, not as an objective fact with which I can reckon or confirm.

181. Cf. K. Barth, *Der Römerbrief*, neue Bearbeitung (Chr. Kaiser Verlag: Münich, 1922; on Rom. 5:17): "that the identification of the old with the new man is only to be carried out in each moment of time; that the judgment of acquittal over us is only *preached*; that no, absolutely no redemption concrete or given in time can correspond to it. Man stands on the *threshold* in this respect as well, on the threshold of the kingdom of God as a realm of the free, of those set free. But he *stands* on this threshold, hoping, and because he hopes he is never quite without the preliminary presence of what he hopes for."

182. Relation between the event (*gnōsthēnai*) and knowledge (*gnōnai*) in the revelation: It belongs to *Dasein*'s historicity that it can understand itself. [o]

183. Ed.: Here the insertion of the altered portion of the lecture ends. It must surely be taken as an oversight that Bultmann did not eliminate the concluding remarks in (the earlier) §8. The remarks read: "Dogmatics must develop further the problems resulting from what we have set forth: Creation and *revelatio naturalis*/original sin/Christology/scripture (canon) and church/the question of Christian ethics." (In the manuscript the *loci* are numbered in column).

184. Cf. R. Bultmann, "Zur Frage der Christologie," *Glauben und Verstehen*, vol. 1, 101–13. [D]

185. Cf. above §12.

186. Cf. K. Barth/H. Barth, *Zur Lehre vom heiligen Geist* (Münich: Chr. Kaiser Verlag, 1930), esp. 45f., 47, 61, 66f., 70ff.

187. Ed.: E adds "in the encounter with fate and. . . ."

188. That for the preacher and hearer this moment also retains its usual claim is beside the point.

189. Ed. E adds "the understanding of fate as God's gift (of the world as creation) as well as. . . ."

190. 133f.

191. Wilhelm Herrmann, "Die Lage und Aufgabe der evangelischen Dogmatik in der Gegenwart," 95–188. 116–18 contain the criticism of Ritschl whose intent is to describe the content of faith as system and thus becomes the last great representative of orthodox dogmatics.

192. Wilhelm Herrmann, "Der Streitpunkt in betreff des Glaubens," *Gesammelte Aufsätze*, 254–74; the quotation is from 268.

193. Wilhelm Herrmann, "Die mit der Theologie verknüpfte Not" (n.149 above), 18f.

194. Despite misleading expressions, for example in "Die mit der Theologie verknüpfte Not," 25; cf. "Grund und Inhalt des Glaubens," *Gesammelte Aufsätze*, 275–94, and 279, ". . . that a fact has appeared to him in his own life."

195. Wilhelm Herrmann, "Die Lage und Aufgabe der evangelischen Dogmatik in der Gegenwart," 111 (cf. n.24 above).

196. Wilhelm Herrmann, "Die mit der Theologie verknüpfte Not," 34.

197. Ibid., 22. But not as though I were related to my experience as such, rather to what I rely on in the experience of trust.

198. Ibid., 24.

199. Cf. R. Bultmann, "Zur Frage der Christologie," 85–113. [B] The experience of the Thou (from another aspect as one-sided in Gogarten as in Herrmann). [O]

200. Wilhelm Herrmann, "Die mit der Theologie verknüpfte Not," 22f.

201. Wilhelm Herrmann, "Die Busse des evangelischen Christen," 33–85; the quotation is from 52f.

202. Ibid., 53.

203. Martin Kähler, *The So-Called Historical Jesus*, 157ff. [O]

204. Herrmann, "Die Busse des evangelischen Christen," 54.

205. Ibid., 54f.

206. Wilhelm Herrmann, "Der evangelische Glaube und die Theologie Albrecht Ritschls," 1–25; the quotation is from 16.

207. Ibid., 17; cf. the entire essay!

208. Nor does the New Testament (cf. especially John!) assert this, but contains either the eschatological idea or the idea of substitution.

209. Further, we cannot see why, in the eventual relation of trust in Jesus, our own will to obedience should not be as uncertain as in other such

relationships, and why—if it should be otherwise—the redemption in that case is not ultimately based on our ability to obey.

210. Cf., for example, Hermann, "Der evangelische Glaube und die Theologie Albrecht Ritschls," 24.

211. Hermann, "Die mit der Theologie verknüpfte Not," 26.

212. Ed.: Italics by Bultmann.

213. Hermann, "Die mit der Theologie verknüpfte Not," 32.

214. Or the authorized preaching.

215. WA 10, III, 354, 15–24, 30–31 (a sermon delivered on St. Michael's at Erfurt on faith and works, October 21, 1522).

216. Cf. also Luther in WA 10, III, 260, 8–9 (a Sermon on the Eighth Sunday after Trinity, August 10, 1522): "So God must say into your heart, 'This is God's Word.'" WA 10, I, 1, 130, 3–6, 14–17 (a Sermon on Luke 2:15-20, Kirchenpostille 1522): "But again, godly faith clings to the word which is God Himself, believes, trusts and honors the word not for his sake who said it, but feels that it is so certainly true that no one can any longer tear him from it. . . . The word alone, without respect of person, must suffice the heart, grasp and seize a person, so that he just feels caught in it, feels how true and right it is, even if all the world . . . yes, even if God Himself were to say otherwise. . . ."

217. And it proceeds from the notion that I would have to resolve to believe when something is put to me. Faith, however, is not based on resolve (*Entschluss*) but on decision (*Entscheidung*), and in hearing I have already always decided. If it were a matter of resolve, then we would be with orthodoxy. [o]

218. Fr. Gogarten, *Ich glaube an den dreieinigen Gott*, 76, and 156: The Word of Jesus Christ can only be heard as binding, that is, only in faith in God the Creator.

219. Ibid., 111: "Where revelation occurs nothing else occurs than usually, always and everywhere occurs, has occurred and will occur. . . . Revelation is nothing but . . . qualified event," that is, in it the I as I, the Thou as Thou become intelligible." [B (perhaps also A)]

220. The law makes the gospel intelligible!

221. Actually, Herrmann is also thinking of experiences which apply to him; in essence, he is thinking of the history qualified by preaching, faith, and love. Incidentally, it is also clear that he does not make Jesus the basis or Lord of the church, but takes him into the church.

222. Wilhelm Herrmann, "Die mit der Theologie verknüpfte Not," 27. (Ed.: The words in parenthesis are Bultmann's insertion).

223. Wilhelm Herrmann, "Religion und Sozialdemokratie," *Gesammelte Aufsätze*, 463–89; the quotation is from 487.

224. "The Christian life is not a structure [superimposed] upon the rest of life. It is quite profanely and banally the life which each must live in his setting. One need not undertake this or that to live the Christian life. We live it in our place, in our situation!—But now this life is claimed by God. There are no areas about which we can say, God has no business there—there God need not interrupt. It is not true that there is a religious sphere where we allow ourselves to be addressed—and alongside it another where life has its own laws and we allow allow nothing of God's light to fall [on it]. Rather, as all of life experiences mercy, so also all of it is set under the severity of grace. God wills and needs nothing less than all!" (Karl Barth, *Vom christlichen Leben*, 22f.). [B]

225. E. Chr. Achelis, "Praktische Theologie," *Grundriss der theologischen Wissenschaft*, 6th ed. (Tübingen: 1912), §62, II, 3, 150.

226. Adolf Schlatter, *Der Glaube im Neuen Testament*, 4th ed. (Stuttgart: Calwer Vereinsbuchhandlung, 1927), 121: "The believer does not seek the efficacy of faith in its strength, but in God's goodness, and does not treat faith as a performance that more surely achieves its goal the greater it is." 149: "But" faith "also brings rest to the passions, because it turns one's gaze from one's own I and what it feels to the one whose word and command will be kept and done." Cf. 176: The believer's reflection may not be bent back upon himself, and may not seek signs of efficacy in himself. 257f.: There are no stories of conversion in the New Testament. Reflection is not directed toward the condition of faith in the soul, but toward its foundation and result. Cf. 278, 283, and 377: "It is precisely faith's sight of the one to whom it is related that gives the apostle's [Paul: R.B.] train of thought its faithful character. . . ." Cf. Martin Kähler, *Der sogennante historische Jesus und der geschichtliche, biblische Christus*, 149ff., 200f. : Christian certainty cannot exist *prior to* Christian faith). I do not know *whether* I believe; but I know in *whom* I believe (formulation by Althaus). [B, E]

227. Wilhelm Herrmann, "Der Streitpunkt in betreff des Glaubens," *Gesammelte Aufsätze,* 254–74; the quotation is from 267.

228. *The Book of Concord*, 171.

229. WA 5, 623, 40 (Operationes in Psalmos 1519–1521, on Psalm 22): "*Agat ergo secundum fidem, idest insensibilitatem.*"

230. WA 18, 526, 33, 34 (Exposition of the Seven Penitential Psalms 1517, 1525).

231. Cf. above, 150f..

232. WA 8, 357, 20–25, 28–30 (Kirchenpostille, Sermon on the 14th Sunday after Trinity, Luke 17:11-19).

233. WA 17 II, 203, 15–18, 29–35 (Fastenpostille 1525, Gospel for Reminiscere Sunday, Matthew 15:21ff.). Cf. also J. Gottschick, "Luthers Theologie," 22.

234. Karl Barth, "Die Kirche und die Kultur," *Zwischen den Zeiten* 4 (1926): 363–84; the quotation is from 374f. Cf. Karl Barth, "Der heilige Geist und das christliche Leben," in K. Barth/H. Barth, *Zur Lehre vom heiligen Geist*, 85f.: "So there is a problem here, because we can only understand ourselves as hearers of the word and as doers, as truly made holy, and thus as living in obedience, and because, on the other hand, our obedience is likewise absolutely hidden from us. . . ."

235. For precisely this reason there is such a thing as theology, since existence has self-knowledge. In developing this knowledge theology is dialectical. In only this way is there an answer to the question of truth, since theology makes clear the relation of the kerygma to existence and the relation of existence to the kerygma, thus making clear the possibility of faith as a possibility of self-understanding, and with it an answer to the question of truth, itself borne by assent to the question. [o]

236. Cf. below.

237. Ed.: Bultmann refers to §6 in parentheses here (in our edition: §7).

238. Cf. Kierkegaard's reproaching Hegel for forgetting his own existence.

239. R. Bultmann, "Die Geschichtlichkeit des Daseins und der Glaube," *Zeitschrift für Theologie und Kirche* 11 (1930): 339–64; Gerhardt Kuhlmann, "Krisis der Theologie?" *ZThK* 12 (1931): 123–46; G. Kuhlmann, Brunstäd, and Tillich, "Zum Problem einer Theonomie der Kultur," *PhG* 18 (Tübingen: 1928). [o]

240. Cf. above, 57f..

241. Cf. philosophy. The understanding of immediacy. Freedom—dependence (answer). Relation of the revelation to the moment. [o]

242. Likewise, the transcendence of revelation is not an external automatic occurrence beyond *Dasein* but an historic event.

243. *Christian* theology is possible because there is (1) revelation, and (2) a natural theology. The relation to philosophy, the formation of theological concepts, the critical significance of philosophy (as *ancilla*). [o]

244. Ed.: ᴇ adds this word (originally "however" in the manuscript) and the previous sentence.

245. Theology as a human, sinful undertaking, must stand under the grace of justification. [o] Bultmann, "Welchen Sinn hat es von Gott zu reden?"; "Kirche und Lehre im Neuen Testament"; "Das Problem der 'natürlichen Theologie,'" *Glauben und Verstehen*, vol. 1, 26–37; 153–87, 294–312.

246. But to contest its possibility would mean that the believer no longer exists but would be changed into an angel or the like. Put in specifically theological terms, it would then be disputed that the *sinner* was made *righteous*, that the justified one was the sinner.

247. No more than a sacred technology!

248. "Let us not disparage thinking, let us not share in the anti-intellectualism of our days! One cannot act without thinking! The great requirement which the mercy of God directs to us, is primarily the requirement of a proper thinking, of a knowing from which then proper action should proceed! Repentance means: the knowledge stirring our will, that we must be thankful to God must seize a place in our thinking" (Karl Barth, *Vom christlichen Leben* [Münich: 1926], 37). [B]

249. Ed.: In the manuscript the conditional sentence is in the plural: "if they have their meaning from the word, if they are *understood*."

250. It *"keeps watch"* over retaining or restoring pure doctrine," Karl Barth, "Kirche und Theologie" (n.174 above), 18–40; the quotation is from 37.

251. Thus theology is never apologetics, as though it had to demonstrate correct doctrine by critical reflection on the basis for faith. Rather, its duty is merely to set forth what the doctrine *states*; it is critical-methodological reflection on what the preacher does when he speaks on the basis of the revelation from God. Cf. Fr. Gogarten in Hermann Herrigel und Friedrich Gogarten, "Vom skeptischen und gläubigen Denken— Ein Briefwechsel," *Zwischen den Zeiten* 3 (1925): 78.

252. That they are not meaningless is due to the fact that even unbelieving *Dasein* has a preliminary understanding of faith; cf. the *revelatio naturalis*.

253. Cf. Barth, "Die Kirche und die Kultur," 363–84. [o]

254. Cf. R. Bultmann, "Das Problem einer theologischen Exegese des Neuen Testaments," *Zwischen den Zeiten* 3 (1925): 334–57, esp. 353.

255. Cf. Karl Barth, "Das Wort Gottes als Aufgabe der Theologie," *Das Wort Gottes als Aufgabe der Theologie: Gesammelte Vorträge* (Münich: Chr. Kaiser Verlag, 1924), 156–78; R. Bultmann, "Die Frage der 'dialektischen' Theologie" (Eine Auseinandersetzung mit Peterson), *Zwischen den Zeiten* 4 (1926): 40–59.

256. Cf. Karl Barth, "Kirche und Theologie," 18–40, esp. 25–27.

257. Cf. ibid., 35.

258. Cf. R. Bultmann, "Das Problem einer theologischen Exegese des Neuen Testaments," 334–57.

259. For this reason, the criticism of scripture! Cf. WA.DB 7, 384 (Vorrhede auff die Epistel Sanct Jacobi, 1522). [o]

260. Here we should recall again that in the first draft the lecture was announced as "Introduction to Theological Study." Cf. Editor's Foreword above.

261. "Synergism"?—indeed, if it meant that the *logos* constituted faith; but it is faith, rather, that constitutes the *logos*. Theology is the understanding of the *logos*. [o]

# Appendix: Truth and Certainty

1. *Marburger akademische Reden* 46 (1927).

2. Plato, *Phaedrus*, 248b: *hē pollē spoudē to alētheias idein hou estin*; cf. 247.

3. Cf. *Phaedrus*, 247: Above the heavens the soul views *autēn dikaiosynēn, sophrosynēn, epistēmēn*. The decisive riddle is how things are with the human being.

4. "Worldview."

5. So also in positivism.

6. Cf. Spitteler, *Prometheus und Epimetheus*.

7. M. Rade, "Wahrheit, Wahrhaftigkeit," *Realenzyklopädie für Theologie und Kirche*, vol. 20, 779–88, esp. 783.

8. Cf. Ernst Troeltsch, *Die wissenschaftliche Lage und ihre Anforderungen an die Theologie*, SGV 20 (Tübingen: J.C.B. Mohr, 1900), 37: "In the religious sphere, ideas, thoughts, and concepts are only symbols which give expression to a content of religious feeling, and which for this reason are subject to the changes of time and individual variety." Cf. p. 38: The religious idea has "subjective and personally conditioned, individual and symbolic character."

9. "Theologie," in *Religion in Geschichte und Gegenwart*, 1st ed., vol. 5, cols. 1197–1205.

10. Georg Wobbermin, "Der Streit um Schleiermacher," *Zeitschrift für den evangelischen Religionsunterricht* 39, 292, describes the task of theology as "setting forth the objective content of the Christian conviction of faith, a content given with the basic Christian conviction, and, so to speak, contained in it." This, it is said, is the theological task in Schleiermacher's terms.

11. Troeltsch, "Glaube III: Dogmatisch," *Religion in Geschichte und Gegenwart*, 1st ed. (Tübingen: J.C.B. Mohr, 1909–13), vol. 2, cols. 1437-1447. The quotation is taken from cols. 1438, 1440.

12. Ibid., col. 1440.

13. Cf. Troeltsch, *Die wissenschaftliche Lage*, 50!

14. For Troeltsch, doubts about the validity of these values in face of an all-devouring nature, are the real enigmas of life.

15. "A comprehensive science of the nature and development of human religious consciousness is the foundation of all scientific theology": Troeltsch, *Die wissenschaftliche Lage*, 39; cf. also 43.

16. The "critique of perception" does not touch the current question, What is true? This question inquires after a fact, while the theory of knowledge analyzes the universal conditions for the possibility of knowing, without taking into account what is true for me. The critique of perception can never determine the limits of possible knowledge, since it always follows knowing. [o]

17. Even Troeltsch saw this. Cf. *Die wissenschaftliche Lage*, 45f.

18. In the manuscript: "which treat, etc."

19. Ms.: "claim" in the plural.

20. Ms.: "they are false."

21. Ms.: "to their observation."

22. Losing historical, temporal character, losing its authentic being. [o]

23. In the margin: "to whom he belongs in love." [o]

24. as belonging to himself, having free mastery of himself. [o]

25. Ms.: "in faith."

26. the question of *the* truth is the question of the claim of the moment. [o]

27. the moment may be understood in one way or another—true, but it *should* not be understood in one way *or* another; only in *one* way! [o]

28. the truth of the moment requires knowledge of all possible truths for the sake of the obligation of the moment. [o]

# Index of Names